Tony C

THE TRIUMPH AND TRAGEDY
OF TONY CONIGLIARO

Tony C

THE TRIUMPH AND TRAGEDY
OF TONY CONIGLIARO

DAVID CATANEO

INTRODUCTION BY LINDA HOUSEHOLDER
FOREWORD BY BILL CONIGLIARO

RUTLEDGE HILL PRESS
NASHVILLE, TENNESSEE

Published in Nashville, Tennessee, by Rutledge Hill Press, 211 Seventh
Avenue North, Nashville, Tennessee 37219.

Distributed in Canada by H. B. Fenn & Company, Ltd., 34 Nixon
Road, Bolton, Ontario L7E 1W2.

Distributed in New Zealand by Tandem Press, 2 Rugby Road, Birken-
head, Auckland 10.

Distributed in the United Kingdom by Verulam Publishing, Ltd., 152a
Park Street Lane, Park Street, St. Albans, Hertfordshire AL2 2AU.

Cover and book design by Harriette Bateman
Typography by E. T. Lowe, Nashville, Tennessee

Library of Congress Cataloging-in-Publication Data

Cataneo, David.
    Tony C : the triumph and tragedy of Tony Conigliaro /David
Cataneo : Introduction by Linda Householder : foreword by Bill
Conigliaro.
        p.   cm.
    Includes bibliographical references (p. 257) and index.
    ISBN 1-55853-532-2 (hardcover)
    1. Conigliaro, Tony. 1945–1990.   2. Baseball players—United
States—Biography.   I. Title.
GV865.C66C38   1997
796.357'092—dc21
[B]   97-26305
                                                                CIP

Printed in the United States of America

1 2 3 4 5 6 7 8 9—00 99 98 97

∾ CONTENTS ∾

~ FOREWORD ~

"Tony C is your brother? He was my favorite ballplayer when I was growing up. What a great player. He was my idol. I remember the time I was at Fenway when your brother hit a homer to win the game. After the game I waited by the players' entrance to get his autograph. . . . Did you play ball, too? Oh, yes, Tony C was my favorite. How is he doing now?"

I can't count how many times over the years I've heard that story or one like it. Still, each time someone says something like that to me, I find it hard to answer without a quaver in my voice. "Tony passed away," I tell them. These are the people who remember Tony's tragic beaning in 1967, completely unaware that he also suffered a heart attack in 1982 that incapacitated him. Then there are those people who know about the heart attack and ask if it had anything to do with the 1967 beaning incident. Of course, it did not.

I have nothing but admiration for Tony's fans. They supported my family long after most people would have forgotten. Still, it hurts me deeply to talk about a family member, *my* idol, my brother, and my teammate. I get mixed feelings of joy and sorrow when I hear people talk about Tony. I have so many wonderful memories of a local boy growing up and becoming a person that people looked up to and worshipped.

Tony's life was a constant battle to overcome adversity, injuries, jealousy, batting slumps, and bad press. This was the price he had to pay for the short-lived success he had at such an early age. Nobody ever expected that the struggles of being a professional athlete would, just a few years later, be exceeded by an all-out fight just to exist on this earth as a normal human being. I would look at my brother—a star in baseball, basketball, and football; a singer with no fear of anything—lie in a hospital bed unable even to eat solid food. I would feel helpless, even angry. This had to be life's most depressing and cruel degradation. It made me wonder about many things in this world, such as religion, God, justice, and whoever it is that selects individuals to suffer like this.

It was in 1982 that Tony returned to Boston to interview for the Red Sox's vacant color commentator's position. A night of celebration when Tony was promised the job ended the next day with the start of a battle to save Tony's life. Try to imagine driving your brother in your car to the airport, in one breath speaking about how great it will be for him to be back in Boston as a broadcaster, then in the next breath looking over and seeing him gasping and writhing in pain as he suffered the heart attack.

I have never been one who panics, and this certainly was not the time to lose control of my emotions. All I could think of was Mass General Hospital and getting Tony there as quickly as possible. To this day I don't have second thoughts about my actions that day, even when people ask, "Why didn't you stop—" And do what? If I had to do it all over again—knowing now what everyone, especially Tony, went through during the eight agonizingly frustrating years of round-the-clock care before his death in 1990—I would pull over to the side of the road and just say good-bye to the brother I loved. This would have saved Tony the pain, the torture, and the horrible existence he would suffer.

Tony, Richie, and I have had the absolute blessing of being children to the best parents in the world. Also, there was my uncle Vinnie Martelli. They supported us boys every step of the way through the ups and downs and pressures that accompany sports. Every action we took on and off the field was meant to please our parents and to make them proud. We three boys have respected and loved them dearly.

In thinking of the pain and torture that Tony suffered over the years, I immediately think of our parents. What price do you have to pay for succeeding at something you love? Do your parents have to suffer to repay all the thrills they have experienced over the years? We were all in pain and had to deal with this tragedy. We realize now that many people are trying to deal with tragedy in their lives, too. No one is insulated from such life-changing events.

I will always remember Tony C as a fighter, a clutch hitter, warm to his fans. He was a brother who made me proud. The "pitch" that hit

Tony in 1982 came from an unknown source, disabling the incredible mind and spirit that had already overcome so much adversity. Tony's ability to fight back was restricted by the damage to his brain. If only he had had a fighting chance that last time, he might still be with us today.

I thank all our friends who helped us during those terrible years. There are a great many people out there, not just sports fans, who helped us greatly. I also want to sincerely thank Linda Householder for her efforts in getting a book about Tony written and published. Without Linda's determination and devotion, this book would not exist. My family appreciates all she has done to see this project through.

—Bill Conigliaro

∼ ACKNOWLEDGMENTS ∽

An accurate, vivid portrait of Tony Conigliaro would not have been possible without the cooperation of the people closest to him. Eternal thanks to Teresa Conigliaro, Billy Conigliaro, Richie Conigliaro, and Vinnie Martelli for sharing their memories.

I'm also grateful to the following for generously digging deep into the past: Julie Markakis, Tom Iarrobino, Jim Magnasco, Lee Thomas, George Thomas, Skip Falasca, Tony Athanas Jr., Dr. Roman DeSanctis, Dick O'Connell, Eddie Kasko, Bobby Doerr, Johnny Pesky, Rick Williams, Carl Yastrzemski, George Scott, Mike Ryan, Milt Bolling, Bill Bates, Jack Hamilton, Dr. Charles Regan, Eddie Popowski, Don Lenhardt, Dick Radatz, Billy Gardner, Dick Johnson, Bob Tillman, Gerry Moses, Alex Markakis, Ed Penney, Rico Petrocelli, Fred Lasher, Joe Morgan, Buddy Hunter, Jerry Coleman, Tom Murphy, Lennie Merullo, Boots Merullo, Albert S. Ruddy, Satch Hennessy, Jim Rice, Gale Carey, Fred Zurawel, Dennis Gilbert, Dave Morehead, Dale Gribow, Bobby Guindon, Ed Kenney Sr., Bobby Mazzarino, Joe Rocciolo, Kazumi Tabata, Jerry Maffeo, and Dick Ellsworth.

Special thanks to *Boston Herald* phenom baseball writer Tony Massarotti and *Herald* copy desk chief John Vitti; also, thanks to *Herald* deputy sports editor Hank Hryniewicz and executive sports editor Mark Torpey; Jim Gallagher, Mary Jane Ryan, Dick Bresciani, Richard Geiger, Tom Lutgen, John Cronin, Betsy Warrior, C. E. Smith, Mike Towle, Larry Stone, Linda Householder, Paul Sullivan, Bob Clark, Andi Clark, Cuddles Carlisto, Mike Lynch, Tim Wiles, Chuck Stevens, and Joe Giuliotti. I am also grateful to Kathryn B. Cataneo and Emily B. Cataneo, whose patience was essential to this project.

—David Cataneo

I have many people to thank for their involvement in and contributions to this endeavor. Former Red Sox players who graciously shared their time and knowledge are Galen Cisco, Frank Malzone, Rico Petrocelli, Gerry Moses, Mike Ryan, Eddie Kasko, Ken Brett, and the last of the true southern gentlemen, Frank "Pete" Charton.

David Gulinello of the Bay State Coin Company in Boston went above and beyond the call of duty in providing priceless information and memorabilia.

The Baseball Hall of Fame Library in Cooperstown, New York, the Boston Public Library, and the Revere Chamber of Commerce were sources for this book.

Dr. Charles Regan provided valuable insight. Dr. Jerry Sell, Dr. Tom Miller, and Cyrus Upton offered me their guidance and support.

My good friends Josephine Cox, Nelson DeMille, and Jaci Koester listened to my joys and frustrations throughout the course of this endeavor.

My parents, the late Robert Nosek and Beatrice Nosek, gave me the strength to continue when I felt like giving up. My brother Gary is always there for me.

My husband, Tom, and my children, Stephanie, Bryan, and Brent Householder, put up with a lot and to them I owe everything.

And thanks to the Conigliaro family, Teresa, Bill, and Richie, for their kindness, support, and, most of all, their friendship.

—Linda Householder

∼ INTRODUCTION ∼

It was a bleak, rainy afternoon in early spring 1994 as I sat inside the Nahant, Massachusetts, home of Teresa Conigliaro, sipping from a mug of steaming coffee. I looked through old family scrapbooks filled with the saga of former baseball star Tony Conigliaro, Teresa's son. In my mind I was piecing together the parts of a puzzle that would become the foundation for this book.

I had arrived in town the day before and found the bustling traffic rotaries of greater Boston to be a far cry from the gently rolling farmlands of Ohio that I call home. Bill Conigliaro, one of Tony's brothers, met my flight into Logan Airport: He had made arrangements for me to stay in a nearby bed and breakfast. The phrase "culture shock" had flashed through my mind as he maneuvered his white Jeep in and out of traffic, pointing out various sights on our drive toward the North Shore. My trip was the culmination of months of research, correspondence, and phone calls, and now I was savoring the reward—a firsthand look at the incredible life and tightknit family of a fallen New England sports hero.

Although I had envisioned a biography of "Tony C" since the previous year, my fascination with the young slugger actually dated back to the summer of 1968, when Tony had made an appearance on *The Merv Griffin Show*. That's when I saw him for the first time. Tall, handsome, and charismatic at twenty-three, he had already lived a tale of tragic misfortune. A fastball had exploded into the left side of his face in August 1967, nearly killing him and, in fact, ruining his eyesight. Tony eventually returned to continue his major-league career, but his comeback, while successful, would be short-lived. The worst for Tony was yet to come a few years after he left baseball.

Upon seeing Tony for the first time on television, I began following his career with a strange intensity. He was relentless in his efforts to overcome lingering vision problems, and Red Sox fans remained hopeful that he would. After a 1970 season in which he produced career bests of thirty-six home runs and 116 runs batted in, Tony, surprisingly, was sent to the California Angels in a trade that reeked of controversy. His brother Bill, still a member of the Red Sox, became embroiled in an ongoing verbal war with Carl Yastrzemski and Reggie Smith; and embittered parents, Sal and Teresa, vowed to discourage their youngest son, Richie, from ever playing professional baseball.

I lost track of him, but I never forgot Tony Conigliaro. When I read about his death in 1990, I was greatly saddened. He was only forty-five years old. I grieved for a stranger. Shocked and dismayed, my curiosity about Tony was again piqued. I began a quest that I hoped would offer solace and closure for a part of me, and which would bring forth something positive from his death.

Many people have asked why someone born and raised in the Midwest would be so committed to a subject whose background was so totally different. I've asked myself that same question hundreds of times and I have no logical answer. It baffles me, too. An acquaintance of mine who claimed to be a psychic told me that my connection to Tony stemmed from recognition. She believed that I had recognized him from a former life. Someone else suggested that I was involved with his story because of emotional empathy and that I unconsciously identified with him. Speculation aside, if someone had told me in 1968 that I would someday be immersed in a project of this magnitude, I would not have believed it.

This book is a dream come true. My intent in conceiving this book and helping to get it published was to award Tony whatever recognition eluded him in life and to maintain his legacy in baseball. Unfortunately, I never met Tony or his father, Sal; but as I sat in Mrs. Conigliaro's living room that gray Sunday afternoon, I felt their presence. Although baseball historians might argue that Tony Conigliaro was a victim of grievous circumstances, I realized how fortunate a man he had been. Not every individual can enjoy the love and support that Tony did, whether the source was his family or baseball fans throughout all New England and much of America.

I felt at peace in the Conigliaro home that spring day in 1994. Stolly, the large white dog that had greeted me earlier at the back door, lay asleep on the kitchen floor. In a room down the hall, Richie busily packed for a golf excursion to Florida. Bill, himself a former major leaguer and now an amateur photographer, was in another room taking formal photographs of a friend's children. He would soon be joining me to begin the first of many hours of conversations that led to the conception of *Tony C.* Teresa, forever the colorful matriarch, sat across the room reminiscing about the lost promise of youth. As I sat looking at the beautiful oil portrait of Tony Conigliaro over the mantle, forever swinging at the elusive ball, I couldn't help thinking, "Wish you were here."

—Linda Householder

⮜ DEDICATIONS ⮞

For KBC and EBC
—David Cataneo

To Robert Nosek, Salvatore Conigliaro, and Anthony Conigliaro.
—Linda Householder

～1～

BAD NEWS ON THE DOORSTEP

BILLY CONIGLIARO WISHED HIS BROTHER WOULD DIE. It was Saturday morning, February 24, 1990, gray, damp, and cold. Tony Conigliaro, again, was in Salem Hospital on the North Shore of Boston, this time with a 104-degree temperature and complications from pneumonia. Billy had lost count of how many times he had rushed his brother to the hospital—twenty or thirty—with high temperatures and breathing problems and foot and leg ailments and when the horrible coughing fits just wouldn't stop. Billy had been raised in a fiercely loyal, eternally optimistic family and he had been taught to never, ever give up. But sometime after Tony's heart attack and subsequent severe brain damage in 1982—perhaps it was the second or third year of watching him suffer and never improve—Billy had abandoned hope. "I went there thinking maybe this was the day he was put out of his misery," Billy recalls.

The wretched, hopelessly impaired forty-five-year-old man in the hospital bed just wasn't Tony anymore. He hadn't been Tony for eight years. Tony loved to eat. Now he was fed through a tube in his stomach. Tony loved to dance. Now he couldn't walk. Tony loved to sing. Now he could barely speak. Tony loved to play. Now Billy tossed a sponge ball to him, and he couldn't raise his hands to catch it. Tony loved life. Now his life had become something grotesque. Tony loved to battle—he was stubborn, tough-as-nails, incredibly willful. Now he couldn't fight back. That's how Billy really knew his brother was finished. Tony had to be gone, because he wasn't fighting back. "It was the only time Tony wasn't able to overcome something," Billy says, "because it wasn't him doing the fighting."

1

In the afternoon doctors came to the room in the intensive care unit and told Billy they didn't know if the medication would adequately treat Tony's infection. His kidneys were failing. They didn't know if Tony would make it this time. At about 3:45, Billy sat in a chair next to Tony's bed and grasped his brother's hand. He could feel Tony's pulse in his wrist. In the course of an hour, as the gray afternoon turned to a dull, winter dusk, Billy held on as Tony's heart gradually beat slower, slower, and slower, like a clock winding down. Then there was one sluggish beat and nothing more. Billy looked at Tony's face. "It looked like he was asleep," he remembers. Billy summoned the nurses, some of whom had treated Tony over the years, and they hugged and kissed the corpse and sobbed. Billy's eyes filled, but not from grief. He was joyful that Tony's torture was over.

Billy telephoned his younger brother, Richie, his mother, Teresa, and his uncle Vinnie Martelli, Teresa's brother who was like Tony's second father. Vinnie hung up the phone and cried. "Every night for three months, I went to bed praying he would die," remembers Vinnie. He thought about Tony, young and strong and brimming with promise, snapping baseballs over the left-field wall at Fenway Park, and wondered if he could ever again think of those home runs and not ache.

By early evening Tony's death had moved on the news wires, and as word spread that Tony C was gone, a lot of people found it hard not to feel a little older and sadder. In East Boston Joe Rocciolo could remember coaching the tall, skinny Little Leaguer who hit the ball clear across Saratoga Avenue. In Greenville, Mississippi, George Scott could remember Wellsville, New York, in the summer of '63, and a double date with Tony and two blonde sisters and how they stayed out extra late and got up the next day and hit home runs. In Lynn, Massachusetts, Julie Markakis could remember her high school sweetheart and his singing love songs to her in a convertible and how neither of them ever married. In Lynnfield, Massachusetts, Rico Petrocelli could remember Tony's smile and the ferocity he brought to every single at-bat. In the North End, Jerry Maffeo could remember how great the kid looked when he stepped onstage wearing a tux. In Branson, Missouri, Jack Hamilton turned off the television news and could remember the night his fastball sailed into Tony's handsome face, and wondered "if in some way I was responsible for him dying. Maybe I started all the bad things for him. You never know." In downtown Boston, Tony Athanas could remember how Tony walked into a room and the place instantly became a little more charming. In Beverly Hills, California, Dennis Gilbert could remember leaving a fancy restaurant with Tony and a car rolling past and a young woman leaning out the window to yell, "Tony C, I love you!"

Baseball fans across the country, especially long-suffering Boston Red Sox lovers in New England, found the bad news on the doorstep when they hefted the Sunday newspapers. Over the years there had been plenty of hardball heroes, but Tony C was extra special. His appeal wasn't in statistics. Jackie Jensen hit more home runs. Vern Stephens had more runs batted in. Pete Runnells had a better lifetime batting average. Billy Goodman got more hits. Ike Delock played more seasons. Ed Romero had more World Series at-bats. But Tony C touched Red Sox Nation deeply and forever, the way Ted Williams and Carl Yastrzemski did.

"I felt like I had lost a friend," says Red Sox fan Gale Carey. She grew up in Natick, Massachusetts, fell in love with baseball in the early sixties, had a slight teenage crush on Tony C in the late sixties, and was all grown up and married and a professor at the University of New Hampshire the day Tony C died. And she felt as if someone had thrown out her baseball card collection. "It felt like, deep inside, that a little heartstring had been cut. He came along just as I was getting into baseball, and I felt like we had both come into this magical scene at the same time. I wished I could talk to his family and tell them how much he touched my life."

Baby boomers who remember Dad cracking open a Narragansett while they watched the Sox on television felt closer to Tony C than they ever did to Teddy Ballgame or Yaz. Ted was born during World War I and Yaz was born before World War II. Tony was born in 1945, and to the boomer generation, he was one of them. He wore dungarees and flipped baseball cards in the fifties. His father had a car with preposterous tail fins. He sang Elvis in the shower. He listened to the Beatles on 45s. He didn't like rules. He said exactly what was on his mind. He wanted to be number one. He could be arrogant. He had doting, indulgent parents. He cried the day John F. Kennedy was assassinated. He didn't believe in waiting his turn. He nearly got married before he was old enough to vote. He collected telephone numbers during the sexual revolution. He got the dreaded draft notice. His best friend was killed in Vietnam. He was disillusioned in the late sixties. He grew funky sideburns in the early seventies. He decided it was time at last to let go of childhood dreams when he hit thirty. He went to California in the late seventies. He felt the tug to come home in the early eighties.

For the Mickey Mouse Club generation, Tony was just right. He came along at the right time. The Red Sox, led by the workmanlike Yaz, had been men in gray flannel suits. Then Tony joined the club in 1964, the year John, Paul, George, and Ringo came to America and added a dash of flamingo plumage. He was a teen dream, young, handsome, audacious. He was sure of himself. He cut a record as if he were Ricky Nelson.

"Conig was always my idol," says Tom Murphy, who pitched in the big leagues from 1968 through 1979. "I was in college in Ohio when he was in the big leagues in Boston. He had a style. He was cool." Tony was intense, yet joyful. He adored being a baseball player—fans could tell that just by the way he strode to the plate. "He loved baseball," says Gerry Moses, Tony's teammate with the Red Sox and the Angels. "I've never seen anyone, to this day, so dedicated to the game."

Tony couldn't wait to hit. He wanted to be a hero. He lived to wallop home runs, because they were the most glamorous thing in the baseball world, and Tony C craved glamour and bright lights. "He was born to play," recalls Rico Petrocelli. "He loved being a ballplayer. He loved what he was."

Tony was in the right place. New Englanders love the Red Sox, and they love local kids, and Tony C was a local kid starring for the Red Sox. He grew up in Revere and East Boston, just a trolley ride away from Fenway Park. He knew a milk shake should be called a frappé and he wasn't afraid of traffic rotaries and he knew the South End from South Boston. He had a wonderful Boston accent—not Beacon Hill like every Bostonian caricatured in the movies, but the blunt, no-nonsense cadence of the blue-collar neighborhoods. He didn't grow up listening to Curt Gowdy or sneaking into Fenway—Tony loved to play, not watch—but it was easy for Red Sox fans to imagine he did.

And he was born for the lyrical, little, rundown home bandbox and its famous left-field fence just 315 feet from home plate. Tony was a right-handed, slashing, aggressive, dead-pull hitter. He lifted baseballs into breathtaking parabolas, turning them into tiny white specks that disappeared into the darkened Victorian rooftops beyond the green wall. "He was built for Fenway Park," says Carl Yastrzemski. "I would say, had he stayed healthy, without any doubt, he'd have hit five hundred home runs playing in Fenway Park. Christ, he could hit home runs in that ballpark in his sleep." Jim Palmer, a Hall of Fame pitcher with the Baltimore Orioles, thought Fenway Tony would have pushed what was then Babe Ruth's lifetime home-run mark of 714.

Tony had the right stuff. He had a truckload of natural talent. He had a nearly obsessive will to work—he wanted to improve and become one of the all-time greats. "He was a consummate athlete," says Bill Bates, a friend of his who was the head trainer for the Boston Patriots from 1961 to 1972. "He worked. He worked. He worked. He was always lifting weights. He was always running. He was always doing things to improve his game. He would have played until he was forty, forty-one. With the designated hitter? There is no doubt in my mind. He had a lot of guts."

"He had tremendous determination," Yastrzemski recollects. "He just kept attacking, attacking, attacking, attacking. That was the key to his success. He never backed off at the plate—*never* backed off at the plate."

Tony was graceful under pressure—when he stepped up to bat in the anxious moments of ballgames and when he stepped onstage in front of television cameras, with a so-so singing voice, to croon in front of millions. "To play in front of thousands of people was one thing, but this was different," Petrocelli remembers. "We all respected him for that. Whether he was good or not, it didn't matter. We thought he really had balls."

Tony was a starting player in the major leagues when he was nineteen. He led the American League in home runs when he was twenty. He hit his one hundredth career home run when he was twenty-two—Babe Ruth was twenty-five before he hit his first home run for the Yankees. New Englanders were sure they had their own home-grown version of Joe DiMaggio. "If I had been a scout and I knew then what I know now," says Lee Thomas, general manager of the Philadelphia Phillies and Tony's teammate on the '64 Sox, "I would have thought, 'My God, what a find!' " In the summer of 1967 he was still evolving, honing, learning. Tony was twenty-two and the future was bright—Yastrzemski didn't pull his game together until he was twenty-eight. "I think in '67, he really came into his own as an all-around player," Yaz reflects. "I think he would have become just as big."

And then, on one pitch, it all went wrong. In an instant he was no longer the right man in the right place at the right time. Tony would go into the record books, but not for chasing Babe Ruth. He would be remembered as the victim of the second-most devastating beaning in baseball history. Carl Mays's submarine ball killed Ray Chapman in 1920. Jack Hamilton's fastball killed Tony C's future of endless possibilities.

"He was Halley's comet," Bill Bates declares, "that just stopped in midair."

Tony was mutated from a symbol of youth and hope to a symbol of dashed dreams. He felt cheated, and so did his boomer legions. Neither wanted to say good-bye, not so soon after saying hello. In 1968 when the Tet offensive stalemated Vietnam and Martin Luther King Jr. and Robert Kennedy were assassinated and Chicago police cracked college kids on the head on national television, they turned their lonely eyes to Tony. "The image that kept flickering was of him working," says Richard Johnson, curator of the New England Sports Hall of Fame. "Swinging at balls a foot outside. Swinging at air. Trudging to the bullpen at Fenway Park. You knew if someone could come back, he would. As long as he had hope, we all had hope."

For longer than anyone thought possible, Tony was gallant amid graceless times. Even Dick Williams, his best manager and his most relentless tormentor, saw it. "Say what you will, the guy was a fighter," Williams wrote in his autobiography. "Between the lines there was nobody who played harder. . . . by having Tony Conigliaro in there fighting every day, the game of baseball was the winner." Bates used to tell his Patriots patients, "If you guys had half the balls Tony Conigliaro does, we wouldn't be 4-10."

Tony C returned to baseball during the summer of Woodstock (1969) and it seemed everything would be all right. He hit twenty home runs, went on *The Dating Game,* and had a fling with actress Mamie Van Doren. The next year he willed himself through his most productive season in the major leagues, but it was clear that everything would not be all right. "He hit thirty-six home runs blind," says Jerry Maffeo, another friend of Tony's. "He couldn't see the ball. That's how much guts he had. He couldn't see and he had the balls to get in there with them throwing ninety miles per hour." In the year of Kent State and the Beatles' breakup, the Red Sox cashed out their folk hero and traded Tony far away. Of course, he unraveled in Anaheim—he was no longer the right man in the right place. Of course, his perfunctory comeback in 1975 fizzled— he was no longer the right man at the right time. He was thirty, and it was somebody else's turn. Tony C was finished, and a generation of Red Sox fans felt they had barely gotten a chance to know him.

"He was baseball's JFK," Dick Johnson maintains.

And a generation could grow old, cut its hair, sell the lava lamps in yard sales, forget the words to "Riders on the Storm," spawn baby boomlets, get flabby, and remember Tony C as forever young. He never took the field old and slow and never played gray and fat in an old-timers' game. He was the guy who got away, and people always remember those types as talented and beautiful and miss them the most. Boomers freely allow their imaginations to run wild. What might have been? After two beers on a sunny day, any middle-aged fan in Red Sox Nation can imagine the plaque in Cooperstown:

Anthony Richard Conigliaro
"Tony C"
Boston A.L. : 1964–1985
Gathered 611 lifetime home runs. Batted .320 with nine home runs in three World Series, including three home runs in Game Seven victory over Cincinnati in 1975. Led A.L. in home runs six times. League Most Valuable Player in 1976. Youngest player in baseball history to win home-run crown in 1965. Totaled 1,568 runs batted in. Named to All-Star team eight times. Known for key hits in clutch situations.

Tony knew his real legacy better than anyone. "I wanted to become the greatest right-handed hitter of all time," he said after escaping the California Angels. "I thought I was on my way at one time. Then I got hit in the head."

After three beers on a sunny day, any middle-aged Red Sox fan can get sad about Tony C. His career was cut short, he had a heart attack when he was thirty-seven, and he suffered terribly for eight years until he died. To the people close to him—his family, his friends, his fans—his life is a story of incredible accomplishment, terrible luck, enormous willpower, but ultimately a tremendous tragedy. "Every time he was the happiest, he was knocked down," says his mother, Teresa. Still, there is something else in his life story, and Rico Petrocelli saw it on the day Tony died, and he has thought about it many times over the years since.

"I think about when I first met him—his laugh," Petrocelli remi-
nisces. "Me, him, and Mike Ryan singing old rock 'n' roll songs together.
Some of the at-bats he had. I think about seeing him before he passed
away. I think of how life is. How it can change so fast. His life really
taught me about life in general. It can change, from one pitch to another.

"The time he had as a ballplayer, he lived. He really lived. I think
about ballplayers and life. We really should enjoy what we're doing. Have
some fun in it. I say that to young ballplayers today, and they look at me
like I'm crazy. We should have some fun."

~2~

THAT TED WILLIAMS KIND OF CONFIDENCE

THE JOYFUL BASEBALL PLAYER IN TONY CONIGLIARO'S PEDIGREE WAS ON HIS MOTHER'S SIDE. Tony's father, Sal, had starred in track and football in high school. It was Uncle Vinnie who was the ballplayer, the *baseball* player.

Vinnie Martelli loved baseball. He grew up in Revere, just north of Boston, in the 1930s, and he was crazy about the Boston Braves. His favorite players were Rabbit Maranville, the eccentric, brilliant shortstop who made vest-pocket catches of pop flies, and Wally Berger, a young outfielder who walloped long home runs into the stiff wind blowing off the Charles River at Braves Field. Vinnie enlisted in the Knothole Gang, a club that admitted kids into certain sections of the ballpark at a discount. He liked to take the trolley into Boston to the big old ugly ballpark on Commonwealth Avenue, just a few blocks west of Fenway Park.

Vinnie was a third baseman and was known in the high compliment of the day as "a pretty good ballplayer."

"The older I get, the better I was then," he laughs six decades later.

Vinnie played on the sandlots of Revere, at Revere High School, for the American Legion, for semipro teams in Revere and Malden, and a couple of times he even worked out with the Chicago Cubs. He dreamed about the big leagues, but then came World War II and four years in the marines and a serious back wound suffered on Peleliu. After the war he returned home to Revere and moved in with his sister Teresa, her husband, Sal, and their baby son, Tony.

Tony, who was born on January 7, 1945, had been nicknamed "Choo," as in "choo-choo," after Sal noted that the boy motored on all fours at full speed, like the Twentieth Century Limited. Vinnie and the little guy became fast pals. As he grew up, Tony began to motor full speed after his uncle. When Uncle Vinnie went to the barbershop for a haircut, to the variety store to get a newspaper, or to a tavern for a cold beer, Tony tagged after him. People around town started to mistake the skinny kid with big brown eyes and a great smile for Vinnie's son.

Inevitably, if he tagged after Uncle Vinnie long enough, the kid ended up on a ballfield. One day, Vinnie doesn't remember exactly when, he and Tony took their baseball mitts, a bat, and a couple of balls down the street to Ambrose Park, a small, treeless lot with a chain-link backstop and a dirt infield. Like millions of dads in mid-twentieth-century America, Sal had outfitted his boy with baseball equipment and he sometimes played ball with him. But Sal was busy with his job at a zipper factory and with assorted business ventures, from manufacturing music stands to raising chickens. Instead, it was Uncle Vinnie who most often played with Tony. He had come back from the South Pacific at twenty-three thinking baseball had passed him by. "I thought it was a young man's game," Vinnie remembers. And here was a youngster dying to throw the ball around with him.

Vinnie was delighted. He played catch with Tony, hit ground balls to him, and pitched to him. They went to the park two or three times a week, and their sessions continued after Uncle Vinnie married, took a job delivering the mail, and moved into his own house five minutes away from the Conigliaros.

With or without Uncle Vinnie, Tony played. Nobody ever had to push him to do that. Teresa loves to tell the story: When he was about four, Tony would get up, dress himself, and head to the ballfield, where he would

Even at the age of three Tony was hinting he was ready to set sail for the big leagues. (Photo courtesy of the Conigliaro family)

play all day by himself until she dragged him back to the house for meals. He threw the ball, chased it, hit it, chased it again—it didn't matter to him, just as long as he got to play. Nosy neighbors gossiped that the skinny little Conigliaro boy in the park with his clothes inside out was a neglected child, such a shame, the poor little boy, all alone all day in the park.

"Now the baseball field at that park is named after Tony," Teresa says. "I wonder what they think of that."

The notion that Tony was neglected was laughable. Sometimes he was terribly indulged, sometimes he was strictly controlled, and sometimes he was harshly disciplined, but Tony Conigliaro was never, ever neglected. A younger brother, Billy, was born in 1947, and baby brother Richie came along in 1951. Tony grew up in an intensely close family, with lots of hollering and screaming and affection—love at two hundred decibels. There were squabbles and fights, but no Conigliaro ever sided against the family with an outsider, whether it was the neighborhood girl who cracked a toy gun over Richie's head or the second-grade teacher who locked Tony in a closet.

The Conigliaros knew their sons weren't angels. One Christmas the boys got a BB gun and used the tree ornaments for target practice. Later, Tony plinked a neighborhood kid in the seat of her pants. And they were forever conking neighbors and passing cars with snowballs. "They very seldom missed," Teresa says with a sparkle of maternal pride. "They had a pretty good eye." But the Conigliaros would discipline their own. When they needed punishment, the boys met the business end of Teresa's wooden spaghetti spoon. They could run, but they couldn't hide. She was skilled at flushing culprits from under a bed with a dust mop. Sal dealt with serious infractions, such as the time Tony was caught cutting kindergarten. And then there was the incident famous in family history: The Day the Boys Wouldn't Go to the Store.

Tony was around ten years old. He and his brothers had spent most of the day squeezing their mother in a three-on-one campaign to drive Mom over the edge. Then she asked Tony to run down to the store for her. He said no, he didn't feel like it. She asked Billy to run down to the store. He said no. Exasperated, she asked little Richie. He followed his big brothers' lead—nope. Teresa burst into tears and called Sal to come home from work. In middle-class, blue-collar, 1950s America, getting Dad out of work was more serious than calling the marines.

Naturally, Sal went for the oldest first, asked Tony the ominous rhetorical question, "So you think you're a big man, huh? Telling your mother you're not going to the store for her?" and proceeded to deliver what was known in those days as a good beating, first with his hands, then with his belt. Sal's brown eyes turned black, which meant he was extra, extra angry. Billy and Richie were next, and soon the three whimpering former wise guys walked to the store. In his 1970 autobiography *Seeing It Through,* written with sportswriter Jack Zanger, Tony noted that "at the time I really hated my father for it," but the incident lived in family lore and eventually acquired a humorous tone. Tony told the story often, with the pride people develop for tough discipline twenty years or so after it was dropped on them. "Sal controlled Tony's life," states his boyhood friend, Jim "Jimmy Maggs" Magnasco. "But Tony needed it. He could be a little devil."

Many times in his life Tony resented and grumbled about his father's discipline, meddling, and manipulation, but no one remembers his ever saying a bad word about him. Tony loved and respected Sal and almost always in retrospect said of his father's directions, "As usual, he was right." Sal was a tremendous influence on Tony. In many ways Tony took after his father and thus found himself in the Red Sox outfield at nineteen. While Uncle Vinnie taught Tony how to field and throw and hit, Sal taught him how to make the big leagues. Sal gave him the attitude—be confident, strut a little, don't be afraid of anything, and if you're afraid, don't show it—that would charm and infuriate people from Little League to Yankee Stadium. Tony was good and he knew it, and that made him better. Uncle Vinnie could not teach that. "I wished I had that confidence," comments Vinnie.

"Vinnie gave him the baseball sense. Sal gave him the aggressiveness," says Joe "Joe Rock" Rocciolo, who grew up with Sal in East Boston. "He got that hard-nosed aggressiveness from his father. In Italian, we call it *capitoso*. That means 'hard-headed.' It means nobody is going to tell you what to do. That was Sal."

In 1953 the Conigliaros moved some five miles to East Boston, where Tony would spend the rest of his childhood. Across the harbor from downtown Boston, Eastie was a predominantly Italian and Irish section of the city. It was mostly middle class, thickly settled with narrow streets, mom-and-pop groceries, close-together single- and two-family homes, and postage-stamp-sized yards. Sal bought a white-clapboard Cape for about ten thousand dollars on Crestway Road in Orient Heights, known as a nicer neighborhood because of an occasional well-to-do home, including those on Pork Chop Hill, so named because residents there were said to be able to afford pork chops on Sunday.

People who lived in East Boston during the Eisenhower years remember it as a good place to grow up. It was safe. In the mornings, fathers went off to work for the MTA or at the General Electric plant in Lynn or to their shoe stores and television repair shops in the square. Mothers stayed home and washed and cleaned and looked after the kids and sat on the front steps to talk to other neighborhood mothers. You could go to Mass at Saint Joseph's (where most of the Irish went) or Saint Lazarus (where most of the Italians went, including the Conigliaros). A cop from District Seven walked the beat and gave scampish kids a boot in the pants—or worse, threatened to go talk to their fathers. You could buy a newspaper at Milgram's and read it next door over a cup of coffee and a doughnut at Steve's. You could get cannolis at Florentino's and the best jelly doughnuts at Gracie's. Small grocery stores strung up slabs of salami and hunks of provolone in the window. Old guys in baggy pants loitered around the barbershops to shoot the breeze or look at the dirty magazines or play the numbers.

And there were a lot of kids. The streets of East Boston teemed with little baby boomers in dungarees, T-shirts, and PF Flyer sneakers, and Tony Conigliaro could always find someone to play with. He liked all sports, but this was the 1950s. The only real game was baseball—or forms of baseball adapted to fit the topography. Tony played a lot of stickball and halfball in the street. "My mother could never find a broom handle. We were always cutting them off for stickball," says Billy. Tony played baseball in the vast parking lot of Suffolk Downs Racetrack, which was just down the hill from the house, where he would run baselines chalked onto the blacktop. And he played baseball at Noyes Park.

Noyes Park was a bike ride away, on the other side of the hill, a few hundred feet from the black waters of Boston Harbor. There was a chain-link backstop, a dirt infield, a chain-link outfield fence, and a big storm drain in shallow center field—when the tide was high, the field flooded. Giant fuel tanks, left over from World War II, dominated the horizon and blocked the noise of traffic whooshing along the busy McClellan Highway. Now and then, there was the drone of propeller planes going in and out of Logan Airport, just across the water. There were enough kids around so that Tony, Richie, and Billy each had his own set of friends. But Tony and Billy often took their mitts, bats, and a couple of battered balls and played for hours at Noyes. Tony pitched to Billy and Billy pitched to Tony. Sometimes, they hit the ball out onto Saratoga Avenue, where it would thump satisfactorily off the bulbous sedans parked on both sides of the street. Sometimes the boys cracked balls clear across the road and against the red brick wall of the Stop & Shop supermarket.

Little League teams played at Noyes, and Tony and Billy liked to climb onto the billboard in center field and watch. Naturally, Tony was enchanted by the snappy uniforms and cleated shoes and the applause from the small crowds. He went to Uncle Vinnie, who was president of the Revere Little League, and asked how to join. Vinnie told him to go to Noyes some day and ask for Mr. Campbell.

Ben Campbell worked at the Boston Fish Pier, had boys of his own, and coached the Orient Heights Sparks. He had prematurely white hair and a gentle way with his charges. Vinnie had already telephoned and told him all about Tony by the time the boy approached him. Mr. Campbell told the skinny little kid that, at eight years old, he was a year too young for Little League, but he was welcome to work out with the team. As he fielded grounders, Tony noticed that the other boys were older and bigger but not better than he. Mr. Campbell noticed, too, and told Tony he could practice with the Sparks whenever he wanted. Tony loved his sessions with the team, especially the way everyone gathered around to watch him hit the ball harder than anyone else. He was a new kid in Eastie, and he was a terrible student in school, but here was something he did well. And this was something he would work at. He played ball with Billy, with Uncle Vinnie, with his neighborhood pals, including Magnasco and Bobby "Muzzy" Mazzarino, and he played with the Sparks. He wanted to hit until his hands bled. He could feel himself getting better.

In the summer of 1954, at age nine, he was old enough to join the team. Tony Conigliaro was issued his first baseball uniform: plain dark purple cap; white jersey, *Sparks* in black block letters across the chest, and red, white, and blue Little League patch on the left sleeve. "This must have been what I was always waiting for," Conigliaro wrote in *Seeing It Through*, "because it felt natural putting it on." He played second base. He remembered that in his very first at-bat, he homered over the center-field fence.

Uncle Vinnie, of course, came around to see his nephew play. The old dream, the one that flickered in the grandstand at Braves Field in the thirties, started to stir again. "To me, he just looked like he could be a ballplayer," recalls Vinnie. "He just had all the moves." In his first season, Tony batted .400. The next year, he moved to shortstop, batted .500, and led his All-Star team to within one victory of the Little League World Series in Williamsport, Pennsylvania. Boots Merullo, whose father, Lennie, played for the Cubs in the 1940s, was on Tony's team. He remembers how well Tony played and how every kid wanted to ride to the games in Sal's brand-new Buick convertible. Tony was already glamorous.

When he was eleven, Tony played shortstop and pitched—the standard Little League positions for superstars—and batted .650 and went 8-0 with two no-hitters. When he came to bat, his teammates would shout at the opposing outfielders to position themselves on the sidewalk on Saratoga Avenue. Even that wouldn't have helped—sometimes Tony lofted home runs onto the roof across the street. He was getting bigger and stronger and smarter. One day Tony was taking grounders in practice and a bad hop barely missed his head. On the next bouncer, he flinched. Mr. Campbell stood over him and held a baseball in front of his face. "Tony, if you're afraid of this little baseball, then forget it. Maybe you shouldn't be a ballplayer," he declared. Tony never flinched again, from Noyes Park to Fenway Park.

Another time, with runners at second and third, Campbell signaled for Conigliaro to take a pitch. The offering was too juicy to resist, however, and Tony smacked a two-run single. "You're on the bench next game," Campbell told Tony, who knew exactly why, but he would always find it easier to follow a fastball than instructions.

Something else was in blossom. Tony could hit and field beyond his years, but he could also strut better than most ten-year-olds. Flashes of a startling self-confidence became more frequent and more audacious. "He would tell the pitcher to get the ball over the plate so he could hit it out of the ballpark," said Rocciolo, who was an assistant coach to

Taller and more confident than most other boys his age, Tony had no trouble standing out among his peers on the East Boston Little League team. Tony, middle back row, is twelve here. (Photo courtesy of the Conigliaro family)

Mr. Campbell. "You could actually hear him out there, talking. When he got a walk, he got mad. He wanted to hit."

The kid was unbelievable. This was Boston in the midfifties, and as crazy as it seemed, the skinny shortstop-pitcher reminded some people around Noyes of another player who used to be skinny and brash. "Tony had that Ted Williams kind of confidence," Joe Rock says. "He was in Little League. He'd say, 'I'm going to hit two home runs and strike out fourteen.' And he'd do it. He'd always do it."

Sometimes even Uncle Vinnie couldn't believe his ears. He remembers taking Tony, who was ten or eleven, to a Revere High School game at Medford to see a hot pitcher. They sat in the bleachers and watched the high school kid throw nasty, sharp deliveries.

"That's a pretty good pitcher out there," Uncle Vinnie said. "What do you think?"

Looking at the teenager on the field, Tony the Little Leaguer said evenly, "I can hit him."

When he was thirteen, Tony's Pony League team traveled to a tournament in Newburgh, New York, five hours west of Boston, to play teams from the New York City area. It was not a pleasant cultural exchange. The New Yorkers didn't like the wise-guy Italian Americans from Boston and the Boston team didn't like the arrogant New Yorkers. For years afterward Tony loved to tell how he surveyed the field and asked a local how far away was the fence in left.

"It's 340, but don't worry, none of your guys is going to reach it," the man replied.

"Oh, yeah?" countered Tony. "Well, I betcha I can hit three out of ten over that fence right now."

He enlisted a pitcher and smacked four over the fence.

"There is no question in my mind that sounds just like something he would do," says Magnasco, who played first base on Tony's Pony League team. "He'd tell you he would do something, and he would do it."

During one of the boys' games the Yankees happened to be throttling the Red Sox, and the New Yorkers turned up a radio so the Boston kids could hear it. What really ticked off Tony and his teammates, however, was the brutal heat and the fact they were issued the only rooms in the hotel without air conditioning. To repay management for the stuffy accommodations, Tony supervised the trashing of his room on the way out.

~ 3 ~

MISTER CONIGLIARO

NATURALLY, SAL TOOK A CENTRAL ROLE IN TONY'S HIGH SCHOOL SELECTION. Lennie Merullo, then a major-league scout, recommended Saint John's Prep in Danvers, about fifteen miles north of Boston. Sal was more interested in Saint Mary's of Lynn. The school had a legendary baseball coach, Nipper Clancy, and, best of all, it was situated near the Triangle Tool and Die Company, where Sal worked. He could drive Tony to school in the morning, zip over to catch his sports practices in the afternoon, and drive him home at night. Saint Mary's Boys High School was the choice.

Years later Tony referred to Saint Mary's as "a school that never really accepted me." People at Saint Mary's say he got it all wrong, that they welcomed Tony just fine. They admit they didn't always know what to make of him. He had strutted around Little League as some sort of half-pint Ted Williams, and he wasn't about to pretend to be the shy new kid in high school.

"As cocky as anybody I ever met in my whole life," says Tom Iarrobino, who was a sophomore when Tony tried out for the baseball team as a freshman in the spring of 1959. "He was fourteen years old. He just came out and said, 'This is easy.'"

"He was the most egotistical athlete—no, he was the most egotistical person—I've ever seen in my life," comments Skip Falasca, Tony's classmate and teammate for four years at Saint Mary's. "He was in love with himself."

Before long most of them came to agree with Tony—they loved Tony, too. Who did this kid think he was? He thought he was handsome, charming, and the best athlete around, and he turned out to be right. "If there was any resentment, it didn't last long," Iarrobino notes. "Certainly not with his teammates. He wasn't offensive. He was funny. You *had* to laugh at that stuff."

"He went out and did everything he said he was going to do," Falasca relates quietly, as if still awed four decades later by the big words followed by the big deeds. "After a while, everybody got to know him and like him."

One person Tony could not charm haunted his thoughts for the rest of his life. White shirts and ties and discipline and Latin were big at the school, which was run by the Sisters of Saint Joseph. One nun who would not indulge the teenager with the big ego, no matter how far he hit a baseball, was Sister Ernestina, who had piercing eyes and a withering, sarcastic wit. *Capitoso* was no more encouraged in parochial high schools than it was at Parris Island.

Sister Ernestina could just say his name, *"Mister* Conigliaro," and make Tony feel two inches tall. She told him he'd never make it as a ballplayer. She kept him after school. She gave him a C on a science project he "really worked hard on." She told him he didn't have the guts to be a professional ballplayer. She belittled him in front of the class. And Tony took it personally. "She hates me," he told friends, not noticing that she was doing the drill instructor routine on many of his classmates as well.

"He wasn't alone," Iarrobino recalls. "He may have had a nun who was all over his case, but he wasn't the only one."

"She used to embarrass me, too," Falasca remembers. "She didn't like his attitude. He was a cocky kid. He was a star. He was God's gift to women. She didn't like it. But she was right on target with him. I think she did it to make a better man out of him."

None of the Conigliaros appreciated the gesture. "Tony and his friends planned to kill her," Teresa says. Well, maybe not kill her. They were going to rough her up a bit. As Tony told the story, he and some buddies plotted to sneak up on the dictatorial nun when she was facing the board one day in class. Tony gave the signal and proceeded up the aisle and noticed that his co-conspirators had retreated to their desks . . . just as she turned around. She lasered him with those eyes and said, "Well, *Mister* Conigliaro, what do you want?" and Sister Ernestina had won another battle.

At Saint Mary's, as generally in his life, Tony was most comfortable on the playing field. As a freshman, Tony made Nipper Clancy's varsity team as an outfielder and batted .370. As a sophomore, he played shortstop, pitched a little, batted .425, and stirred up a lot of interest from major-league scouts because of a star-is-born moment during a game in Danvers. Tom Iarrobino remembers riding the bus to the game that day filled with excitement because Saint Mary's was going to face the senior superstar pitcher from Saint John's Prep, Danny Murphy, a stocky right-hander with the kind of raw fastball that scouts adored.

"Tony, you're going to see something today that you've never seen before," Iarrobino told Tony.

"Yeah, yeah."

"Tony, you're in for a shock."

Iarrobino recalls that Tony, in his first at-bat, pulled one of Murphy's fastballs for a double. Tony remembered that Saint Mary's got four hits that day, and he got three of them. (Relating the game years later, Tony left out that Murphy drilled one of his offerings for a home run.) The scouts stuck with Murphy, who signed with the Cubs for one hundred thousand dollars. But the scouts also asked how to spell the name of that Saint Mary's kid. They wanted to keep their eye on him.

"He was not in awe. He was not afraid," Iarrobino relates. "I remember thinking, 'Nobody's going to stop this kid.' "

In the summer after his sophomore season, Tony was fifteen and had already shot up to six-foot-two, 175 pounds. He played in the then-prestigious Hearst sandlot tournament on Cape Cod. The big leagues were watching there, too. "That kid really looks like something," Milwaukee Braves scout Doc Gautreau told a reporter from the *Boston Record*. "He can run, throw, and field. And how about the way he hits that ball?"

In his junior year Tony batted .545 while playing shortstop and third base, and pitching. In June he told a reporter his favorite position was third base, but more than anything, at age sixteen, "I have one big objective and that is to play big-league baseball."

Sal, more and more, also believed his son was a special ballplayer. But he was smart enough to know that there was plenty that could stop him, or any prospect, no matter how strong the talent. There were pitfalls everywhere—stupid injuries, bad work habits, girls.

*Tony's favorite position while playing for Saint Mary's was third base. He's sixteen here. (*Boston Herald *archives photo)*

With Tony, he didn't have to worry about work habits. Tony applied himself harder than anybody else, showing up early for practice, staying late, and going into the basement at night to swing a weighted bat until his blisters burst. Sal worried a little less about injuries after Tony gave up hockey. Tony played basketball and football at Saint Mary's and was superb at both. He loved hockey after teaching himself to skate on frozen puddles in the parking lots at Suffolk Downs and playing pickup games with older kids in the neighborhood. But Sal was always cool toward his son's ice exploits. When Tony entered high school, Sal told him he wasn't going to tell him what to do, that he was free to play any sport he wanted, but playing hockey was dumb because it was a rough sport and could hurt his chances of becoming a ballplayer. Tony gave up hockey. In *Seeing It Through,* he assessed the decision and wrote, "As usual, my father was right."

Sal didn't worry about women. The girls had been crazy about Tony since junior high school and Tony liked them, but he wasn't crazy. Magnasco remembers going out with Tony and two girls who were cousins on a double date—in those days this meant taking a walk together—when Tony looked at his watch and said, "C'mon, we've got to go play ball." In high school, with his athletic exploits and tall good looks and that smile and those brown eyes, he was considered a dreamboat. "He was a real Romeo," states Teresa. "The girls chased him like you wouldn't believe. They were always coming to our door." He didn't get serious about any of them, so he could always keep his mind squarely on baseball, until he met Julie Markakis in his senior year in 1961.

Saint Mary's was engaged in its annual grudge football match with Lynn English on Thanksgiving. Tony played quarterback, and years later he remembered he was "on the thirty-yard line in a light rain" when he first noticed the petite Lynn English cheerleader with shoulder-length black hair and striking hazel eyes. She noticed him, too. "Our eyes sort of met," says Julie.

The next day Tony and a friend were at the Lynn public library and there she was, studying at a table with a schoolmate. He waited until she went into the stacks to get a book, caught up with her, and struck up a conversation. Julie liked him right away. He was tall and handsome all right, but he also had a nice, wry sense of humor and an ebullience about him, without being frivolous. "He was charming," Julie recalls. They

For Tony C, it was love at first sight with Julie Markakis. (Photo courtesy of Julie Markakis)

started to date, and on New Year's Eve, he asked her to be his steady girl. Sal didn't say anything—directly, at least—but he wanted his son getting serious about a girl about as much as he wanted him to play hockey.

They had a blast together on the North Shore teen scene. Those were the *American Graffiti*-like days: cruising in convertibles and doo-wop on the jukebox. Boys wore chinos and crew cuts. Girls wore tight sweaters and artichoke hairdos. Tony would pick up Julie in his '56 Chevy Bel Air, which Sal had purchased for him, and there was always someplace to go. They could squeeze in among the tightly packed bodies at Hannessey's, the after-school hangout in Lynn, which was a mom-and-pop place with booths and a soda fountain and a loud jukebox. They could get ice cream at Roland's, where Tony could eat a million banana buckets and never gain an ounce. They could have dinner at a spot inappropriately named the Ritz, a pizza parlor in Revere that featured checkerboard tablecloths and sawdust on the floor. They could catch a movie and make out at the Lynnway drive-in. Julie thought Tony was the most romantic boy in the world. When one of his favorite love songs would come on the car radio, he'd sing along to her. She remembers his crooning "In the Still of the Night" and "I Can't Help Falling in Love with You."

Tony was fun to be around. Although intensely driven and furiously ambitious, he saw no sense in not enjoying himself on the climb. He loved to dance and sing, and Richie remembers his big brother bopping around the house singing "Hound Dog" and "At the Hop" (the syrupy ballads being reserved for Julie in the car). He loved to eat. One time when Tony was at the Markakis home, Julie's mother fried a piece of meat for the family's pet poodle.

"Oh, Mrs. Markakis, what smells so good?" Tony asked.

"I'm cooking this for Jean-Pierre," Mrs. Markakis answered.

"Forget Jean-Pierre," Tony announced, grabbing a plate and taking a seat at the kitchen table. "I'm taking it." And he did, relishing the dog's dinner.

Tony was not a joke teller, but his humor surfaced in pithy comments when he saw irony in situations. He also enjoyed a good practical joke and was a lively audience for class clowns. Skip Falasca, a cutup at Saint Mary's, perfected a drop-dead imitation of Crazy Guggenheim, the drunken barfly played by Frankie Fontaine in the popular *Jackie Gleason Show.* "Tony used to go nuts over that," Falasca says. "He'd love it."

One day when the Saint Mary's team bus was parked in Malden Square, a huge Cadillac convertible stopped alongside at the traffic light and in the driver's seat was . . . Frankie Fontaine!

"You gotta do it. You gotta do it," Tony begged Falasca. Tony slid open the school bus window and called out, "Hiya, Joe!"

Falasca leaned out and did it right, with the trademark slur, "Hiiiiya, Joe."

Fontaine looked up, contorted his face, and slurred back, "Hiiiiya, fellas. How're ya dooooin'?" The bus exploded with laughter. Tony laughed so hard he could hardly get the words out when he told Falasca, by way of compliment, "You are *so* crazy."

Tony could get crazy, too. One night, he and Alex Markakis, Julie's older brother, went out for pizza, and near the end of the meal realized neither one of them had any money.

"How are we going to pay for this?" Alex asked.

Tony gave him a let-me-handle-this look, produced a coin, and pried a nail out of the stainless-steel trim on the Formica table. He placed the nail in his mouth, steadied himself, and erupted in a fit of loud coughing and gagging. While the restaurant fell silent, the panicked owner—wearing a tall chef's hat—darted out from the kitchen and tried to hush Tony, who by now was making horrid guttural sounds.

"Shhhhh," said the owner, placing his finger to his lips. Tony barked and spit the nail onto the table. "There was a nail in my food and I almost choked on it," he sputtered. The owner gave them the meal on the house and threw in two free sodas—anything—to get them out of the restaurant.

Tony's high school contemporaries say you either loved him or you hated him. Tony had many acquaintances but few close friends. According to Tom Iarrobino, "He was careful about who he let himself get close to." Tony's best pal was Freddie Atkinson, a tall, dark-haired kid from Lynn who was not athletic but was the student manager of the football team. "They were as thick as mud," Iarrobino says. "They were always together." Tony, Freddie, and Alex would shoot pool together. Tony and Julie would double-date with Freddie and his girlfriend. "Freddie had a great sense of humor, a dry sense of humor, like Tony's," says Julie. "Tony was very close to Freddie. He was crazy about him." He kept almost everybody else at a distance.

Tony was not popular among Saint Mary's intracity rivals, Lynn Classical and Lynn English. He got a lot of publicity and he loved every bit of it. He was cocky, and he was always beating their teams in basketball, football, and baseball. There was plenty of tough *West Side Story*-type talk and near-fights when Tony ran into English and Classical kids around Roland's or at school dances. Tony often told stories of being challenged by gangs of English kids in parking lots or being followed by carloads of Classical kids on the Lynnway. One time Tony came out of a dance at Saint Mary's and found the windows shattered on his father's white 1959 Cadillac Eldorado convertible. Julie Markakis routinely found herself defending Tony to her Lynn English classmates.

"He's a jerk," English football star Charlie Campbell once told her.

"You don't know him," Julie retorted.

"I don't like him."

"Wait until you meet him," pronounced Julie, who went out of her way to introduce the pair at a party.

"Julie, you were right," Campbell told her next time they met. "He is a great guy."

Everyone who knew Tony knew his ambition. "All he ever wanted was to become a professional baseball player," Julie says. "He just lived for baseball. That was his dream." To reach the big leagues would not be good enough. Even in his teens, before he got out of high school, Tony wanted to be a big leaguer and he wanted to be one of the all-time greats. Sal had taught him well: There was no sense doing anything unless you were going to be one of the best. "He told me he wanted to be another Ted Williams," Alex Markakis states. "One day he just came out and told me that."

In his senior season in the spring of 1962, Tony batted .560 and the scouts thought he was pretty good. Considered a good prospect, he would have been a first-round pick if the baseball draft had existed at the time, but he was not a can't-miss phenom like Danny Murphy (who jumped straight from high school to the Cubs—and missed, batting .174 with four homers in four seasons). Still, there was something special about him. Many superior athletes don't mind stepping up with the game on the line, some really enjoy it, and Tony Conigliaro craved it, as if the pressure and intensity were a drug.

"I couldn't wait to get to the plate, either, but if it was 2-2 in the ninth, I'd have this doubt, this hesitation, this nervousness," says Falasca. "With Tony, if it was 2-2 in the ninth, he'd be saying, 'Please let me get to the plate.' "

Tony recounted that fourteen of the twenty teams then in the major leagues expressed interest in him, with the Baltimore Orioles and the Red Sox paying closest attention. Boston assigned scout Milt Bolling to keep an eye on the Conigliaro kid. "I almost lived with that family the whole spring," Bolling remembers. He enjoyed spending time with them. There was always plenty of food and wine on the table, and Sal was an interesting character. If Tony played a good game that Bolling missed, Sal made sure the scout knew about it, greeting him every time with, "You should have been here . . ."

"I really liked Sal," Bolling says. "He was a hard-nosed guy to deal with. He ruled the roost. He had more confidence in his family than any man I've ever known. He always built his kids up."

The Conigliaros appreciated the Red Sox's courtship for three reasons: Fenway Park was a fifteen-minute ride from the house, and having Tony play in the big leagues so close to home would be a dream; Fenway Park had its famously close left-field wall, perfect for Tony's right-handed swing; and other than Carl Yastrzemski, the Red Sox outfield (Gary Geiger, Lu Clinton) was short on Hall of Fame candidates. There would be room for a hot rookie.

However, Tony would not sign with the Red Sox out of sentiment. When he was growing up, he was not a Red Sox fan. He might have attended one game at Fenway Park when he was a kid, and he did not listen to Red Sox games on the radio or follow them in the newspapers. He had baseball cards, but not to look at the pictures or to read the statistics. He flipped them with neighborhood kids, to see who could come closest to the wall—which was pure Tony, who thought baseball was something to play, not to read about or watch.

After graduation, Tony signed up for one last summer of American Legion ball with Connery Post No. 6 in Lynn, which prohibited him from a professional contract until the legion season ended in September. He later explained, "I felt I owed the team one more season," but more likely he wanted more time to impress the scouts and inflate the bonus money. College was even an option—Providence was said to be a possibility—despite Tony's apathy toward academics.

The Red Sox wanted to see more of him. They brought him to Fenway to practice with the team before a game. Not surprisingly, Tony made no mention of this workout in his autobiography, as he was dreadful. "He couldn't even hit one off the wall," Bolling says. Red Sox manager Pinky Higgins grumbled about the kid—"How in the hell can you want us to sign this guy?"—and Bolling worried Tony's shot at the Sox was ruined. "I thought it might have blown us out of the water," Bolling confesses.

Red Sox director of scouting Neil Mahoney knew better than to judge a player on a single workout. Tony was summoned for another look, this time without the Red Sox on hand. He auditioned with a muscular seventeen-year-old prospect from California named Tony Horton.

"Horton, you pitch to Conigliaro for a while," Mahoney told them. "Then switch."

Horton pitched and Conigliaro sprayed line drives all over Fenway. Conigliaro pitched and Horton smashed the first offering into the center-field bleachers, the second one into the Red Sox bullpen, and a couple more into the left-field screen. "They both put on quite an exhibition," recalls Ed Kenney Sr., who witnessed the workout as the Red Sox's assistant farm director. "But Tony was not as impressive as Tony Horton. I'd never seen an explosion like the one Tony Horton put out." The Red Sox signed the California kid for $125,000.

In August Tony got another chance to impress scouts when he was selected a *Boston Record-American* All-Star, which won him a trip to New York for the prestigious and closely watched Hearst All-Star series at the Polo Grounds. Teammates remember Conigliaro walking into the old ballpark, which was then home to the fledgling New York Mets, surveying the locker room, and saying, "I'm going to be back here in two years, playing for some big-league club."

He was back in New York just the next week to play for Hearst's United States All-Stars at Yankee Stadium. Skip Falasca, Tony's teammate from Saint Mary's, was also a United States All-Star. On their first visit to Yankee Stadium, Falasca and Tony bounded off the bus, found their way to the locker room, passed through the dim tunnel to the dugout, clambered up the steps into the sunlight, and hurried out across the vast lawn to the historic tombstone-shaped monuments in deep center field. The outfield at the old Yankee Stadium—with the majestic facade overhead and the grass of DiMaggio, Ruth, and Mantle underfoot—was one of the most hallowed sports locales on the planet. Tony and Falasca stood and stared and it was one of the few times anyone saw Tony Conigliaro awed by anything. Awed, but not cowed.

"I'm going to be here," Tony announced while standing in center field at Yankee Stadium.

"Yeah, Tony, sure," Falasca said.

Tony loved New York. It made perfect sense. He was drawn to the spotlight like a moth, and the brightest spotlights in the world were in Gotham. He also enjoyed a good time, and to be seventeen years old and on a road trip to New York City was a great adventure. He didn't care to attend games at Fenway, but he watched one at Yankee Stadium and saw Detroit Tigers slugger Rocky Colavito hit two home runs. He went to see the musical *Carnival* at the Imperial Theater. He enjoyed the fancy room and the coffee shop breakfasts at the Hotel New Yorker, where he and Falasca shared quarters on the twenty-fifth floor. One night they decided to put the altitude of their room to good use by filling condoms with water and dropping them out the window.

"Gee, if this thing hits somebody at this height, it might kill them," Falasca observed, pausing at the window in an unusual flash of sensibility.

"Naw," said Tony. "A penny would kill them. This will just shock them."

To his friends on the trip, Tony was carefree and soaking up New York. There was another side to him, however. One morning Tony found a quiet moment, took a couple of sheets of hotel stationery, sat up in bed, and leaned on a Manhattan telephone book to write a letter to Julie. "I miss you already," he wrote. "If I do go away to college, I don't think I will be able to stay away from you . . ."

When the American Legion season ended, Sal wrote letters to the major-league teams that had scouted his son and informed them that

September 11 was the big day. They were invited to the house to bid, one by one, to sign Tony. "Well, Choo," Sal told Tony before the first scout arrived that Tuesday morning, "we're really going to do it today."

Tony recalled the first scout's sitting down and saying, "Mr. Conigliaro, we'd like to offer your son $8,000," and Tony was sure he must have heard wrong. Danny Murphy had signed for $125,000. The year before, the Sox had signed a local kid named Bobby Guindon for $125,000. Maybe the guy said $80,000.

Nope. It was $8,000.

While their colleagues waited outside in their parked cars, scouts paraded into the house one by one. Through the morning, into the afternoon, and into the dinner hour, it was clear no team would offer anything near $100,000, or even $50,000. The rules had changed, they explained. Teams were scaling back, paying big money to only one prospect and going small on all the others. (One must also wonder if, in those sweatshop days before Marvin Miller, there might have been collusion on the Conigliaro front walk.)

The Red Sox were the next-to-last bidders. Neil Mahoney and Milt Bolling sat at the dining room table and offered $22,000. They were worried about Tony's lack of power—certainly, he didn't have Horton's pop—but Bolling remembers exactly why he wanted him. "You can judge the physical abilities, but you can't always tell about the intangibles," he explains. "His intangibles, his drive, his confidence in himself, were just incredible."

Sal told Mahoney and Bolling they would think about it, sent them away, and ushered in representatives from the last suitor, the Baltimore Orioles. They offered the same as the Red Sox. "For another $5,000, you can have him," declared Sal, not in the least emotional about the hometown Red Sox. Like the car salesman checking with the sales manager, the Orioles scout said he would telephone Baltimore for permission to increase the offer. The Orioles brass, feeling stingy after spending $35,000 in the spring on a skinny shortstop from Pittsfield, Massachusetts, named Mark Belanger, wouldn't budge. Sal telephoned the Red Sox and said it was a deal.

Bolling and Mahoney returned to the house about 10:00 P.M. and Tony signed. Wearing a short-sleeved shirt, a tie that ended two buttons short of his pants, and a Red Sox cap, he posed for photographs and Sal broke out the champagne. Then he went out for a ride with Julie. "You never saw a happier person in your life," she remembers.

Uncle Vinnie, who had dreamed of the big leagues three decades earlier, stood in the dining room and could hardly believe it. The dream had come true for the little kid who used to play catch with him at Ambrose Park. But, geez, the money could have been a little better.

"You just stole him," Vinnie told Mahoney amid the celebration.

"What do you mean?" inquired Mahoney.

"You gave some guy, Guindon, in West Roxbury $100,000, and he couldn't carry Tony's shoes."

"You're prejudiced," Mahoney retorted.

"Prejudiced or not," said Uncle Vinnie, playfully but pointedly, "I'm right."

Less than three years later, Uncle Vinnie ran into Neil Mahoney in the Red Sox clubhouse.

"You were right," Mahoney told him.

~4~

THE ONLY GIRL IN THE WORLD

LATE ON A FALL AFTERNOON EVERYONE GATHERED AT LOGAN AIRPORT TO SEND TONY CONIGLIARO OFF INTO THE WORLD. Sal and Teresa, Uncle Vinnie and Aunt Phyllis, and Richie and Billy delivered embraces, handshakes, or kisses on the cheek. Tony toted a suitcase filled with new clothes. Now he was a professional ballplayer on his way to Bradenton, Florida, to report to the Red Sox's team in the Instructional League, an off-season prep and remedial camp for rookies and other young players. He was also still a kid, just a heartbeat out of high school: He wore a sharp dark blue suit, black shoes—and a pair of bright, white athletic socks.

As Tony walked toward the plane, a husky young man introduced himself as Mike Ryan, also on his way to the Red Sox team in Bradenton. They had heard of each other but had never met. Ryan was a catcher from Haverhill, Massachusetts, three years older than Tony, and, more importantly, in his second year of professional baseball. Tony was glad to know someone who had gone through this experience before, and they took seats next to one another on the plane. As the jet climbed into the dusk, Tony received an unglamorous introduction to life in pro ball: Ryan, a notoriously queasy flyer, lunged for the airsick bag, threw up, and splashed vomit onto the pants leg of Tony's sharp blue suit. "He looked at me out of the corner of his eye like he wanted to hit me," Ryan remembers.

After they landed in Tampa, Tony was grateful to keep Ryan, nausea and all, at his side. It was a warm, muggy night, and somehow being far away from home at age seventeen seemed spookier after dark. Other players milled about waiting for cars to carry them to Bradenton. They all seemed to know one another. Tony later said he looked up at the stars and thought, "What the heck am I doing down here?" A few hours later he pulled the sheets up around him in his bed at the Hotel Dixie Grande in Bradenton. He told Julie Markakis in a letter, "I did cry my first night here."

The Hotel Dixie Grande—despite its advertised four shuffleboard courts, steam heat, free television, and fireproof construction—was a glorified seven-story flophouse. "It was built around 1900 and they hadn't done a thing to it since," Ryan insists. He and Tony moved to an apartment, which was furnished with a big bed and a small bed. As the veteran of the pair, Ryan plopped onto the big one. "That really got to him," Ryan says. Conigliaro was to wear the same simmery glare when Ryan speared the larger pork chop or thicker steak during meals and when older players hogged the batting cage during practice. Like anybody in a hurry to get somewhere, Tony didn't like standing in line.

The Instructional League featured spring-training-like workouts and exhibition games, and for the first time in his life, Tony wasn't the best baseball player on the premises. A rite of passage is for prospects straight from high school to have their knees buckled and their confidence shaken by the first hard, biting sliders, darting curveballs, and knuckle-jarring inside fastballs they see in pro ball. Tony ducked from pitches that seemed to bore in at his head and then felt silly when they spun in for strikes. He also began to suspect maybe Neil Mahoney was right: He didn't have much power. He got hits in practice games, but most of them were singles. Tony was discouraged.

As always, he tangled with his doubts in private. Only years later, after he had nabbed his dream and reached the big leagues, could he admit, "I got so depressed several times that I felt like packing my bags and going home." Ryan noticed that his roommate was quieter and that he telephoned home more than usual. He knew exactly what the kid was going through. Ryan never sat Tony down to give him a heart-to-heart; real guys didn't do that sort of thing. Instead, he encouraged him with small asides: "Don't worry about it" and "I've gone through it" and "You hit it right on the nose that time."

Ryan saw his roomie's wobbliness, but nobody else did. Tony swaggered the same as he did in Little League, at Saint Mary's, and in legion ball. He was batting .200 but he walked around as if he were batting .600. It elicited the customary reaction, a bit stronger in the status-obsessed world of professional baseball: Can you believe this kid? Bobby Guindon, the West Roxbury outfielder who had signed with the Sox for $125,000, watched with wonder as Tony pranced around as if he were the bonus baby. "Even if he wasn't doing well, if he didn't have the numbers, he carried himself as if he were great," Guindon says. "I had a problem with his attitude. He was number one. He was the best who ever played in his mind. And he didn't care much about how other people perceived him."

Guindon wasn't the first or last to misread him. On November 1, Tony, the guy who needed no assurance, wrote to Julie from Bradenton: "Today we played the White Sox. I had one hit in three times at bat. During the game we were winning, 2-1. I was playing right field. The batter for the White Sox hit a line drive over the second baseman's head and I came running in and dove and caught the ball. The bases were loaded at the time. I saved the game and everyone told me I did a great job. It made me feel real good."

And three weeks later, Tony, the guy who didn't care what others thought of him, wrote, "All the players like me a lot. Every time we go on a road trip they ask me to sing. Me and Bob Guindon sing together. We have a lot of fun together."

Gradually, Tony's baseball playing evened up with his ego. With perhaps Mr. Campbell's Little League lecture resurrected in his head ("Tony, if you're afraid of this little baseball . . . ") he willed himself to hang in stubbornly on the inside stuff. If the pitchers tested him, no way would Tony Conigliaro give in. So when a fastball hissed an inch from his chin and pushed him off the plate, he'd step back in just as close, if not a little closer. He knew that to move farther away from the plate was to move further away from the major leagues. "He didn't budge an inch," Ryan states. "He just stood his ground and didn't give an inch. The makeup was there. No fear. He was fearless."

Off the field he got comfortable quickly, too. Ryan saw no homesick tears on his roommate's pillow. Ryan says, "The living away from home—it fell right into place for him." Tony missed his mother's cooking and he desperately missed Julie, now a senior at Lynn English, but he was seventeen years old and getting paid to play baseball in a sunny place. He thought the beach on the gulf was beautiful (he mailed shells to Julie) and got a kick out of consuming oranges straight from the trees after practice. He enjoyed the camaraderie with Ryan, who was impressed by the rookie roomie who could cook Italian and knew all the words to the top hits. "I'd say, 'Sing me to sleep, Roomie,' and he'd sing 'What's Your Name?' or something and I'd be out in a couple of minutes," Ryan recalls. The pair hit it off, despite Ryan's outranking him at dinner and Conigliaro's *capitoso*. "He did not like being told what to do," according to Ryan, who remembers suggesting that his roomie make his bed once in a while. "Go f--- yourself," Tony retorted. "You make it." Ryan was amused.

The roomies were different in many ways. For example, Ryan liked to drink and Tony had only an occasional beer. (Once in high school, Tony and Julie took a bottle of orange juice and a bottle of vodka to a drive-in, consumed a great deal of both during the movie, then returned to their respective homes to throw up. Recalling the incident a year later, Tony pronounced, "Never again.") Nevertheless, the roommates became pals, mostly because they shared a natural exuberance. "You felt like something was going to happen when you were with him," Ryan observes. "He was fun to be around. Tony enjoyed. He enjoyed a good meal; he ate very slowly. He enjoyed a good song. He enjoyed a good woman. He enjoyed a good car. He just enjoyed."

Sometimes Tony enjoyed going off on his own. Part of him was a loner, which over the years would confound friends and teammates who were less understanding than Ryan. "He had his way," Ryan reflects. "It made no difference what anybody thought." Tony made some of his solitary expeditions to Bradenton High School dances; he was, after all, just seventeen. At Halloween, Ryan tagged along to see his roomie in action. Tony took over the floor and a crowd gathered to watch the smooth, handsome Yankee demonstrate all the latest dances, including "the Mechanical," accompanied by the "the Monster Mash."

The southern girls loved the tall, dark charmer with the funny accent. "He had every girl in Bradenton at our door," Ryan asserts. "He had every girl's boyfriend in Bradenton at our door, too. I'd say, 'Damn, Roomie, are we going to have a fight every night?' " Tony wasn't shy. Ryan shook his head every time he watched his roommate stroll up to a girl who was standing with her boyfriend and whisk her away to dance. "Like I said, he was fearless," Ryan notes.

Not really. He was terrified of losing Julie. The belles of Bradenton were fine for a dance and a date, but Tony was crazy about the girl back home. His letters to Julie were filled with the anguish and longing of a teenager in love, faraway and insecure. He wrote: "You don't realize how much you love a person until you leave them a short time. It's only been four days now and I miss you so much I could cry" and "I never said you didn't love me. But I did say that I love you more than you love me" and "I just got done talking to you and I am feeling great. Your voice was what I needed. I love you more and more every day" and "I live for your letters."

He had always been the jealous type: Julie was forbidden to wear a two-piece bathing suit to the beach without him. Distance made it more intense. He demanded Julie report, in excruciating detail, any amorous advances made toward her. He hated the idea of her being alone at dances and parties and football games, surrounded by North Shore smoothies who knew her boyfriend was two thousand miles away. His jealousy sometimes injected inelegance into his love letters: "If you went out with boys, I'd shit." He assured her over and over he stayed far away from girls in Bradenton, which was untrue. It was also a not uncommon double standard for a macho-class American male in 1962. A guy could play alley cat while the "good" girl he would marry waited at home.

Tony made it clear to Julie that he wanted to marry her. He wrote: "With all my heart I wish we were married. As far as I'm concerned, you are the only girl in the world" and "When we get married we will have everything." He also knew this sort of talk was his father's worst nightmare. Sal didn't forbid his son to marry Julie because he understood hard-headedness—that would be like telling him to make his bed. Sal took the passive-aggressive path, prodding his son with such teases as "I'll bet you three hundred dollars you'll end up marrying Julie before you're twenty." Reflexively, Tony would respond, "No way, Dad. You're wrong."

Far away in Bradenton, listening to "All Alone Am I" in his hotel room, Tony wasn't so sure. In bed watching television (*The Tonight Show,* with its new, young host Johnny Carson, was a favorite), he wrote to Julie: "I don't think I can wait until I'm twenty to marry you" and "In a way, we can't blame my father. He wants me to be the best and he feels that if I am going with a girl my mind won't be on baseball. I'm proving that I can be quite a ballplayer even though I'm going with Julie Markakis. By the way, my father likes you very much. He realizes that there is no breaking us up."

Tony C and Julie Markakis had been high school sweethearts, although they went to rival schools. Tony's love for Julie would last well beyond their steady dating days, as evidenced in the many letters he wrote her during his travels. (Photo courtesy of Julie Markakis)

In letter after letter he counted off the days until he would see her again. He was seventeen and everyone told him he had all the time in the world, but Tony hated to stand in line—for the batting cage, for the bigger pork chop, for the major leagues, for Julie Markakis. Just before his Eastern Air Lines flight home to Boston, he wrote: "While watching TV I just heard that a plane carrying seventeen people crashed and all seventeen were killed. I hope to Christ I come in okay. I'd hate to die after all this waiting."

Tony's plane landed at ten at night, and despite the late hour, an elaborate Italian feast was spread out for him at the house. He was glad to be back, eating Teresa's cooking, seeing the pride in Sal's face, hearing about the athletic exploits of Billy and Richie, holding Julie's hand. A couple of months far from home had helped him be more appreciative. "It's worth being away because there is nothing like coming home," he had told Julie in his final letter from Bradenton.

Spring training was just three months away and there was so much to do. Nine days before Tony went to Florida for the first time, the family had moved to a new house on Parsons Drive in Swampscott, a shore town north of Lynn and a lot more suburban than East Boston. Tony loved poking around the place. He enjoyed visiting old high school haunts with Julie, this time with the clout of a returning professional baseball player. He went pheasant hunting with Alex Markakis in the high grass around Suffolk Downs.*

At 10:45 on New Year's Eve, Tony and Julie celebrated one year of going steady. He dipped into his bonus money and bought himself a dream cruiser, a white 1963 Ford Galaxie convertible. One night when Alex was sleeping over at the Conigliaro home, he awoke at 3:00 A.M. when he heard noises in the garage. There he found Tony in the car with a rag, Q-tips, and toothpicks, polishing the floor shift and meticulously cleaning the chrome around the radio.

---

*Their single rabbit-hunting expedition to Georgetown, Massachusetts, ended in disaster when Tony merely wounded the first bunny he shot at. The animal's terrible cries badly shook Tony, who chased it down, beat it to death with the butt of his rifle, and vowed to stick to birds.

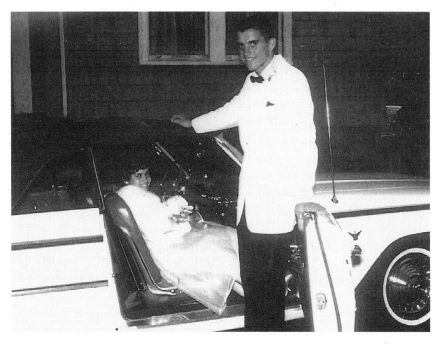

Tony C celebrated a year of going steady with Julie by using part of his signing-bonus money to buy himself a dream cruiser, better for him to show his best gal a great time on Prom Night. (Photo courtesy of Julie Markakis)

Tony also worked on his baseball. The new home in Swampscott had a finished basement outfitted with a weight set, and Tony put himself on a training regimen. For long hours every day he lifted weights and swung a leaded bat. Lifting was rare at the time among baseball players, who were heavily discouraged from weight training—they were warned they'd get muscle-bound and lose flexibility. But Tony had to make himself stronger, and he was going to do things his way. Embarrassed in Bradenton, especially by his lack of power, he was thankful it was just the Instructional League and his lousy statistics hadn't gone into the books. Now he pumped iron and hefted the heavy bat, promising himself he would never be embarrassed like that again.

In March, Tony reported to the Red Sox's minor-league spring-training camp in Ocala, Florida. To leave home and to play pro ball were easier the second time around. Although the Hotel Marion was a lot like the Hotel Dixie Grande, he was no longer the greenest player in the clubhouse. When a teammate named Denny Price got discouraged and homesick and packed his bags to leave, it was Tony who soothed the kid and convinced him to stick. The competition no longer daunted him. At last, his letters back home to Julie Markakis excitedly recounted home runs: ". . . my second home run. *What a blast!* Today I hit the ball good again" and "I knocked the crap out of the ball yesterday. I sure hope I can keep it up."

The weight work paid off, and Tony kept it up. In those days before account executives and legal secretaries did a Nautilus circuit at lunchtime, Tony's techniques were primitive. He thought his right arm was crucial to generate power with his bat, so he worked on it almost exclusively. "Hey, Rico, take a look at this," Tony called one day to infielder Rico Petrocelli. He made a muscle with his right arm. "It looked like a tennis ball popping out of his arm," Petrocelli relates. "The definition in his arm was just incredible; his right arm. His left arm was sort of atrophied."

Tony separated himself from the pack. Ocala was managed by Eddie Popowski, a compact, lovable baseball lifer whose career had started by barnstorming in the 1930s with the bearded House of David team. Pop noticed the kid put a lot of extra time in the batting cage and was getting stronger. "He loved to swing a bat," Popowski remembers.

Ocala's hitting and outfielding coach was Don "Footsie" Lenhardt, who had played for the Saint Louis Browns, Red Sox, and Orioles in the early fifties. Lenhardt took one look at Tony's sweet swing and knew exactly what he had to do: nothing. "You don't fool with something like that," Lenhardt declares.

Tony's outfield play, however, needed tinkering. His obvious flaw was throwing: He brought his arm around at the ten-o'clock position instead of over the top at twelve o'clock. Throwing with the arm at three-quarters made the ball spin and tail away from infielders. Lenhardt told Tony he had seen only one outfielder, Kenny Wood of the Browns in the 1940s, throw three-quarters and survive in the big leagues. Only one. Tony got the message and worked endlessly on proper throws.

"We went through so many drills," says Lenhardt. "He wanted to get to the big leagues, that's what he wanted to do. I think he was very driven, more so than some of the others."

Tony could see his dream take shape. He wrote to Julie: "You wanted to know about how I'm doing in baseball. Well, honey, I am doing great. I am hustling more than anyone here. I look as good or better than all the guys here. I love baseball. It is a tough but great life."

Ocala was a quiet town, too hot for Tony's tastes (he got an extra-short haircut to stay cooler) with too many mosquitoes at night. But he enjoyed baseball life. He felt comfortable enough amid the team to pull practical jokes. One time he sent a telegram to a pitcher inform-ing him that he was wanted with the big club right away, and he howled when he saw the poor fellow lugging packed suitcases through the cafeteria. Tony shot pool, went to the movies, and, of course, chased girls. They chased him, too. In *Seeing It Through,* he described going to a doctor's appointment in Ocala and striking up a conversation with a woman who was "about forty-five years old, but she was really a good-looking woman." When he came out of the doctor's office, she was waiting for him and asked him if he wanted a lift. "I wound up staying with her for the next two weeks," he wrote. The women's age and the duration of his stay were likely exaggerated, but the essence of the story rings true.

Tony stayed in his own room long enough to write love letters to Julie Markakis: "There's people all around but I don't here [sic] a sound, just the lonely beating of my heart. You know them words, don't you? It's just how I feel right now," and " 'Two Young Lovers' is on the radio now. It drives me up a wall. It seems that song was maid [sic] for us" and "We'll get married because we love each other, we love KIDS, we love being with each other for the rest of our lives."

At the end of camp players received their minor-league assign-ments. Tony hoped to go to the Red Sox's Double-A team in Pittsfield, Massachusetts, in the western part of the state. Instead, he drew the lower, Single-A team in Wellsville, in the western part of New York. Tony was hardly disappointed, for at last the practice and prep were over and he would get to play a real season of professional baseball. The Red Sox chose the lower-class minor-league competition to give Tony Conigliaro, of all people, a chance to build his confidence.

～

Before he headed north, Tony asked Red Sox scouting director Neil Mahoney for permission to report to Wellsville by way of Swampscott. Tony wanted to swing home to pick up his beloved Ford Galaxie convertible, which was perfect for cruising a minor-league town on hot summer nights. Mahoney agreed but warned him not to be late. He had three days to get to Wellsville.

One afternoon while he was home, Tony and Alex Markakis were cruising the North Shore in the Ford and decided to run up to Lynn English to give Julie a ride after school. Tony rolled the car to a stop in front of the high school crowd, and soaked up the admiring glances—for himself and his car. Then he glanced at the front door of the school and could barely believe his eyes. Julie was walking out alongside some guy named Dave.

This was too much. While he was in Ocala, Julie had been elected Miss Lynn English and Dave had been elected Mister Lynn English, and they were required to accompany one another to a dance. When Julie dutifully reported this to Tony—assuring him the arrangement was strictly platonic—Tony was predictably enraged. Now here was Julie, his girl, walking out of school right next to this Dave character.

Julie climbed into the convertible and Tony glared at Dave, who glared back. Tony started the car to leave. Dave passed in front of the car, blocking Tony's exit, and took his sweet time as he ambled past.

"Just go, just go!" Alex said to Tony, who took his friend's sound advice and squealed away from the curb, all the while shooting a hateful stare at Dave, who shot a hateful stare right back.

Tony drove to Julie's house and told her he wanted to run some errands with Alex. As soon as the front door closed behind her, Tony swiveled his head toward Alex, looked at him with blazing eyes, and muttered through clenched teeth, "I can *not* let him get away with that."

"What are you going to do, Tony?" asked Alex.

"We'll go to his house. We'll go to his house. I got to talk to him."

As the convertible roared down the causeway to Dave's family's home in Nahant, the pair concocted a plan. Alex would slide into the driver's seat, in case a quick getaway were needed, while Tony went up to the door.

"What if he hits me?" Tony wanted to know.

"You've got to hit him first," declared Alex.

When they reached Dave's house, Tony bounded up the front steps, rang the bell, and banged on the door. From behind the wheel of the convertible, Alex watched the inside door open, then the screen door open, and Dave step halfway onto the porch. Words were exchanged, and suddenly Tony reached back with his right hand nearly to his ankle and delivered a devastating punch to Dave's face.

"Tony used the same power he used to hit the ball over the fence," Alex remembers. "Dave's face exploded. It sounded like somebody threw a cabbage against a stone wall. There was blood everywhere."

Dave staggered backward into the doorway as Dave's mother suddenly appeared and stepped over her son, yelling and swinging at Tony, who backpedaled and screamed back. Alex jumped out of the car, ran onto the porch, half-dragged Tony down the steps, and pushed him into the passenger seat. Alex floored the Ford and careened wildly down the causeway.

Tony was far from calm, too. His chinos were splattered with Dave's blood. Worse, he cradled his right hand against his chest. His thumb was twisted at a strange angle and bone poked up through the skin. "What's my father going to say? What's my father going to say?" Tony wailed. A half-hour later, Tony sat in a doctor's office, a wet cast on his right thumb, and sobbed, "What a mistake I made."

Sal and Uncle Vinnie were at a ballfield in Swampscott watching Billy play, when they saw Alex approaching. Immediately, they knew something was wrong.

"What happened? Where's Tony?" Sal demanded to know.

Alex brought them back to the car, where Tony sat with bloody pants and plaster-encased thumb. Sal and Vinnie threw a fit of operatic proportions.

"My stomach dropped," Vinnie remembers. "It was one of the worst days of my life."

They sped off in their cars, leaving Alex alone on the sidewalk to find his own way home. Sal would place a huge chunk of blame for the disaster on Alex—something always seemed to go wrong for Tony when he was with Alex. "I was persona non grata after that," Alex observes. And Sal was convinced more than ever that having a steady girl would only get Tony into trouble. "It didn't do our situation any good," Julie admits.

The broken thumb put Tony Conigliaro through six weeks of hell. His father concocted a story to tell the Red Sox, that Tony suffered the break on a backyard batting practice pitch from Uncle Vinnie; then he refused to even speak to his son. Sometimes when Tony first awoke in the morning, it would cross his mind that the whole disaster had been a terrible dream. Then he'd look at his cast and he'd feel crushed and stupid all over again. In Wellsville, New York, the season played on without him. Tony had always hated to wait, yet now, on the verge of his big chance, he must wait, and it was all his fault.

At one point the thumb was x-rayed by a Red Sox doctor, who shook his head and put a real scare into Tony. The doctor didn't like the way the thumb was set. He speculated that it might need surgery, or maybe even to be broken and reset. Tony couldn't open his thumb wide enough to hold a baseball. There was concern he wouldn't be able to throw again. Then he went to another specialist, who ruled out surgery and told Tony to exercise the thumb by gripping a towel and twisting it as tightly as he could. Gradually, Tony was able to hold a ball. There was nerve damage—his thumb clicked every time he threw—but at the end of May, Tony stood in his kitchen with his bag packed for the ten-hour drive to Wellsville.

Sal took a look at his son and burst into tears. "I'm sorry I've been so hard on you," he said. Then he hugged Tony closely and continued, "I'm sorry about what's happened, but you know how much I love you, how much I want you to make good. Let's forget about all that now. I want you to go out there and play the hell out of that league."

~5~

THE ROAD TO WELLSVILLE

WELLSVILLE PRESENTED EVERY CLICHÉ OF BUSH-LEAGUE BASEBALL. The town was dead—the players called it Dullsville. The decrepit team bus had mushy suspension, hard-rubber tires, and a sputtery engine. Once, after a collision with a deer on a secluded back road, the bus quit and left the stranded players to listen to crickets and swat mosquitoes until daybreak. The team quarters were in Cook's Motel, which reminded visitors of the Bates Motel from *Psycho.* The home field was a cow pasture and a few wooden bleachers.

The good news was that it was within driving distance of Boston. Sal, Teresa, and Richie made the ten-hour journey and sat deep in their chairs around Cook's staring at one another and complaining that there were only three stations on the television. Then a thunderstorm rolled through and knocked the television out altogether. The family went to the only theater in town to see *Viva Las Vegas,* attended one game at the cow pasture (Tony homered as they walked into the ballpark), then couldn't take it anymore, not even for Tony. "It's not like we don't love you," Sal explained as they packed to hurry back to civilization. "But we've got to get out of here."

Tony was amused. "Now you know why I'm working so hard," he told his father. "So I don't have to play in a place like this again."

After his postponed arrival, Tony waited to crack the Wellsville outfield, wobbled to an oh-for-sixteen start, then made it clear he wouldn't have to play in cow pastures for long. He fed on the Single-A pitchers. And he was vintage Tony, older and stronger and getting paid good money to play, but still the Little Leaguer telling the pitcher to put one

45

over the plate so he could swat it onto Saratoga Avenue. He charmed and annoyed his teammates with astonishing lack of humility—and to the dismay of his detractors, he did what he said he would do. "Tony and I hit it off right away, because I was the same way. I understood him," recalls George Scott, who played shortstop and shared the third and fourth slots in the lineup with Tony that summer. "I thought I was confident. But I've never seen an athlete with the kind of drive and determination he had. I don't think a lot of guys on the ballclub liked him because he was cocky. He would tell you what he was going to do and he would go up to the plate and do it. People resent that. They get jealous of that. They wonder why they're not able to do it."

One night in Geneva, New York, the wind wailed straight in from center field and fastball pitcher Bob Lee started for the home team. The Wellsville players agreed no one would hit any home runs that night. Around the sixth inning, Tony approached Scott in the dugout. "I'm going to go up there and I'm going to look for one of his fastballs and I'm going to turn it around and hit it into that wind and hit it out of here," Tony said. "Oh, sure," muttered Scott, who watched Tony step to the plate and line a home run to dead-center field.

In another game, in Jamestown, New York, Tony misplayed two ground balls in center field, each for a three-base error. He stomped into the dugout after the inning, angry at himself, and ranted to the bench, "I'm going to hit a home run on the first pitch that guy throws me. I don't care where he throws that first pitch, I'm going to hit it out of the ballpark. He can throw it over my head, I'm going to hit it out of the ballpark. He can throw it on the ground, I'm going to hit it out of the ballpark. I just don't care." The first-pitch homer sailed deep into the night to left-center field. "Tony was that kind of a guy," observes Scott. "If he did something to hurt the team, he wanted to redeem himself."

Tony prospered, but by the second week of July he was learning the huge difference between high school and the pros. There were a lot more games and a lot more pressure. And even a dream job can be a job. "Day after day of bus trips and games can get a guy real tired," he wrote to Julie Markakis. "People really think that baseball is all fun. When you play pro ball, everything is for keeps. It's just like any other job—you have to work to keep it." Tony, the ultimate battler, would not surrender easily to tedium of any sort. He wanted to play. He made sure there was fun, even in Dullsville. He moved from Cook's Motel into a bungalow with team-mates Mario Pagano, Dave Casey, and Bill Nagle. More than three decades later, Pagano remembers Tony's dragging him onstage at the town hot spot, the Hotel Wellsville, to accompany him on "Where or When."

Tony participated in the team's standard practical joke for new-comers, the Girl in Room 504. The victim was told that there was a woman, the mythic minor-league pushover, in the room who agreed to have sex with a portion of the Wellsville lineup, one at a time. The vic-tim was maneuvered to fourth in line. One by one, the guys in front of him entered the room, made a racket, and emerged disheveled, panting, and mumbling, "That was the best ever." When it was his turn, the vic-tim eagerly entered the darkened room; but the lights flicked on, and instead of a baseball roundheel, he was faced by his teammates convulsed in laughter. In his autobiography, Tony tells of being party to the joke but not falling for it. George Scott remembers that *everybody* fell for it.

Like anyone who watched him turn on the charm, Scott mar-veled at Tony's brilliance with women. "Tony was tall and he was good-looking and he was cocky and he loved women," says Scott. "He went out with a different woman every night." But Scott, fresh out of high school, had never been on a real date in his life, and he didn't expect that to change in Wellsville. He was the only black player on the team, and there were practically no blacks in Wellsville or anywhere else in the New York-Penn circuit. Then one day at the ballpark, Tony came up to Scott and pointed out a blonde woman in the stands. "She's got a twin sister," Tony told him. "You want to come out on a double date?"

Scott could hardly believe what he was hearing. He had grown up in Greenville, Mississippi, in a poor, segregated part of the Delta where black men dared not even look too long at a white woman. Now he was being asked to date one, in public. In the summer of '63, that was rare, even way north in Wellsville, New York. A few months earlier Sammy Davis Jr. had been snubbed at the Kennedy White House because he was married to a white woman.

Tony convinced Scott to go. "I saw the girl. She was gorgeous," Scott says. "My legs felt like spaghetti. I've never been so humble in my whole life. Tony put me at ease. They all put me at ease. They could see that I was out in left field. Let me tell you, there weren't too many people like Tony." Tony, Scott, and the twin sisters went to dinner and dancing in

Olean and stayed out late. "It didn't slow us down any," says Scott. "I think we both hit home runs the next day."

As for his romantic future, Tony still had no doubt he was going to marry Julie. Twin sisters and the Girl in Room 504 were fun, but they couldn't give him what Julie did. He wrote her: "Love is great, isn't it? I don't know how you feel but I feel good that I have someone to love. Just to know I've got you waiting makes me feel real good. I've been writing every day lately and I'll keep doing it because I feel like I am talking to you. I like to tell you my problems. I like to tell you when I'm happy."

He was crazy about her. Tony wanted Julie to accompany his family on a visit to Wellsville. When Sal dragged his feet about it, Tony sent her twenty dollars—ten dollars for gas and ten dollars for food along the way—to come on her own (suitably chaperoned, of course, by another player's girlfriend from Rhode Island). He told her to invest in some pots and pans for when they got married. He was happy to hear she had learned how to make meatballs. "We will be married and we will live with each other and love each other forever," he wrote. Tony never let his teammates see this side of him. If he were on the phone to Julie and any of them were in earshot, he wouldn't say "I love you" to her, because he didn't want his teammates to tease him about it and he enjoyed his reputation as a serial seducer.

For Tony the worst thing about Wellsville was that it was too far from the big leagues, and he made sure he would never see the place again. The season that started with his brooding at home with a broken thumb ended with his batting .363 with twenty-four home runs and seventy-four runs batted in over eighty-three games. He was named the New York-Penn League Rookie of the Year and Most Valuable Player, and he treasured the acclaim. "I am going to get my trophy on September 1. This night is called Tony Conigliaro Night," he wrote to Julie. "I can't wait."

Tony was home just a few weeks before he shipped out for another hitch in the Instructional League, this time in Sarasota, Florida. As his plane prepared to land in Tampa, Tony thought back a year earlier, when he was just out of high school on a night flight to Florida, skinny, scared, and wiping Mike Ryan's vomit off his pants. Now he was strong and comfortable and, as far as he was concerned, on the verge of the big leagues. Ironically, as the plane descended, he was also a little airsick.

He had cause—not that he needed any—for optimism. The Red Sox placed him on the forty-man roster, which meant he would go to spring training in 1964 with the major leaguers in Scottsdale, Arizona. No one told him he was close to making the big club, but he could feel it. "Well, honey, I'm on my way," he wrote Julie. "I have a Big League contract and all I have to do now is work hard and hope for the best."

In his first game in Sarasota, he hit a four-hundred-foot home run to left center. That night he assured Julie in a letter, "I will love you when I'm in the majors." Neil Mahoney, general manager Mike "Pinky" Higgins, and manager Johnny Pesky dropped by the team for a few days, and Tony, as usual, rose to the occasion. He wrote to Julie, "I did real good today. I got two hits in front of the big boys, Mahoney and Higgans [sic]" and "Today I did great. I only got one hit but I hit the ball extra good. I hit two balls that would have been out at Fenway Park. Neil Mahoney, Higgans and Pesky remarked on how good I looked. It's quite a feeling to get a compliment from them." On the day he left Sarasota, Pesky—who lived in a house not far from the Conigliaros in Swampscott—took the kid out to dinner and told him how impressed he was.

For Tony compliments were an invitation to push harder. In hours of extra practice, Eddie Popowski hit fly balls to him in right field—high pops, twisty liners, one-hoppers, and anything else Tony might encounter in a real game. Popowski stationed Tony at third base to get him accustomed to fielding grounders. He also drilled him on the fine art of smart base running. Tony was grateful. He knew he would make the majors, but he wanted more than that. "You know how much I want to make the Big Leagues," Tony wrote Julie. "It's got to happen and when it does I'll be one of the best Major Leaguers that ever played ball in Fenway Park. I don't want to be just a Big Leaguer. I want to be a great one and the only way to be great is by working."

In Sarasota Tony watched a lot of television (he enjoyed the movies *The Blackboard Jungle* and *Hercules*) and went to the movies (he gave two thumbs-up to *Jack the Ripper* and *The Naked and the Dead*) and lounged around the pool a lot. The Hotel Sarasota Terrace was a dream, mostly because it was air-conditioned. Tony and a teammate bought a beat-up 1953 Ford for seventy-five dollars for running around town. In the meantime, Tony daydreamed about the car waiting back home for him: Just before he left, he had ordered the ultimate teen dream ride, a red Chevy Corvette.

Julie also waited back home. His letters to her from Sarasota were slightly less plaintive, but he still counted the days until he would return home to her (and the Corvette and his mother's cooking). He still talked about getting married, but he and Julie wrangled bitterly over a trivial matter, the way only teen lovers can. She wanted a hope chest, and he didn't want to get one. He wrote, "As for us getting married, there is no doubt in my mind. I want to marry you. I'll always want to marry you. The only thing that bothers me is that I don't want to get a hope chest. I asked my mother about it and she thought it wasn't necessary to get it."

He was young, tanned, and strong, on the threshold of fame, with a loving family, a pretty girl wanting to marry him, and a sporty car waiting back home. "I didn't go to church today," he wrote Julie. "In fact, I haven't gone at all. Just one Sunday. When I get back home, I'm going to go every week. I should because God has given me a lot and I should be greatful [sic]."

In camp on a Friday afternoon Tony and a handful of teammates were sunning themselves around the hotel pool when someone ran up to announce that President Kennedy had been shot. They sat in silence and prayed for him. For Tony and the rest of his generation, it was the first inkling that, in an instant, everything can go terribly wrong. "Kennedy is dead," he wrote to Julie the next day. "What can I say? I cried the same as you cried. He's gone and God has a great man by his side. . . . It just goes to show you. Anyone can die at anytime, so while we're alive we should be grateful and enjoy life."

Not long after Tony returned to Swampscott, Sal was driving down Western Avenue in Lynn when he rolled past Young's furniture store and thought he saw someone familiar in the window. It was Tony and his best pal from Saint Mary's, Freddie Atkinson. Sal parked and went into the store to find out what on earth the boys were up to. He didn't like what he discovered: Tony was purchasing a cedar hope chest for Julie.

Tony couldn't wait to get to Scottsdale. Although he was only nineteen (on January 7), he felt overdue for the big leagues. He kept thinking about Pesky's compliment in Sarasota, and he read in the newspaper that Mike Higgins, while attending the winter meetings, had said Tony "stands up to the plate like Kaline." Tony loved that. Al Kaline had broken into the Detroit Tigers outfield when he was eighteen. In February, Larry Claflin of the *Boston Record* led a story with a prediction: "If Lou [*sic*] Clinton and Roman Mejias fail to hit as well as they are expected to for the Red Sox this summer, they are going to find an ambitious kid from Swampscott named Tony Conigliaro in right field some night while they fret on the bench."

Sal and Uncle Vinnie watched Tony's expectations soar and worried about him. They sat him down for a talk. "Look, Choo," Sal began, "I just wonder if you wouldn't be better off going to the minors next season and playing every day, rather than sticking with the Red Sox and sitting on the bench. I wouldn't want you to be too disappointed if you don't make it."

"Just don't get your hopes up too high," Uncle Vinnie added.

Tony looked at them as if they were crazy. "I don't know what you guys are worrying about," he declared. "If Pesky gives me a shot, I'll come back with the big club."

Tony loved Scottsdale, with its dry air, pink desert, and orange mountains. And, at last, it was the big leagues. The team quarters in the Ramada Inn were strictly top drawer, certainly a long way from Cook's Motel. Long road trips would no longer be by yellow school bus—the Red Sox flew by jet to far-flung Cactus League outposts.

It was the big leagues, but he was only a rookie. Early in camp Tony was introduced to the irritating major-league caste system. Major-league clubhouses, like military academies and English boarding schools, are ruled by status, class, and rank. Tony was a plebe. He discovered this firsthand when veterans—such as Carl Yastrzemski, Bill Monboquette, and Dick Radatz—acted as if he didn't exist. He *really* knew it the day he emerged from the dugout with his head down and a baseball whizzed past his ear. Tony looked up and saw Dick Williams leering back at him. Williams was a well-traveled, thirty-five-year-old outfielder hanging on with the Red Sox. He had come up in the Brooklyn Dodgers system, which always seemed to ratchet up a fellow's arrogance a notch or two.

"Watch where you're going, bush," Williams hollered.

Tony, a true baseball democrat, didn't like the hazing any better than he liked Mike Ryan's grabbing the bigger bed in Bradenton. A few days later, he was playing catch with veteran first baseman Dick Stuart when he saw Williams emerge from the dugout with his head down. Tony fired a baseball at his head.

"Watch where you're going, bush!" Tony yelled at him. Williams trod across the lawn to set the rookie straight. Stuart, himself not popular among veteran players critical of his sometimes lackadaisical and selfish play, sided with the kid and shooed Williams away.

Tony was never strong on protocol, and he wasn't about to change now—not for Dick Williams, not even for Ted Williams. A highlight of every Red Sox spring camp was the grand arrival of Ted, who as special batting instructor dropped by for a week or so, checked out the hitters, spoke at the top of his lungs, held court, and generally poured legend all over everybody. This spring his arrival date was uncertain because he was in New Zealand—perfect for a mythic figure who could have been written by Hemingway and played by John Wayne.

After he showed up, Williams was hitting fungoes to Tony when Ted shouted, "See if you can catch this one, bush, and I'll give you a Cadillac."

Tony playfully yelled back, "I already have a Cadillac," which was exactly what Ted Williams would have shouted when he was a young, skinny, brash rookie.

Later the Red Sox took batting practice under Williams's critical eye. When Tony stepped out of the cage, he heard the magic words from Teddy Ballgame: "Don't change that solid stance of yours, no matter what you're told." Tony was flattered. He was not upset a few days later when he read Williams's quote about his chances to make the big club: "He's just a kid. He's two years away." It couldn't bother him; Tony knew better.

Scottsdale was the first place Tony and the Boston press had a chance to spend a lot of time together, and they hit it off. In those days the written word still ruled, and correspondents from the *Boston Herald, Boston Globe, Boston Record, Boston Traveler,* and *Boston American* made Scottsdale the hub of the New England sports world.

Tony was in the right place at the right time. Red Sox fans were starved for something to cheer about: The team hadn't fielded a serious

It's spring training, 1965, and the Splendid Splinter, Ted Williams, is giving Tony C a few pointers. In this case Williams appears to be showing Tony how to break in a glove. (Boston Herald archives photo)

contender since 1950 and hadn't won more than it lost since 1958. The Boston press was starved for something to write about: Ted Williams had retired in 1960 and took all the color with him. The only star on the Red Sox was Carl Yastrzemski. He was a first-rate player who had won the American League batting title the year before, but he didn't hit a lot of home runs (fourteen in '63), and he approached the game as if it were grim work. There wasn't much to fill inky headlines. And then came Tony.

The newspaper boys loved him. He was a local kid, which went a long way in the most parochial big city in America. He was a slugger, a right-handed power hitter on deck for the coziest left field in baseball. He was tall and handsome and charming and having fun. He was young and outspoken, brimming with ego and ability. He was good copy. Instead of walking away from the spotlight like Yaz, Tony ran toward it. The writers pulled for him, which didn't hurt a rookie trying to leapfrog up the Red Sox's ziggurat.

Tony hit a lot of home runs in batting practice. At the start of the exhibition season he played part-time, did everything right, and the writers started to ask Pesky about the kid's chances of sticking with the club for Opening Day in New York. "He's got a lot of base hits to get between now and April 14," the manager observed.

During an exhibition game against the San Francisco Giants in El Paso, Texas, Tony didn't play but saw exactly what he wanted. "Willie Mays hit a home run out of sight," he wrote Julie. "It cleared the right-field wall by one hundred feet. He's great. Some day I'd like to be like him. The people love him. The thing I like most about him is that he hustles just like any other ballplayer. Some ballplayers tend to get a little lazy. He's good to watch."

Two weeks into the exhibition schedule, Pesky—who was getting nothing from his veteran outfielders Clinton, Mejias, and Dick Williams—granted Tony his first start against the Cleveland Indians in Tucson. Tony doubled three times. When he returned to Scottsdale, twenty-five fan letters from Boston waited for him and adoring dispatches began to arrive steadily. "The fan mail is still coming in," Tony wrote Julie. "The people are great to me. I hope I can live up to what they want."

Teresa, who had never flown in a plane before, and Sal traveled from Boston for a visit. On their first day in Scottsdale they watched from the third-base seats when Tony, who had entered the game as a defensive replacement in the seventh inning, batted against Indians fire-baller Gary Bell in the eighth. Tony crushed the second pitch to dead-center field. The ball flew over the fence, at a spot marked 430 feet, landed in the road that ran outside the ballpark, and rolled until it struck a barrel on the Scottsdale rodeo grounds across the street. A couple of stadium workers, who were fixing the scoreboard, marked where the ball landed. Baseball writer Larry Claflin of the *Boston Record* got a tape mea-sure and calculated that the blast had traveled 572 feet in the air. Sal exclaimed, "I have never seen Tony hit a ball that far." Tony wrote Julie that it was "the thrill of my life." The home run got everybody's atten-tion: Pesky, Higgins, and newspaper readers back home. "The fan mail is still coming in," he wrote Julie. "I guess the people in Boston really like me. It makes up for all the jerks in Lynn."

Everything was different in the big leagues, even the women. Tony roomed with Tony Horton, the California bonus baby who had worked out with him at Fenway Park in the summer of '62. Horton was eccentric and a little on the wild side: Years later, when he was playing for the Red Sox, Horton took a seat, arms folded, in the Boston dugout next to staid manager Billy Herman, his head decorated with a huge hairdo and beard fashioned out of shaving cream (Horton's baseball career ended with the Indians in 1970 when he suffered a nervous breakdown). Still, they became friends. Both Tonys liked a good time and both had large appetites for fleeting romances.

In Scottsdale the pair visited a nightclub called J. D.'s and were pleased by the large number of pretty young women. Later Tony described how he and Horton met two women and invited them back to the hotel. Doubting that the girls would actually show—the percentage had been low in minor-league barroom encounters—they met another pair and invited them back to the room. Eventually, they invited eight women to the room, and two by two they began to show up. With each knock at the door, Tony and Horton hid their guests somewhere on the premises. In his autobiography Tony wrote that they stashed two visitors in the closet, two on the patio, two under the bed, and had two sitting on the couch chatting before the jig was up. "I guess I realized after that when you're a major-league ballplayer and you ask a girl out, she'll go," Tony wrote. The story seems too pat, like something out of a Matt Helm movie. But people who knew Conigliaro and Horton are sure they had plenty of girls in their room and at one time or another probably had to hide them in a closet.

Tony also renewed his friendship with Mike Ryan. One night in Scottsdale, Tony, Ryan, and Bobby Guindon went to a club and Tony found himself onstage, singing with the band. Tony cajoled Ryan and Guindon into joining him, and Tony sang "In the Still of the Night" while his teammates provided the background ooooo-wah-wahs. "Tony was a person who loved to be onstage and loved to have his friends with him," says Guindon.

Back home, Julie was a little uneasy. Tony was becoming a celebrity, and now it wasn't just the girls in Lynn who swooned over him, but girls all over New England and pretty soon New York, Chicago, Baltimore, and the rest of the American League. She didn't want to be just another high school sweetheart abandoned by a famous boyfriend. Tony didn't waver about getting married, but he was less specific about when. "It's true when you say I don't want to talk about marriage," he wrote to her. "But when the time comes, Julie Makarkis will be Julie Conigliaro." Sal, who couldn't forget seeing his son in the window of Young's buying a hope chest, was likely working on him. But Tony's mind was also on baseball, without prompting from his father. It looked like he was going to make it. Late one night in camp, he listened to the Beatles' "Twist and Shout" on the radio, then wrote to Julie, "If I keep it up you just might see me starting in Yankee Stadium. That will be the greatest thrill I could ever have."

The newspaper guys joined the chorus. Claflin wrote in the *Record,* "It would be quite an experiment if this product of East Boston were to open the season in the Red Sox outfield. Imagine what a boost it would be to Red Sox attendance." Higgins, the general manager, wanted to ripen Tony a little longer in the minors. Pesky, who thought Tony was the best young hitter he had seen since Ted Williams, wanted to keep the kid. "Let's give him a chance," Pesky told Higgins. "Let's give him a month or six weeks, and if he doesn't do it, we'll send him out."

Pesky found Sal at poolside and told him his son would be in Yankee Stadium on Opening Day. "I don't know if there were tears in his eyes or not," recalls Pesky. "But he was close."

Tony broke the good news to Julie in a letter, but he didn't mention making the big club until the fourth paragraph, as if he had known it all along. He underlined, "Honey I am coming back to Boston."

Bobby Guindon, the bonus baby who stayed in the minors as Tony rocketed to Fenway Park, assesses him: "He carried himself like he was above us. By God, then he went out and proved it. He *was* better than us."

~6~

A ROOKIE WHO HUGGED THE PLATE

ON TUESDAY, APRIL 14, 1964, HIS FIRST DAY IN THE MAJOR LEAGUES, TONY CONIGLIARO OVERSLEPT. His friends and family took this as testament to Tony's utter grace under pressure. What a cool customer! He was nineteen, about to debut at Yankee Stadium, and he snoozed. It was like Gordon Cooper's falling asleep in his Mercury capsule, but it was also testament to Tony's devotion to sleep. He awoke in the Hotel New Yorker, saw a heavy rain falling, rightly assumed Opening Day would be washed out, and simply stayed in bed.

He forgot there was a mandatory team workout. His roommate—veteran third baseman Frank Malzone—had bunked overnight with his family in the Bronx, so he wasn't there to remind the kid. Clubhouse attendant Don Fitzpatrick telephoned from the stadium and told Tony the sickening news: Everybody is here except you. Tony dressed in a hurry and grabbed a cab (in later accounts, Tony alternately said the cab ran out of gas or got a flat tire on the way uptown). When he finally arrived, he got a fatherly lecture from manager Pesky.

"For Chrissake, you've got a chance to play," Pesky said. "Don't screw it up." He fined Tony ten dollars.

Per custom during a rainout, baseball men loitered around the stuffy clubhouses and damp dugouts. On the Yankee bench the new New York manager, Yogi Berra, asked Boston reporters about this Red Sox rookie.

"How do you pronounce that new outfielder's name?" Berra wanted to know.

"Yogi from Dago Hill in Saint Louis asking a Bostonian how to pronounce *Conigliaro*? You'll be ostracized by all Italians," a newsman replied.

"Mine is a small name," Berra observed. "That new boy in Boston has a long one and it's tough to pronounce. They tell me he's a tall, skinny kid."

"Yes, and so were DiMaggio and Williams when they broke in," retorted the reporter.

Opening Day was postponed again on Wednesday because of wet grounds. On Thursday the outfield was still soggy, but the game went on. Lefty craftsman Whitey Ford started for the American League champion Yankees, looking for his two hundredth career victory. Bill Monboquette started for the Red Sox. Tony was penciled in at center field and batted seventh behind Chuck Schilling, Eddie Bressoud, Yastrzemski, Malzone, Stuart, and Clinton.

Tony was back at Yankee Stadium, just as he had predicted in 1962 when he played there with the Hearst All-Stars. (He could not keep his promise to return to the Polo Grounds as demolition on the hallowed ballyard was underway across the Harlem River as the Red Sox and Yankees played.) Somehow the place looked bigger. After two days of rainouts the crowd was small—only 12,709—but that was ten times what he had ever seen in Wellsville. On his way out to center field, Tony spied Mickey Mantle on his way in. They passed at second base, and the Mick said, "Hi, kid, how're you doing?" Even the unflappable Tony was awed. "Fine," he rasped.

Tony got his first chance in the first inning when he caught Phil Linz's routine fly ball. He got his first at-bat in the second inning with the bases loaded and none out, a perfect scene for the kid to become an instant hero. Instead, he nearly became an instant goat. He slashed a hard shot to third, where Clete Boyer stepped on the bag for one out and threw to second base for the second out. Bobby Richardson's relay to first base barely missed nabbing Tony for a triple play. He scored all the way from first, however, on catcher Bob Tillman's bloop single to right. Eddie Popowski had taught Tony to run the bases right.

In the Yankees second, Tom Tresh nailed a long line drive to the wall in right center and Tony made a nice running catch. The play brought him a warm round of applause and a four-shot photo sequence in the next day's *New York Times*.

In his next at-bat Tony singled for his first major-league hit. In his next at-bat, he showed that it took him about ninety minutes to get completely comfortable in the major leagues. Ford threw a pitch that bounced in the dirt. Tony thought he saw a moist spot on the ball—a spit ball. The rookie turned to the umpire and gestured out at Ford, 199-game winner and World Series hero.

"For crying out loud," Tony griped. "Why don't you make him wipe that stuff off the ball before he throws it?"

The Red Sox won, 4-3, in the eleventh inning. It wasn't Tony's style to debut quietly. He went one-for-four, got a photo spread in the *Times,* nearly hit into a triple play, and insulted a future Hall of Famer. And he was merely saving the real dramatics for the next day, when the Red Sox opened in Boston.

The scene begged Tony, who craved center stage, to do something big. The Red Sox played host to the Chicago White Sox. Fenway Park was

Before he would make history, Conigliaro took a few moments to learn a little about it. Here he is as a rookie visiting Yankee Stadium, inspecting the plaques of Gehrig et al. (UPI/Corbis-Bettman)

decorated with red, white, and blue bunting for the Friday afternoon game. For those days, the crowd was good: 20,213 (the Sox only averaged 10,904 that year). The game was dedicated to the martyred President Kennedy, with proceeds going to the Kennedy Library Fund. The box seats were packed with dignitaries: Saint Louis Cardinals legend Stan Musial, American League president Joe Cronin, former boxing champs Jack Dempsey and Gene Tunney, Massachusetts governor Endicott Peabody, Boston mayor John Collins, actress Carol Channing, actor Fredric March, Crazy Guggenheim himself, Frankie Fontaine, and the dead president's brother, the attorney general Robert Kennedy (who inadvertently amused the crowd when he thanked "all the Redskins, er, Red Sox" for their support). Tony's VIPs were there, too: Sal and Teresa, Billy and Richie, Uncle Vinnie and Aunt Phyllis, Julie Markakis, and even his old Little League coach, Ben Campbell.

Tony again batted seventh. There were two outs and the bases were empty when he strode to the plate for his first Fenway Park at-bat in the second inning. The public address announcer mispronounced his name and the fans gave him a nice stretch of applause. The Conigliaros had stood and clapped and were checking behind them to sit back down when they heard the crack of the bat and a roar. Tony smacked the first pitch from Joel Horlen way over the left-field wall. As he ran between first and second, Tony saw the ball leave the ballpark and gave his head a quick, nearly imperceptible shake. Even he didn't believe himself sometimes—the first pitch he saw at Fenway Park and he hit it for a home run! The television camera followed him into the dugout, so the folks watching him could see his great, handsome smile as he was congratulated by his teammates.

The Conigliaros erupted in joy. Julie cried. Uncle Vinnie was stunned. He opened his mouth to holler, but nothing would come out. "A lot of nights," he declares more than thirty years later, "I still lay awake in bed, thinking about it." After the game, Tony joked with reporters that hitting a home run was the least he could do, since all those dignitaries had come out to see his Boston debut.

Alex Markakis, who had watched the game from a third-base seat, on the opposite side from the Conigliaros, rode home with Tony after the game. They had trouble getting the red Corvette out of the players' parking lot—fans mobbed the car, trying to touch Tony and begging for autographs.

Alex signed a few autographs, too. Later, at around nine o'clock on the spring evening, Tony and Alex roared down Union Street in Lynn in the Corvette and passed a newsboy hawking the evening newspapers. The headline read: "Conigliaro Homers." Tony slammed on the brakes, backed up the car, and rolled down the window.

"You want a paper, mister?" the kid said.

"Give me all of them," Tony announced.

Tony Conigliaro was becoming Tony C or Conig, depending upon how the headline writer felt at the time. Young, dashing, and fun to watch, he livened up a perennially moribund team. "He was a breath of fresh air," remembers Red Sox pitcher Dave Morehead. "We needed it."

Tony kept swatting home runs. One month into the season he had hit five, and even hit for average. Of course, he lived at home in Swampscott, where the phone rang so often and sometimes so late that the Conigliaros switched to an unlisted number. Neighborhood children steadily appeared at the door for autographs. Teresa helped handle fan mail, which averaged twenty-five letters per day, and by midseason had filled five hundred requests for Tony's photograph. A twelve-year-old girl wrote and asked if he would marry her.

Newspaper readers learned about Choo and Ambrose Park and how Uncle Vinnie had broken his thumb with a backyard pitch just before Wellsville and that Teresa fixed Tony juice, cereal with bananas and strawberries, and a glass of milk for breakfast and how Tony's teammates liked to come to the house for spaghetti and lasagna. Baseball writers calculated how he might stand up to other teen wonders in baseball history, such as Kaline, Mel Ott, Bobby Doerr, Jimmie Foxx, and Freddie Lindstrom, who all ended up in the Hall of Fame. Red Sox coach Billy Herman called him "the best nineteen-year-old hitter I've ever seen, bar none."

Residents of East Boston complained that Tony was too often identified as a native of Swampscott. "The kid is our boy," asserted Francis Vesce, who posted a photo of Tony in the window of his liquor store in Orient Heights. "We all watched him growing up playing ball. So what is this about him being from Swampscott? Okay, his family moved there a couple of years ago, but he's an East Boston kid. You can't change that." At Santarpio's Cafe on Chelsea Street, barkeep Frank Santarpio said, "Everybody around here has fallen in love with Conigliaro, like he was their son or brother. Guys who don't care anything about baseball run to the TV set when he comes up to bat." Mayor Collins issued a proclamation: "We lay claim to Tony as a product of East Boston. I hereby invite him to visit us at City Hall and we'll reestablish his affinity with Boston."

On the Red Sox, the rookie celebrity got a mixed reaction. As always, he acted sure of himself. Milt Bolling, the scout who had signed him, remembers running into Tony in the Fenway Park parking lot when the kid was in the middle of a little slump. Bolling kindly offered a pep talk.

"Hang in there, Tony. Keep being aggressive," Bolling suggested. "Don't get discouraged. It'll come around."

Tony gazed at him as if to say, "Are you done?"

"Look," said Tony. "I'm hitting the ball hard."

During a game against the Angels, some Red Sox marveled at young Bob Lee's impressive fastball.

"I hit ten homers off him last year in Wellsville," Tony scoffed (and exaggerated).

"Why don't you hit one now and show us?" somebody challenged.

Tony smashed the first pitch Lee threw him out of the park. He returned to the dugout and faced the bench, hands on hips, waiting for comments.

"Well, kid," commented pitcher Gene Conley, "that's eleven off Lee."

Some veteran Red Sox thought the kid ought to have more than a month or two in the big leagues before swaggering. In June, Yankees pitcher Bud Daley told the newspapers he thought that Tony was cocky and that he had heard many Red Sox thought so, too. "I do pop off," Tony replied. "But I'm not trying to do or say the wrong thing."

That was true. Tony was forthright, said what he thought, and was not manipulative. Sometimes he was truly innocent about how others perceived him. Bobby Guindon, who was brought up from the minors late in the season, recalls a game in Washington against the Senators when Tony was at the plate. Tony swung and missed. Thinking intently, Tony called time, walked to the on-deck circle, and took a couple of practice swings with a leaded bat. According to baseball's delicate etiquette, that was like thumbing his nose at the pitcher. And the simmering hurler buzzed the next pitch at Tony's head. Tony got up, perplexed, and smashed the next pitch for a double. "I know he did that innocently," says Guindon. "But it appeared to the pitcher and others that he did it arrogantly."

Smarter players took Tony's style for what it was, a genuine part of his personality or shtick, and they saw another side of him. Tillman, for instance, remembers Tony listening more than talking. "He was dedicated to his trade," Tillman says. "He loved the game. He was curious. He'd sit with some of us on the bus and ask a lot of questions. What do you do on the road? What do you do on game days? He wanted to make sure he was doing things right. He was genuine. He was young. Sometimes his questions were even a little naive. It was great to see a young man who was in awe of the sport he was in. He was very unassuming. Possibly, he was a little cocky with the kids he came up with. But I wasn't introduced to that side of him. He was not a snot."

As usual, Julie saw the deepest part of him. Tony was no more or less devout than the average Catholic school product, but when he first found himself in the big leagues and a hometown hero, when he felt that weight that came with the celebrity, he made a leap of faith. In his letters to Julie, he did not sound as cocksure as he had earlier. He wrote: "I'm going to church every Sunday. I can't miss with God on my side" and "Pray for me if you will. I need all the help I can get. I'd like some help from God."

Around the league Tony developed a reputation as a tough out. "You learned that if he was hot, you should just pitch around him," explains George Thomas, who played outfield for the Detroit Tigers that summer. He was also known as a hitter who crowded the plate. A rookie who hugged the plate and hit home runs was a red flag—or a bull's-eye—to pitchers. It was a simple maxim of pitching, especially in those more ruthless days, when intimidators like Bob Gibson and Don Drysdale ruled: The batter must be moved away from the plate. Throw at him, bean him, hurt him, but move him back or he'll be taking money out of your pocket.

Tony, of course, would not budge, and the duel was on. Early in the season White Sox manager Al Lopez was asked what he thought of Tony. "He's one of those rare naturals," pronounced Lopez, a baseball sage after nineteen years catching in the majors and thirteen years managing. "He's very impressive at the plate. He attacks the ball. Those are the guys who are great hitters. But I must say this. If he continues to stand as close to the plate as he does and his reflexes and reactions don't become much sharper, he's going to get hit often and will be in danger of getting seriously injured. The pitchers simply aren't going to let him keep on challenging them the way he does right now. They'll throw in on him."

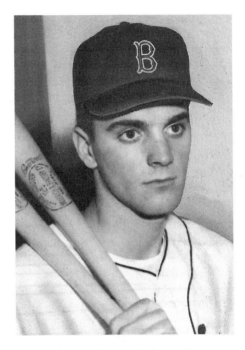

Tony looks somewhat pensive here as he prepares to take a little batting practice, perhaps wondering just how close to the plate he should be standing. (Boston Herald archives photo)

When they did, Tony did not flail or jump, if he could help it. In the intimidation game, you show no fear. "He was fearless of the ball," says Pesky. "He would just move his head, like Williams did. A ball up and in, Tony would just move his head. He thought the ball would never hit him."

Remembers Lee Thomas, a first baseman who joined the Red Sox from the Los Angeles Angels during the season: "He had a little air about him. He thought he was going to lead the league in home runs. They were always throwing him inside, and he never backed off. You always thought, 'One of these days, he's going to get nicked.' "

In May, Kansas City Athletics right-hander Moe Drabowsky hit Tony on the left wrist. He suffered a hairline fracture and was sidelined for four games.

By June, Tony had learned a lot about the big leagues and about himself. During a game at Fenway Park against the Orioles, he was thrown out by shortstop Luis Aparicio on a close play at first. Tony griped and umpire Al Smith ejected him from the game. A few days later against the Yankees, he was called out on another close play at first. Red Sox first-base coach Harry Malmberg protested, but Tony didn't say a word.

In an interview with *Boston Globe* baseball writer Clif Keane, Tony said: "I've learned one thing that's very important. I'm a lousy ballplayer if I don't play hard every second. A few times I've tried to coast and I've looked like a real bush leaguer doing it. I may get tired faster by racing around the best I can. But I have to play that way or I'm going to be in a lot of trouble."

Hustling could cause trouble, too. Tony was not suited to play center field, so Pesky had moved him into Yastrzemski's place in left.* During a night game on June 24 in Chicago's Comiskey Park, Tony ran hard after a long drive down the foul line by White Sox shortstop Ron Hansen. Tony missed the catch, careened into the concrete wall, and toppled into the seats. Hansen legged out an inside-the-park home run, and Tony was carried off on a stretcher as Comiskey's traditional posthomer fireworks burst overhead. He had injured his left knee, his right hand, and his back. He would be out for nine days.

It was not his most painful moment of the month. Before the Red Sox left on their road trip, after a game at Fenway Park, Tony drove Julie home, walked her to the door, and said he had something to tell her.

"We have to break up," he announced.

"What?"

"Julie, I love you more than anything. I'll always love you. But I have to do this."

Julie started crying. Tony cried, too.

"What did I do?" Julie pleaded.

---

*Tony quickly discovered the hardest thing about left field for the Red Sox was getting guff from the home fans, perched cozily alongside the leftfielder at Fenway; Tony couldn't understand why the same people who razzed Ted Williams would razz him, too. "I haven't been around long enough to get it, so I wish it would stop," he said.

"I have to concentrate," Tony stammered. "I have to—" He kissed her and ran from the house. Julie called after him, but he didn't come back. She stayed in the house for days, by the telephone, crying.

"I was shattered," she states more than thirty years later. Eventually, she gathered all the letters he had sent her over the years and placed them in the cedar hope chest from Young's. Three decades later, they are still there.

In *Seeing It Through,* Tony wrote that he broke up with Julie because he thought he was too young to marry, that he wanted to "date other girls and find out more of what life was all about. I haven't had enough running around yet. I hated to think about being married at only nineteen."

Sal couldn't have said it any better. "My husband broke them up," Teresa remembers. "He told Tony it was either Julie or baseball."

Completely untethered, Tony ran around with vigor. Once again, he was in the right place at the right time. In the summer of '64, the Fabulous Sixties kicked in and the sexual revolution stirred. Suburbanites sneak-read *Tropic of Cancer.* Movies started to show a little flesh. Baby boomers came of age with plenty of time and money on their hands, and the male boomers embraced the *Playboy* philosophy: an obsessive pursuit of fast cars, fast women, bachelor pads, and a new playmate each month. The Pill was at the drugstore, making it easier for women to sign up for sex as recreation. Secretaries read *The Feminine Mystique.* Tony never read it, and never would have bought it. He maintained that when he did marry, he would forbid his wife to work. But if *liberated* came to mean "easy sex," he was all for it.

The Red Sox were a perfect team for young men who liked to party. Owner Tom Yawkey, himself a monument to inherited wealth, had long run his franchise like a country club, where the living was easy, lights burned into the night, and no one paid too much attention to the score. Pesky was not strict. He had played infield for the Red Sox for eight seasons, most of the time setting the table for Ted Williams (Pesky batted .307 lifetime), and greatly admired the legendary Joe McCarthy, who managed Boston from 1948 through 1950. "You've got to treat a person the way you want to be treated yourself," Pesky believes. "I learned that from Joe McCarthy." Pesky's supporters say he is a nice man and was a good manager who would have won more games with a decent team. Pesky's critics say he was too nice, and the good-time Red Sox took advantage of him. "The saying around the league was, 'If the hotel where the Red Sox are staying burned down, it sure wouldn't kill any Red Sox,' " says pitcher Pete Charton, Tony's teammate in '64. "Back then, Johnny Pesky said if you were going to be late getting in at night, leave a message in his box at the desk. His mailbox was always overflowing with notes and papers."

Management had seen Tony C in action with Tony Horton in the spring and tried to simmer down their young rookie by rooming him with Malzone, fifteen years older and married. "We had very little in common to be roommates," recalls Malzone. Next, they bunked Tony with Dick Williams, which proved the Red Sox were no better at matchmaking than they were at winning World Series. "I was ordered to room with young Tony Conigliaro, to provide him with a veteran influence," Williams wrote with Bill Plaschke in his autobiography, *No More Mr. Nice Guy.* "The setup lasted just two months, because during that time, I never saw him. Not late at night, not first thing in the morning, never. I was providing veteran influence to a suitcase. I told management they were wasting their time, and I began rooming with Russ Nixon." Tony switched to pitcher Ed Connolly, who was five years older, but a fellow rookie.

Tony built on his already formidable reputation as a womanizer. "He was a very outgoing young man," relates Lee Thomas. "He was not bashful in any way. No matter who the girl was, he wasn't afraid to ask her for a date. I remember we were in Kansas City and it was around noon and all the secretaries were out on their lunch breaks. We were in the old Muehlebach Hotel and Tony was leaning out the window hollering, 'Hey, sweetheart, I'm Tony Conigliaro of the Red Sox!' I haven't seen too many guys do that sort of thing."

Tony's night moves inevitably spilled out in the newspapers. In late July, on a Saturday night in Cleveland, Tony missed the 12:30 A.M. curfew—in fact, he didn't return to his room at all—and Pesky checked several times in the night and found an empty bed. Before the game the next day, Tony trotted out for pregame practice, tucking in his shirt.

"Where the hell have you been?" Pesky shouted.

"Johnny," Tony said with a straight face, "I've been to Mass."

In the clubhouse Tony wasn't so flip. "Girls will ruin your life sooner or later," Pesky scolded. "You've got a chance to be another Joe DiMaggio. You're hurting the team by staying out all night."

Tony contritely explained that he had visited the Flemings, wealthy friends of Red Sox announcer Curt Gowdy, in a Cleveland suburb, had a lobster Newburg dinner, and was invited to stay the night. Tony said he told the Flemings he would stay over, "provided there was a Catholic church in the neighborhood and they would get him to the park on time." Tony told Pesky he didn't telephone because he didn't think it was necessary. He also promised he got at least ten hours' sleep. Pesky told him that whatever he was doing, he was required to call, and because he didn't, he would be fined $250—not insignificant to a player making seventy-five hundred dollars a year.

Pesky remembers: "I looked at it like he was my son. He said, 'If that's the way it is, that's the way it's got to be. It won't happen again.' And it didn't. One thing you could always do with Tony is you could talk to him."

But it wasn't over. In the first game Tony smacked his twentieth home run off Lee Stange. The newspapers pointed out that Tony was on pace to challenge the all-time record for homers by a rookie, thirty-eight, set by Boston Braves outfielder (and one of Uncle Vinnie's boyhood heroes) Wally Berger in 1930. In the fifth inning of the nightcap, Pedros Ramos plunked Tony on his right arm, fracturing the ulna, likely putting him out of action for six to eight weeks. Then the story of the missed curfew and the fine leaked, and people offered the preposterous theory that Tony got hit because he was so sleepy, he couldn't see the ball.

Tony was getting a playboy image, which nettled him for the rest of his career. He thought it was unfair. In the old days the press stayed away from a player's private life, as long as the player stayed off the police blotter. How many New Yorkers picked up their *Times* in the morning and read about Mickey and Whitey's escapades? And now, with practically the entire Red Sox team roaming the city after hours, he was getting singled out as a carouser. Because Tony was single, newspaper guys could write about his wanderings—married guys still got protection. Tony's complaint was legitimate, but he was also the ultimate baby boomer who wanted it both ways: He wanted to party and he wanted a choirboy image.

Tony went to the newsmen to set the record straight. "I'm not a playboy," he announced. "I hate liquor. I've never been drunk. In fact, I hate the taste of beer, but I have two bottles of beer after the game because the fellows tell me it's good for you, medicine like. . . . I'm really shocked at the things I've heard since I returned to Boston. I want all to know that I'm not a playboy and that my heart and soul are set on being an established big leaguer. I have no interest in girls." At least the part about liquor was true.

Tony was well enough to play again in September. In his first game back, he appeared as a pinch-hitter and homered. He hit three more before the season ended, to finish his rookie year batting .290 with twenty-four home runs and fifty-two runs batted in, in just 111 games. (Minnesota Twins outfielder Tony Oliva, who led the league in hitting at .323, was the league's Rookie of the Year. He was also five years older than Tony.) The Red Sox finished eighth, twenty-seven games behind the first-place Yankees, and Pesky was fired. Years later Tony called 1964—his first season in the big leagues—his favorite year.

~7~

YOUNG, HANDSOME, AND FAMOUS

IN THE WINTER OF 1964–65 GOOD THINGS HAPPENED QUICKLY, ONE AFTER THE OTHER FOR TONY CONIGLIARO. Sometimes it was still hard to believe. Just a year earlier his uncle Pat had set him up with a job in the sporting goods department at the Sears in Saugus, so the kid could pick up $1.25 an hour in the off-season. Now the last thing on this teenager's mind was minimum-wage work.

Soon after his rookie season ended, Tony visited general manager Mike Higgins at Fenway Park to negotiate a new contract, an encounter Tony gleefully recounted in *Seeing It Through*.

The Red Sox had offered a raise of $1,500, to $9,000 for 1965. "I want more," Tony stated.

"You still have to prove yourself," Higgins countered, delivering the standard line to young players who had turned in one or two good seasons. "You do well next season and we'll make it up to you." He was asking Tony to be patient, to wait his turn. "I'm not interested in next year, Mike," Tony declared.

Higgins rose from his chair, paced the room, and announced he would increase the deal to $12,000. Without waiting for an answer, he called to his secretary to draw up a contract.

"I want more than that," Tony asserted.

Higgins said he wouldn't go any higher. Tony said he wouldn't sign. Higgins huffed and puffed and asked what kind of money Tony had in mind. Tony said $17,500. Higgins said that was insane, offered $14,000, and called to his secretary again to draw up a contract.

"No, I'm not signing for that," Tony decreed.

Higgins replied he wouldn't budge.

"Look, don't you want me to be a happy ballplayer?" Tony demanded. "I'm from Boston. If I play well, we'll be drawing more people. You'll see."

"Who do you think you are?" asked Higgins, who grumbled and griped and gave the kid exactly what he wanted. Tony knew precisely who he was. He went out to his car, rolled up the window, screamed for joy, started for Swampscott, and had a sickening thought: Higgins gave in so easily; maybe he would have sprung for $30,000. Even so, Tony was nineteen and about to make $17,500 for a summer of baseball. The average construction worker in the United States was making $7,195.76 per year.

After getting his raise, Tony landed a big promotion. On November 29, the Red Sox traded first baseman and cleanup hitter Dick Stuart to the Philadelphia Phillies. On December 1, new manager Billy Herman declared: "Tony Conigliaro is my cleanup hitter as of right now. If this were Opening Day and I had to make out the lineup, Tony would be in the number-four spot." When Herman was asked if cleanup might be too much responsibility for the kid, he said: "Not for that youngster. You know him. He has all the confidence in the world. He loves pressure."

A few weeks later Tony picked up a second career. Public relations man Ed Penney, a Cambridge, Massachusetts, native, got in touch and said he had heard about Tony's hopping onstage to sing in clubs around the league. Penney—age thirty-nine, tall, thin, with receding hair and black horn-rimmed glasses, a former disc jockey on WTAO on Boston—took Tony to a studio in South Boston and listened to him sing with a piano accompaniment. "It was obvious we could cut a record that we wouldn't be ashamed of," Penney recalls. "It was worth a shot."

Penney and Tony each put up money and went to New York in the third week of December to cut a record on the Penn-Tone (as in Penney and Tony) label. Charlie Calello, who had done arrangements for Frankie Valli's Four Seasons, oversaw Tony's recording of the rollicking, benign, but catchy "Playing the Field" ("Now, I'm no rookie at love, I know what a girl's made of . . .") and the mournful "Why Don't They Understand?" backed up by a New York group, the Angels. Tony sounded vaguely like the then-popular Ricky Nelson. "He had a good voice," Penney says. "He could carry a tune. He wasn't Sinatra, of course."

*Tony loved music almost as much as he did baseball. Like any aspiring singer or musician, he made it a point to diligently study his sheet music before performing. (*Boston Herald *archives photo)*

Not that it mattered. Beatlemania had struck and young Americans were hot for singing teen idols. Tony was young, handsome, and famous, and teeny-boppers in greater Boston scooped up all fifteen thousand copies within a month of the record's release. "We had a good ride with it," says Penney. "It ended up being profitable." Tony, who a year earlier was buying a hope chest for Julie, made sure his swooning young fans knew he would never break their hearts. "I'll tell you when I'm going to get married," he declared, "when I'm eighty-five or ninety years old." Before he left for spring training, Tony signed a deal, said to be worth twenty-five thousand dollars, with RCA-Victor to produce records nationally. Penney, hamstrung by Tony's insistence on not doing musical work during baseball season, was also wheeling to get him on *The Ed Sullivan Show* and *Shindig*.

By the time he got to Scottsdale, Tony, at age twenty, was the kid who had everything: fame, fortune, girls, a red Corvette, and his own hit 45. Mike Ryan saw his old pal and couldn't help but think back to when they had met in Bradenton, which seemed like a million years ago. "Now he was the one who got the bigger steak and the bigger bed," Ryan comments.

Tony C was hot. The Boston sporting press was often compared to a snarling lion, but it really resembled a mercurial great aunt, alternately heaping lavish undue praise and bitter undue criticism. In the training camp and exhibition season preceding the 1965 season, Tony was the darling boy of "the Great Aunt." Tony had unlimited potential. Tony was the key to Red Sox attendance. Tony was another Ted Williams.

The Great Aunt loved that one: Tony as Ted. He was "gangly" and "brash," just like Ted. He was outspoken, just like Ted. In January when a newsman asked Tony the secret of his making the club as a rookie the previous spring, Tony replied it was because he came to camp in good shape. The comment was interpreted as a slam against lazy, gooey teammates. The ensuing brouhaha (during which Carl Yastrzemski and Dick Radatz admitted, yes, they were too chubby the previous year) angered Tony, who went back to the newspapers and said, "I didn't criticize any of the Red Sox players. I'm just a punk. Who am I to point the finger at anyone? It burns me to a crisp when stories might get me on bad terms with the other guys on the club." And this made Tony "misunderstood"—just like Ted.

Claflin of the *Record* began a spring training story from Scottsdale: "When you sit down to figure out what's good about the Red Sox this year, you must start with the name of Tony Conigliaro. Not since Ted Williams was a kid in pre-war days has a player had the chance to dominate the Red Sox as Conigliaro has." Three days later Claflin began his story, "Tony Conigliaro will be a better ballplayer than Ted Williams," and attributed that remarkable conclusion to an American League rival's scouting report on the Red Sox. Claflin quoted from the report: "With all due respect to Ted Williams, Conigliaro should at his present progress exceed the great record that Williams established. Not in batting average, but in home runs and runs batted in and certainly in defensive play."

Adoring quotes about Tony appeared in the papers regularly. Comparing him to Ted was the highest form of praise, but not the only one. Herman said: "Eddie Mathews hit twenty-five home runs his rookie year and forty-seven his sophomore season. Tony can match that." Chicago Cubs third baseman Ron Santo said: "I find it hard to believe he is only twenty years old. Conigliaro is the most aggressive hitter I have ever seen in baseball in any league. I have never seen a hitter glare at the pitcher the way Tony does and dare the pitcher to throw the ball. He defies them, and they don't like it." Indians manager Birdie Tebbetts predicted the kid would someday smack sixty-two home runs in a season and Yankees outfielder Roger Maris, who held the record with sixty-one, agreed.

At last the rest of the world thought as highly of Tony as Tony did. Exalted expectations naturally turned up the pressure, but Tony was used to it. "It makes you bear down," Tony observed during spring training. "And either you do or you're all done." He had worked hard all winter, including indoor sessions at Tufts University in Medford with Red Sox pitcher Bill Monboquette and at the Chelsea Armory with Uncle Vinnie. He reported to camp, as always, in top shape (which was rare among ballplayers in those days, and as Tony had pointed out, even rarer among the Red Sox). He took extra practice on high and tight pitches, including an exercise where Tony assumed his stance and coach Bobby Doerr pitched tennis balls, trying to hit him in the hands. They wanted the kid to practice getting out of the way. More and more people worried about his nearness to the plate and the growing irritation it caused pitchers. "He's going to get nailed," Santo declared at the end of his soliloquy. Commented Tony: "People tell me I'm going to get hit a lot because I crowd the plate. Well, that's my style."

And it worked, didn't it? Basking in worship, attention, and high hopes, Tony-the-kid-who-had-it-all sparkled in the exhibition season. He hit for power and average. He was the talk of the Cactus League. He even outshone Willie Mays. "There's no such thing as a sophomore jinx," Tony pronounced as the Red Sox broke camp.

Long before a game early in the season, Tony appeared in the nearly empty Red Sox clubhouse at Fenway Park with a stack of his own Penn-Tone records. He delivered one to each teammate's locker and headed out to the field for a workout. When he returned, the clubhouse was filled with Red Sox amid their pregame rituals, pulling on uniforms, reading mail, drinking soda, playing cards. No one said anything about the records. Tony peeked into a few lockers. No sign of "Playing the Field."

"What happened to the records?" Tony said to no one in particular. Someone pointed to the trash barrel. Tony walked over, peered in, and found the records—all of them—in the garbage. The clubhouse erupted in laughter, and no one laughed harder than Tony.

A good laugh was rare on the Red Sox in the summer of '65. The team stunk: It would go on to lose one hundred games and finish ninth, forty games out of first place. Even Tony struggled to have fun. He had it all and he cherished it, although that sometimes was a lot to carry. "I saw two things that year," said Rico Petrocelli, who joined the big club full-time to play short-stop and resumed his friendship with Tony that summer. "I saw him love what he was in—playing ball in the major leagues, the celebrity status. He really loved that. I also saw how he started to feel the pressure, playing and producing in his own hometown, living up to something that was developing —him as a star."

It unraveled fast. Tony tried too hard to live up to his stardom and stumbled to a terrible start. He hit home runs, which was his greatest wish, but his average dipped sickeningly near .200. He thought too much about home runs. He also made too many mistakes in the field. Herman had shifted him to

*As intense as he was, Conigliaro also knew how to have fun. Good thing for him here, though, is that taciturn Dick Williams is not yet the Red Sox manager: Otherwise, the cap wouldn't be on backward. (*Boston Herald *archives photo)*

right—Tony's third outfield position in two seasons—and the quirky angles in that part of Fenway Park confounded him.

Red Sox fans, who had read the enthusiastic accounts all spring, including comparisons to Ted Williams, started to treat him the way they often did Ted—they razzed him. Tony responded in the worst possible way—he razzed back. In the newspapers, he called them "the worst fans in baseball," a quote that was eagerly played up in inky headlines in the next day's papers. Tony was distraught over the horrible publicity. He went to Ed Penney's office in the Saint George Hotel near Kenmore Square and said he could barely bring himself to show his face at the ballpark that night. The Yankees were in town, and Penney impulsively picked up the telephone, dialed the Statler Hotel, asked for Mickey Mantle's room, spoke for a moment, and handed the phone to Tony, who heard the famous man's Oklahoma twang over the line. Mantle had always impressed Tony—to a child of the fifties, the Mick was the ultimate hero ballplayer. And here he was, telling Tony not to worry, that Boston fans and media were tough, but they were nothing compared to New York's, and just let this be a lesson to keep your mouth shut. Tony hung up and felt better and a little amazed. "He couldn't believe Mantle would even speak to him," Penney notes. Soon, however, Tony learned he didn't have to say a word to generate bad press. For the first time, but not the last, his romances drew snide remarks from the Great Aunt. During a Red Sox visit to Minneapolis in early July, Tony dated Elizabeth Jane Carroll—Miss Minnesota, who had a great white smile, blonde hair in a flip, and plenty of eyeliner—on four consecutive nights. Tony made two costly errors in the series and the Red Sox dropped all four games. A Boston headline read: "Sox's Tony C, Losing Games, Gains a Girl."

Slumping, Tony got advice from all over. Fans wrote letters to tell him he pulled his head out when he swung. The milkman in Swampscott said he dropped his hands. The toll taker on the Tobin Bridge told him his footwork was all wrong. Finally, Mike Higgins, the general manager from whom he had wheedled the big raise, advised him to let up on homers and build up his average. It worked. Tony was hitting .270 with ten home runs before he slumped again at midseason. And then another avalanche of troubles hit. Just as one good thing after another had happened to him in midwinter, one bad thing after another befell Tony in midsummer. In both instances, he deserved it.

During a trip to Baltimore in July, Tony was out on a date when Herman phoned his hotel room right at curfew. "He's sleeping," Tony's roommate, Mike Ryan, told the manager, who knew better. "Well, wake him up," demanded Herman, and Ryan had to admit Tony was absent. Tony showed up thirty minutes later, phoned Herman's room, and was told he was fined.

"Billy, for being thirty minutes late?" queried Tony.

"That's right," decreed Herman. "You weren't in your room on time, were you?"

"No. But Billy, it was only thirty minutes. Will the papers find out?"

"Yes, I guess they will," said Herman, who then sensed Tony's distress and relented. "All right, look. You're being fined. But if the writers ask you about it, tell them no, you were in your room on time."

The next day word of Herman's dragnet of AWOL Red Sox—and there were plenty—spread through the hotel. Writers asked Tony if he were among the fined. "I wasn't one of the guys," he declared. "I got tipped off that it was coming and was in my room. If I am involved in this thing, may my head fall off." Sox players who had been nabbed were furious and squealed on him to reporters. The newsmen went to Herman, who admitted Tony had been among the missing. Around the batting cage at Fenway, one teammate snapped at Tony, "Why don't you grow up and act like a big boy? If you get fined, take your medicine and keep your mouth shut." Then the Great Aunt, who did not like being lied to, pulled out her hat pin and retaliated. Will McDonough of the *Boston Globe* trotted out an anonymous quote from a Red Sox player, who claimed Tony "only thinks about hitting home runs. He doesn't care if we win or lose as long as he hits homers." McDonough threw in his own opinion that Tony's "fielding has slipped terribly and despite his fifteen home runs hasn't helped the ballclub much."

While the press spanked Tony, the relationship between Herman and Tony started to crack. It had never been great. Herman was a nice man, and he admired Tony's talent, but he just didn't know what to make of the kid. It was a scene being played out across America in the summer of '65—it was the Generation Gap. Parents couldn't understand their budding boomers. The kids didn't want to be hassled. Herman and Tony were not from the same world. Billy Herman had been born in 1909, was named after 1890s populist William Jennings Bryan, played second base for the Cubs the day Babe Ruth called his home run in the 1932 World Series, and hadn't managed a big-league club since he skippered a crew of World War II veterans on the '47 Pirates. Tony was born in 1945 and liked to play rock 'n' roll music—loudly.

Loud music—the flash point of many generational battles in the sixties—pushed Tony and Herman into open combat on July 15. On the Thursday morning plane ride from Boston to Cleveland, Tony cheerfully toted along a battery-operated record player. Shortly after takeoff, he assumed his customary seat in the last row of the plane alongside Ryan, Petrocelli, and Tony Horton and spun 45s. Music pounded throughout the cabin and older members of the eighth-place team grumbled about it.

Herman was in his usual seat near the front of the plane playing bridge with the writers. The Great Aunt didn't like rock 'n' roll much, either, and she goaded Herman about the awful racket. Herman scowled toward the rear seats and observed, "I wonder how that thing will sound on a bus going from Toronto to Cleveland?" And there it was. Tony C, who in the spring was the key to Red Sox attendance, the new cleanup hitter who loved pressure, the kid who upstaged Willie Mays in the Cactus League, the next Eddie Mathews, the next Ted Williams, was threatened with a demotion to the bush leagues.

On Friday night the Red Sox lost to the Indians, 4-3. Tony struck out three times, bringing his total to an astonishing eighty, just over halfway through the season. On Saturday, Boston papers carried stories of the record-playing incident and Herman's dark hint of minor-league bus rides. Teresa telephoned Tony at his hotel and told him to cut out playing records on the plane, for Pete's sake. Tony got to the ballpark in the rainy afternoon and saw that his name was not in the lineup. He was benched. Herman had not said a word to him.

Tony retreated and brooded during a twenty-minute run in the outfield in the rain. When he returned to his locker to pull off his soaked clothes, Henry McKenna of the *Boston Herald* wisely waited for him. The kid poured out his frustration, and it was great copy, if poor form. Public humiliation always brought out the worst in Tony, and now he pouted, made excuses, took it personally, and lashed back.

"Baseball is everything in my life and it looks like somebody's trying to get rid of me," Tony said as McKenna scribbled furiously. "I'm so down in the dumps I can't get out of it. I don't know what to do. I'm really hurt.

"All these stories about me not trying to help the team are unfair. Sure, I've struck out a lot, but I've also hit some good shots. What about the single last night that tied the game? It's nice to get a pat on the back, but I never get one. Never.

"They've written stories about my terrible fielding and I think that's unfair. I've made some good catches, but they're never mentioned. I've been trying to hit the cutoff man with my throws and last night I'd have thrown Rocky Colavito out at third if the throw had not been cut off.

"Right now, I'm so low I don't know whether I want to go out there again."

Then, as if he hadn't said enough, he complained that Herman seemed uninterested in tutoring him out of his slump. "Why doesn't he come to the batting cage and help me?" Tony said.

It was a lame performance, and Tony knew it the moment he stopped to catch his breath. He begged McKenna not to print the story (a request any self-respecting newsman had to turn down). Sal knew it was lame, too. He telephoned Tony and asked, "What, are you crazy?"

On the flight from Cleveland to New York, Tony played his records again. Since the team had won, Herman approved the music, but that didn't stop older players from complaining. "Hey, bush," shouted relief pitcher Arnold Early. "Do you think we just won the pennant or something?" An anonymous voice called out, "I don't know the dope on these kids. Maybe it's because they didn't have to work as long and as hard as I did to get here. But when I broke into this league, I kept my mouth shut." In New York, Herman learned of Tony's wailing speech to McKenna and fired back. "Five days in a row, I talked to him in my office and tried to help him with his hitting," said the manager, who was also frazzled that day by a near fistfight between pitcher Earl Wilson and out-fielder Lee Thomas on the team bus. "When Tony says in the newspapers that I have not tried to help him, it is his biggest lie yet."

Tony was miserable, which wasn't supposed to happen once your dreams come true. When Horton approached him after one of the games in New York and told him about a great party in Manhattan, at an East Side apartment complex known as "Stew Zoo" because of the great number of stewardesses quartered there, he was more than game for a little fun. He finished his customary second postgame beer and struck out for the heart of Gotham. When Tony and Horton reached the party, they couldn't believe their good fortune: The place was packed with young, pretty women, most of them employed by airlines. "I felt like a kid in toyland at Christmas time," Tony remembered. He resumed drinking beer, then proceeded to become inebriated the way only a true nondrinker can. He gulped shots of Canadian Club whiskey and pretty soon was holding an empty bottle up to the light. One of the last mist-shrouded moments he remembered was leaving the party with a woman on each arm.

At about six in the morning, the phone rang in Mike Ryan's room at the Hotel Roosevelt. It was a woman's voice. "We want you to come and get your friend," she said. She gave an address in Greenwich Village. Ryan got dressed, grabbed a cab, and went downtown to find Tony stinking drunk, half-dressed, and rolling around on the floor. "He looked bad," recalls Ryan. "He was sick. It wasn't like him. That kind of thing happens to all of us, but for him it was way out of character."

Ryan hauled his legless pal back to the hotel, where Tony spent the early morning throwing up and wishing to God the room would stop spinning. Breakfast was out of the question. Ryan helped guide him aboard the team bus, where Tony vomited on a writer. At Yankee Stadium, Tony resumed throwing up. Then somebody came to him while he dangled his head over a toilet and said Billy Herman wanted to see him—right away.

Herman slammed shut his office door after Tony entered. "You're drunk!" he shouted. Herman's face would turn red when he was angry, and now his face was the same shade as Tony's Corvette.

"No, I'm not," answered Tony. "I'm just a little sick to my stomach."

"Well, I say you're drunk," hollered Herman, who told Tony he was fined five hundred dollars.

"I am not drunk," insisted Tony, who in times of great stress was a devoted student of the Eddie Haskell school of preposterous denial.

"Okay," announced Herman. He had played big-league ball in the thirties. If he knew anything, he knew how to deal with whiskey-soaked baseball players. "If you're not drunk, then you won't mind playing right field today. How's that?"

It was a punishment commonly used by old-time managers against intoxicated or hungover players—make them run around in the hot sun for a few hours. And it worked. Bleary at the plate against Yankees ace Mel Stottlemyre, Tony grounded out, flied out, popped out, and drove home a run with a sacrifice fly. Sweaty and miserable, he patrolled right field with the dry heaves. When Joe Pepitone smashed a double to right, Jim Gosger had to hurry over from center field to retrieve the ball while Tony wobbled after it. The newsmen were suspicious about the pregame lineup switch and Tony's erratic play and grilled Herman, who said Tony was "sick to his stomach" and added, "I am still investigating the cause of the ailment."

Back in Swampscott, Sal was fed up. Morning after morning when he picked up his newspaper, there was a story about Tony's breaking the rules or playing his records too loud or sassing the manager or coming down with a sinister stomach ailment. When the Red Sox returned to Boston, he loaded his son into the car and, like a father going to meet the school principal, hauled him to a sit-down at Fenway Park with Neil Mahoney, Mike Higgins, and Herman. "And keep your mouth shut unless I tell you to say something," Sal told Tony. "Understand?"

What transpired during the one-hour, forty-five-minute meeting was never clear. Newsmen who camped outside Higgins's office assumed Sal issued some sort of apology on his son's behalf and joined the team brass in coming down hard on the kid. The official press release appeared to support that conclusion when it stated that Tony was fined five hundred dollars for "past mistakes" and had apologized to Herman. But another part of the statement was murky: "Mr. Conigliaro assured Mr. Higgins and Mr. Herman that he naturally had the same interest in his son's future that the Red Sox have and wanted to work closely with the club to avoid any future difficulties involving his son." It didn't say whom Sal blamed for the difficulties. In Tony's account of the meeting in *Seeing It Through,* he said Sal admitted Tony had been wrong but mostly upbraided Herman for mishandling his son. This version rings true. When Tony had trouble with a teacher in grade school, Sal mostly blamed the teacher. When Tony had trouble with Herman, Sal would mostly blame the manager.

Tony and Sal had no comment after the meeting. The newspapers revealed that Tony's stomach ailment was the result of "a late Monday night party" but didn't play up the incident since Tony, as far as the Great Aunt knew, was sufficiently contrite. Herman would only say that some players have maturity "at eighteen. Others don't get it until they're twenty-three or twenty-four." He also pointed out that Tony never failed to hustle on the field and that "the boy has great potential. He could be an All-Star." Whatever Sal had said during the meeting, as usual it was just the right thing for Tony. In a doubleheader that night against the first-place Twins, Tony went five-for-ten and smacked his seventeenth home run.

The next day Red Sox owner Tom Yawkey conducted an informal chat with Tony in the empty box seats at Fenway and asked him what happened in New York. "Tell me, was it worth it?" Yawkey asked after Tony finished. "Believe me, Mr. Yawkey, I was so drunk and so sick, I don't even remember," Tony said. Yawkey laughed and told the kid to forget the past (a fellow is bound to get a little tight now and then at a country club).

Public sentiment on the affair was, like so many issues of the time, split along generational lines. Middle-aged sportswriters used the occasion to mock those crazy kids and their wacky music. One called rock 'n' rollers "shaggy-headed goons who can't tell the difference between noise and music." A female teenager from Canton fired back with a letter to the editor: "Do you call George Washington a shaggy-headed goon because he had long hair? You probably would answer that it was a different generation. Yes, it was, and so is our generation different from yours. That is why our taste in music is different and our ideas on how to spend our free time."

Tony followed the controversy with a batting surge. He smashed four more home runs and hit nearly .500 in the next week. But then another plague nabbed him. On July 28, Kansas City Athletics right-hander Wes Stock plunked him on the right wrist. Tony suffered another hairline fracture, his third bone broken by a pitch in two seasons, and missed twenty-four games. Baltimore Orioles executive Frank Lane observed that perhaps Tony would suffer fewer broken bones if Red Sox pitchers would retaliate by hitting a few more opposing batters. He also said any big-league general manager would die to have the kid on his team.

Tony returned in August and raised his final batting average to .269 with eighty-two runs batted in and led the American League in home runs with thirty-two. At twenty years and nine months, he was the youngest to win a home-run title. Still, somehow, it wasn't a very good year. He slumped, he was benched, he was publicly branded a liar, he showed up drunk for work. In the summer of '65, Tony lost a little

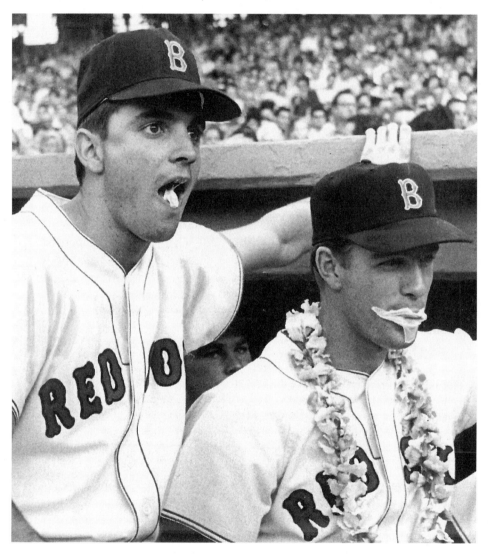

Tony is joined by Red Sox pitcher Jim Lonborg as bubblegum-blowing partners during a special night at Fenway Park. (UPI/Corbis-Bettmann)

innocence. "The dream of making it, the glamour of when you first came up, starts to wear off," Petrocelli observes. "It becomes a job. I think that's something Tony fought."

It was no fun to be jaded at twenty. The sweet spring of '64 seemed long ago, and near the end of his disenchanting second season, on a hot night at Fenway Park, Tony was revisited by his innocent past. He kneeled in the on-deck circle and allowed his eyes to scan the mostly empty stands. He glanced at the box seats near the home dugout and did a vaudevillian double take: Julie Markakis was there with her mother. He had heard through the North Shore grapevine that she was leaving soon for Eastern Air Lines flight attendant school in Miami.

Near the end of the game Tony stuck his head over the dugout roof and tossed a tightly folded piece of paper into Julie's lap. The crowd around her buzzed and wondered who she was and what Tony Conigliaro threw to her. "Open it," said Mrs. Markakis. "Not yet," Julie said. She held the paper in her hand and waited for the crowd's curiosity to fade. Then she unfolded the paper and felt tears fill her eyes and tickle her cheeks. The note said, "I love you."

In the fall of 1965 healthy twenty-year-old American men had something else on their minds besides women and cars and rock 'n' roll. They had to think about Vietnam. As the ground war and the United States's combat role intensified, President Lyndon Johnson doubled the draft rolls. This was not the all-out, all-popular World War II, and a lot of people searched for ways to fulfill their military obligation while keeping their hides out of the Southeast Asia bush. Many professional athletes chose the Army Reserve, which allowed them to be off-season and weekend warriors while keeping their careers, and their bodies, intact.

Tony had enlisted for a six-year hitch in the reserves on August 19. He nearly flunked the physical because of a deformity in his right thumb, a memento from the day he slugged Dave on the front porch in Nahant. Cleared for duty, Tony arrived for basic training and supply school at the army's sprawling installation at Fort Dix, New Jersey, on October 4. From the perspective of the late 1990s, when many big-league ballplayers think roughing it means a ride in a limo that doesn't have a hot tub, Tony's ordeal is remarkable. They shaved his head. They marched him in the rain. They made him peel potatoes for sixteen straight hours. They got within an inch of his face and hollered insults. They made him get up at 4:00 A.M. and clean the bathrooms. They gave him five minutes to wolf down each meal, which was nothing like Teresa's cooking. They even succeeded where Mike Ryan had failed: They made him make his bed.

One day, a sergeant eyed the name tag "Conigliaro" over Tony's right shirt pocket and asked if he knew Tony Conigliaro.

"I *am* Tony Conigliaro," Tony said.

"Yeah, sure," laughed the sergeant and walked away.

"They treat you like dogs out here," Tony wrote to Julie, in a letter he scribbled on the sly during KP duty. "All they do is scream at you and run and march you. The only thing that's killing me is lack of rest. The other stuff doesn't bother me. You know how much I like to sleep. I miss home so much it's killing me."

At some outposts GIs were literally getting killed, which made a reserve unit at Fort Dix seem at least safe, if not cozy. But no one in uniform could really feel safe in the sixties: Around Fort Dix that winter there were strong rumors the reserves would get called up for active duty and shipped to Vietnam.

Even if some sergeants didn't believe it, he was still Tony C. On his twenty-first birthday he received two cardboard boxes filled with cards and letters. During a leave he went to the RCA-Victor studio in New York to cut a record that would be released in February and was introduced to jazz trumpeter Al Hirt, who revealed

Scrubbing garbage cans in the Army Reserve wasn't exactly Conigliaro's idea of fun, and you can bet that sergeant eyeing Tony is about to politely ask him to wipe that smirk off his face. (AP/Wide World Photos)

that he grew up on the same street in New Orleans as ex-Red Sox pitcher Mel Parnell. In February, Tony was released from duty, went home to Swampscott for some of Teresa's gnocchi, took a vacation in Puerto Rico, and reported to the Red Sox's new spring training site in Winter Haven, Florida. He was joined there by his brother Billy, an outfielder who had signed with the Sox after graduating from high school the previous June. Tony bragged about his kid brother to anyone who would listen and guaranteed he'd reach the big leagues soon. The brothers didn't mix much on the field. "He pretty much kept to himself," Billy says. "He was busy getting ready for the season." But Sal and Teresa came to Florida and took a room with a kitchenette at the Holiday Inn where the team was quartered, so mother, father, and the two ballplayer sons were often together for evening barbecues.

Tony knew exactly what he wanted out of the summer of 1966. He wanted to hit forty home runs, bat .300, and drive in one hundred runs. He thought RBIs were most important. "I'm thinking I can help the team more with one hundred RBIs than a good batting average," he said. He wanted to improve his fielding and worked tirelessly with former Sox centerfielder Dom DiMaggio on getting a jump on the ball and backing up infielders. He also wanted to go a whole season without a tussle with the press, without a fine, and without a broken bone from a pitched baseball. The big leagues were his dream, and at twenty-one he was tired of seeing his dream go bad. This was supposed to be fun.

More than anything Tony wanted to win. Playing ball becomes work when you lose, and Tony openly admitted he was depressed after the Red Sox finished eighth and ninth in his first two seasons. Ever since Noyes Park in East Boston, he had most enjoyed batting with the winning run on base, and dreadful teams seldom have the winning run on base. "It would mean so much to Boston to have a winning ballclub," he said. "I think a lot of the problems I had last summer would have seemed much less important if we had been winning."

Tony avoided fines and Canadian Club whiskey, but otherwise 1966 was a lot like 1965. Tony got off to another horrible start: He ended May batting .206. His weight was down—possibly because of his two months of chowing down Fort Dix slop—and his energy was low. "I'm twenty-one years old and I feel like an old man," he complained, before embarking on an all-steak diet. And the Red Sox kept losing. They would finish ninth, twenty-six games out of first place. "We were struggling every game," Petrocelli says. "I remember Tony's coming in after we would blow a game, and he would sit there and just shake his head, as if to say, 'How can we be this bad?' It was very frustrating for him."

Tony loved attention, and with the team losing, the only theater left was personal glory. He passed the summer dueling with his old Wellsville buddy, George Scott, for the team home-run lead. Tony was competitive and was clearly peeved whenever the Boomer passed him. The Great Aunt clucked her tongue at this and resurrected the complaint that Tony was selfish. "This is a moody, unfriendly kid, a kid who can't stand anybody else but himself in the spotlight," Al Hirshberg hissed in the *Boston Traveler.* "You know how you can tell the boys from the men? The boys have to be first." Tony, as always befuddled by sharp criticism, thought that was the whole point—to be first.

Sometimes, as other people his age wondered where had all the flowers gone, Tony thought everything was destined to go wrong. In July he returned from a road trip and went home to Swampscott. His mother looked grim when he walked in the door. "I've got something to tell you, but I don't want you to take this too hard," Teresa began. Tony's heart quickened. He thought another grandparent had died. His mother told him that Freddie Atkinson, his best pal from Saint Mary's, the kid who had helped him pick out the hope chest for Julie at Christmastime in 1963, had been killed in Vietnam. Tony fell to the floor, crying. In his autobiography he wrote, "It hurt so much I was gasping for air and I thought I was going to have a heart attack."

There certainly wasn't anything about the 1966 baseball season to cheer up Tony, although his final numbers (he played 150 games) consisted of twenty-eight home runs, ninety-three RBIs, and a .265 batting average that further substantiated his progression toward true stardom. As for the Red Sox, they stumbled across the finish line at 72-90. At least Tony was around to see the finish—manager Billy Herman was fired with sixteen games left in the season.

In the winter of 1966–67 baby boomers everywhere waded into young adulthood and took stock of themselves. Some went to Tibet to sit cross-legged, some went to San Francisco to wear flowers in their hair, and some went to college to drop acid. In early December, one month before his twenty-second birthday, Tony went on a ten-day safari to Kenya. He

Tony and George "the Boomer" Scott carried their friendship from the minor leagues to the
Red Sox and beyond. This 1967 photo was taken approximately two weeks before
Conigliaro's tragic beaning. (UPI/Corbis-Bettmann)

kept a diary on the trip, and amid accounts of Land Rovers bouncing across the plain and great white hunters bagging impala, cape buffalo, zebra, and gazelle, he looked over his life.

"Tonight we plan to sit by the fire eating barbecued eland (the one I shot)," he wrote. "My beard is getting very long.

"Camp is really peaceful. Relaxation has been a problem for me, but it seems as if this is the place for it. No traffic jams, no girls, no tenseness, no problems. Just fine food, plenty of rest, and good hunting. Relaxing really pays off. For the first time in a long while my stomach feels at ease.

"At times back home in Boston I never have time to think. Everything is go, go, go! Here, as I relax, I think about many things; for example, my family and how lucky I am to have such a close-knit family. I think about my future. I'm in a talkative mood right now and there's no one to talk to. The natives don't understand English.

"Out here there is no jealousy. I don't mind saying I'm afraid of jealousy. . . . I hate people who talk behind my back. It seems people who are down and out are never talked about. People in the limelight get hit head-on. Boy, it sure feels good to get away from jealousy. I'm no angel, but I would like to be treated honestly. If I do something wrong, I don't mind being talked about. But I hate people who make up stories.

"My best friend died—Frederick Atkinson. It's lonely not having a friend you can talk to."

~8~

SISTER ERNESTINA WITH A CREW CUT

FOR 1967 THE RED SOX HAD A NEW MANAGER, ONE WHO DIDN'T PUT UP WITH NONSENSE. The new manager didn't coddle. The new manager was a dictator, with piercing eyes and a sarcastic wit. The new manager was Dick Williams, and Tony Conigliaro could barely believe it: The new manager was Sister Ernestina with a crew cut. "They didn't hit it off," recalls Mike Ryan.

Of course they didn't hit it off. Williams called the team together in spring training in Winter Haven, Florida, and declared the country club closed. He announced the fine for missed curfew was five hundred dollars. He belittled players in public. He drilled them over and over on fundamentals. He told them, "I can make you proud to be a baseball player. And I can get rid of you and I can embarrass you. You pick." He instituted a strict dress code. He didn't tolerate back talk or even a dirty look. He yelled like a drill instructor. He warned players not to go over his head to benevolent rich-uncle owner Tom Yawkey. He made Ted Williams, special batting instructor and schmoozer, feel unwanted in spring training, and the legend got the hint and went fishing. That's the way it would be—do it Dick Williams's way or get lost. He was in charge. End of discussion. No one who knew Williams could imagine Tony's playing rock 'n' roll in the back of this airplane. No one could imagine Sal calling a meeting at Fenway Park to lecture this skipper.

Williams was toughest on the hipsters, such as George Scott, Mike Ryan, Rico Petrocelli, Joe Foy, and Tony. These were the youngest Sox, and the softest—they were brought up in the Boston system and had known nothing but losing and smiling about it. "He came in with an

91

attitude: 'I am the manager. You are the player. Now you're going to learn how to win,' " Scott remembers. "He turned around our thinking. We were babied a bit in the Red Sox organization. Dick Williams didn't hit it off with nobody. He butted heads with everybody."

He butted extra hard with Tony. It was inevitable. Williams was a control freak. Tony hated to be told what to do. Williams scolded everybody. Tony was sensitive, thin-skinned, and took the barbs personally. Williams didn't like Yawkey. Tony loved Yawkey.

Their backgrounds were completely different. Williams had grown up poor during the depression with an angry, mean father. He rode the decrepit, bush-league buses for five years before making the Brooklyn Dodgers, then injured his shoulder diving for a ball and lost his stardom forever. He had to work hard and use his wits as he bounced among six teams in thirteen seasons. And there was Tony, a big-league hero with a red Corvette at nineteen, handsome, having a good time, and still on the way up: Before the season, Athletics owner Charlie Finley had telephoned Red Sox general manager Dick O'Connell and offered five hundred thousand dollars for the kid.

In other respects Tony and Williams were too much alike. "They were both hard-headed," says Ryan. They were both brash—before the first pitch, Williams guaranteed the '67 Sox would win more than they lost. It was exactly the kind of thing Tony would say. "He was a fighter and so was I," Williams wrote in his autobiography, "and that's probably why we got into so many verbal scrapes." Something else was also at work. Tony's most devoted supporters believe Williams, like Sister Ernestina, needled him out of jealousy. More likely, the tough nun and the tough manager nagged Tony to make him better. "Dick Williams was especially hard on guys who had some talent," says Scott.

For Tony, the season started with a disturbingly familiar incident: During batting practice in Winter Haven on March 18, Sox reliever John Wyatt drilled him in the back, causing a hairline fracture in the left shoulder blade. "It sailed and Tony had time only to turn away and take it on the shoulder," catcher Russ Gibson said. "Otherwise, it would have hit him in the face." The medical staff doubted Tony would be ready for Opening Day at Fenway Park, but he was in right field on April 12 for the victory over the Chicago White Sox.

Tony shakes hands with Red Sox General Manager Dick O'Connell while new Bosox manager Dick Williams looks on, on the occasion of Tony's signing a new contract with Boston. (Photo courtesy of the Conigliaro family)

This summer would be nothing like all the others. The stagnant, sleepy, sad-sack Sox were gone. On April 29, Williams's crew trailed the Athletics when Tony led off the bottom of the fifteenth with a single. Jose Tartabull's bases-loaded single won it, and the Sox poured out of their dugout and celebrated near home plate. They were tied for first place. Not many of them could remember occupying first place or having reason to jump around on the field in a Red Sox uniform.

They weren't fond of Dick Williams, but they responded to him. And New England baseball fans would forever set their watches by the summer of '67. It was the year the Red Sox were reborn. For the first time since 1950 the team fielded a bona fide contender and a new generation got hooked on the Sox, and they were hooked for life. In the public's heart, Fenway Park was transformed from rundown relic to precious architectural delight, as much a part of Boston as the Freedom Trail.

In 1967 the world was getting turned inside out and upside down. The Beatles grew mustaches and dressed like hippies. *Bonnie and Clyde* was a hit gangster movie, except now the gangsters were the good guys. The Smothers Brothers were television comics, but they wanted to get political. Much of America was taking off its tie, letting its hair grow, and cranking up Jim Morrison and the Doors. Much of the country was falling apart—students were burning draft cards, rioters were burning Newark and Detroit, and flower power blossomed in California, but Boston was united behind its beloved Red Sox. The usually cushy, hapless Red Sox were banning blue jeans, listening to Jack Jones's "The Impossible Dream," and winning. Anything could happen next.

Everything was changing, fast. None of the Red Sox were counterculturists—they all kept their hair short and neat and dated girls who wore sweaters and pressed skirts. But something different was happening in the bleachers. Tony noticed the Friday night crowd wearing its hair longer and razzing him harder than in the old days. One night his shaggy tormentors were riding him when an eighty-year-old woman stood up and hollered, "They're just jealous, Tony. Just to show we're all for ya: Hip! Hip!" And the long-hairs booed and pelted the old woman with garbage.

And the Red Sox kept winning and Tony felt like a kid again. For all the Great Aunt's unfair carping about his selfishness, he better than anyone in a Red Sox uniform appreciated the difference. "Living in

Boston like I do makes it tougher on a guy when he's on a losing team," he had said in spring training. "You can't imagine how many people give me the needle about the Red Sox. I go out for dinner somewhere and a fan will recognize me and make some sort of wisecrack about the Red Sox. The only way to stop that is for us to win."

Good times brought out the best in him. Now, for the first time in his professional career, he was playing in big games in front of big crowds. More than ever, he got to step to the plate with the winning run on base. And he loved it. In many ways he could be his old self. "Oh, man. He had that little swagger in his walk," Scott remembers. "He wanted to be the man. In the eighth and ninth inning, he wanted to be up there. He was a clutch player. He was the best I've ever seen. Tony and Frank Robinson— I'd like to know who was ever more aggressive and more determined than those two." Says Petrocelli: "Tony always wanted to be the hero."

In mid-May, Tony had to step away from the party. The tumultuous real world called again, as it did for many healthy single twenty-two-year-old males. The Vietnam war dragged on and antiwar sentiment spread, and Washington was starting to wince over the inequities of the selective service system. The Department of Defense cracked down on reserves and national guardsmen and ordered that all of them join an active unit by May 11—or be thrown into the draft pool for the regular army and risk a hitch in Vietnam. Tony signed on with the Army Reserve 412th Engineering Company in Lynn, and on May 19 he reported to Camp Drum, New York, for two weeks' training. Private First Class Conigliaro slapped out meat and potatoes in chow lines and scrubbed garbage cans. He was not happy about it. He injudiciously grumbled to a reporter for the *Syracuse Herald-Journal* that many Red Sox were allowed to do their reserve duty in the off-season. "What are they trying to do, pick on the bigger name players?" he asked, which drew a minor rebuke from the fervently patriotic Great Aunt back in Boston. Tony rejoined the Red Sox on June 2, meeting his teammates on the tarmac as they stepped off the charter flight in Cleveland. Some of them greeted him with cheery mock salutes.

When he returned to the lineup, Tony lapsed into a slump—army life had left him reeling again. And slumps could be hard on him. Most of his teammates remember Tony relentlessly cool and collected, even when he struggled. "I don't think I ever saw him down," says Scott. "I don't think I ever saw him have a letdown when he was oh-for-four or something." But he was too intense to shrug off failures, even momentary ones. He knew a lot of people expected big things from him. He expected bigger things from himself. "He'd put on a cocky air to hide it," says Bob Tillman, the veteran catcher and Tony's wizened confidant. "But he was very hard on himself. He was always down on himself."

Now Tony pressed himself harder than usual. During his reserves service, there had been an important development on the team: Carl Yastrzemski was erupting into a star. Tony and Yaz, the two best players on the team, had always been competitive, but each had stayed out of the other's territory. Yaz hit for average. Tony hit home runs and racked up runs batted in. Now Yastrzemski was getting into power and glamour, too. "In '67, I just completely changed my hitting style, from a straight-away hitter and hitting the ball the opposite way to a dead-pull hitter," Yastrzemski says. "He always hit home runs. He hit them the first day he came in the big leagues, whereas I didn't." Yaz also produced astonishing game-winning hits—another Tony C specialty. He even made terrific plays in left field. With the Red Sox in a throbbing pennant race, Yastrzemski emerged as the biggest hero since Ted Williams. There were Yaz buttons and Yaz pennants and Yaz songs. Eventually, there would be Big Yaz Bread and Yaz on the cover of *Life* magazine. And Tony was not in center ring. "Tony wasn't getting the top billing. I think that ate at him," says Mike Ryan.

As during George Scott's power surge in '66, Yastrzemski's outburst turned up Tony's intensity. When it didn't make him try too hard, it made him better. "They were competitive in a good way," Petrocelli says. "When Yaz started hitting home runs, they really became competitive." It helped Yaz, too, having the kid play catch-up with him. "He wanted to be the best player in the majors and I wanted to be the best player in the majors," Yastrzemski remembers. "Which was great. It was a great rivalry. It keeps pushing you and pushing you and pushing you. We probably both reached higher goals by having this rivalry."

Later developments led observers to believe there was friction between the two sluggers, but that was not true in the summer of '67. They had a good, professional relationship and greatly respected each other's talent. Yastrzemski and Tony, who usually batted third and fourth in the lineup, often discussed opposing pitchers and their tendencies.

This was a welcome sight to Red Sox followers in the mid-1960s: Tony C crosses the plate and shakes hands with Carl Yastrzemski following another Conig homer. Although each player had a professional respect for the other, there was an underlying tension between the two. (UPI/Corbis-Bettmann)

They had a lot in common. They were both ego driven and both as tough as gladiators with the game in the balance. "On the field, we both wanted to win," Yastrzemski says. "We had tremendous, aggressive personalities. We were very much alike. Very aggressive, very demanding of ourselves. *Very* demanding of ourselves." Teammate George Thomas observes that "Tony wanted to drive the winning run in to get his name in the papers; Carl wanted to drive in the winning run to win the game," but that is unfair to Conigliaro. He wanted to win as badly as Yaz. After the big hit, Tony would bask in the glory; Yaz would merely endure it.

They had never been pals: Yaz was married, a product of rural Long Island, New York, quiet, and six years older. Tony was single, a city boy, and outgoing. "Off the field, he went his way and I went my way," says Yastrzemski. "Off the field, we were completely different." Yaz was promoted to the big club in 1961 and inherited left field from the freshly retired Ted Williams. But comparisons to the Splendid Splinter made Yaz wince. A television interviewer asked Tony, "When you finally retire from baseball, would you like it to be considered that you were as good as Ted Williams was?" Before the question was finished, Tony began to shake his head no—and it seemed he was about to deliver a young player's customarily humble response to such a preposterous query. But this was Tony C. "I don't think I'd like to be as good," he said. "I'd like to be better than Ted Williams."

In 1967 most differences were easy to put aside. And in this rare moment in Red Sox history, everybody on the team remembered the real enemies were in the opposing clubhouse, not the Sox clubhouse. In June, Chicago White Sox manager Eddie Stanky, an adherent to the old-time philosophy of needling the other team's big stars, called Yastrzemski "an All-Star from the neck down." This made Yaz want to beat the stuffing out of the White Sox every time they played. Two weeks later Chicago was in first place when it visited Fenway Park, where fans were eager to throw abuse and debris at Stanky. On the second night the Red Sox trailed, 1-0, in the bottom of the eleventh. Yastrzemski led off, anxious to tweak the impertinent White Sox manager, but made an out. With two outs and a runner at first, Tony stepped up. "Carl was on the top step pulling for Tony to get a base hit," recalls George Thomas. Tony cracked one of his trademark artillery shots into the night over the left-field wall. Says Thomas: "Carl was the first to greet him at home plate." No one remembered seeing that happen before.

For one summer there was simply too much fun being a member of the Red Sox to waste time on pettiness. The team swirled in the thrill of what would be the tightest four-team pennant race in baseball history. At the midseason break, the Red Sox were 41-39, six games out of first. Yastrzemski and Petrocelli were voted All-Stars in player balloting (Tony received three votes, which brought merciless kidding from Ryan, who got four). Starting pitcher Jim Lonborg, already a ten-game winner who had displayed a welcomed willingness to protect his teammates by plunking opposing batters, and Tony were added to the team by American League manager Hank Bauer of the Orioles. The National League won the midsummer classic, 2-1, in the fifteenth inning at the Big A in Anaheim,

California. Tony went oh-for-six, including strikeouts against future Hall of Famers Ferguson Jenkins of the Chicago Cubs and Bob Gibson of the Saint Louis Cardinals. But he did give the folks back home—watching the first All-Star game televised during prime time—something to talk about. In the tenth and fifteenth innings Tony made sensational catches in right field, both on long drives by Saint Louis Cardinals slugger Orlando Cepeda.

After the break Tony and Yastrzemski raced off on simultaneous hot streaks. At last they were the one-two punch Red Sox fans had dreamed about. The Red Sox won ten straight. By then the crowds at Fenway Park were enormous and New England was in love. Ken Coleman and Ned Martin's radio broadcasts of Red Sox games were background music at the beach, on front porches, in backyards, and in office buildings. Red Sox game stories appeared on the front page of newspapers. Twenty years of pent-up pennant fever was blowing out: One day a massive traffic jam backed up when a man listening to an exciting moment in a Red Sox game stopped his car and refused to enter the Sumner Tunnel, where his radio would black out, until the inning ended. After winning its tenth in a row in Cleveland, the team returned to Boston and was greeted at Logan Airport by ten thousand screaming admirers. It was like something out of a Beatles movie. Hundreds of fans spilled onto the runway, blocking the assigned gate for the team's flight. After the Red Sox boarded the team bus, fans banged on the sides and pressed their faces against the windows and joyously rocked it back and forth.

Boston was in the middle of a wild summer party, and Tony was literally at the center of it. Before the season he and Tony Athanas Jr., whose father owned the restaurant Anthony's Pier 4 on the waterfront, had taken a bachelor pad together at 566 Commonwealth Avenue, a modern high-rise planted tall amid the red-brick Victorian buildings in Kenmore Square. From the balcony Tony could see his office—right field at Fenway Park. Kenmore Square was becoming a hot spot. Area nightclubs and bars were packed with summer students from the many nearby colleges, suburban kids looking to meet hippie girls, and spillover from suddenly busy Fenway Park. This was one summer, when Tony was out on the town, that nobody heckled him for playing for the Red Sox.

Tony, Athanas, and Bill Bates, who was the trainer for the Boston Patriots professional football team, sampled the newly vibrant nightlife together. Athanas, who was three years older than Tony, was known as

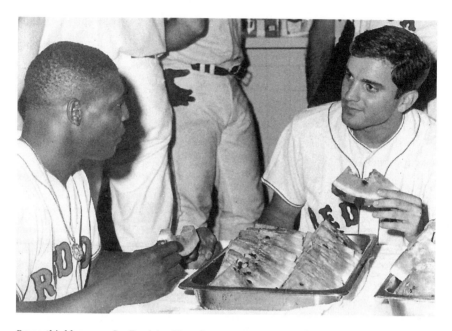

*Bosox third baseman Joe Foy joins Tony for a postgame watermelon party after both had hit ninth-inning home runs to help lead the Red Sox to a dramatic extra-inning victory over the California Angels. (*Boston Herald *archives photo)*

"Mr. A." Bates, who was twelve years older than Tony, was "Mr. B." Tony was "Mr. C." The trio hit the Playboy Club in Park Square, or the Improper Bostonian, or the Kenmore Club. On a typical night they'd nurse a cocktail or two—none of them was a serious drinker—and stand against a wall and check out the women.

Tony would amaze the other two with his brazenness. When he saw a woman he liked (he was especially attracted by buxom females), he'd swoop next to her in an instant, introduce himself, flash that great smile, fix her with those liquidy brown eyes, and switch on the charm. Once Bates was riding with Tony in the red Corvette in Kenmore Square—one of Boston's busiest, most madcap intersections—when a female pedestrian caught Tony's eye. He shut off the car in the middle of the street and zigzagged his way through traffic to the sidewalk to catch up with her.

Now and then there was a party at the bachelor pad. Tony, Athanas, and Bates would carry around blank invitations for weeks and issue them to every pretty woman they came across. "We'd give them to thirty-five or forty women—BU students, models, stewardesses, show girls," Bates recalls. "Then we'd invite fifteen guys."

The apartment would finally get tidied—Tony and Athanas were personally immaculate, but they decorated their digs with prodigious mounds of dirty laundry—a caterer would be lined up, a bartender would be hired, and a pancake stack of albums would be balanced on the turntable. Then the doorbell would keep ringing as the bouffant hairdos, tight sweaters, and Pepsodent smiles arrived. They were not wild nights. Once a Red Sox player sat on a coffee table and shattered the glass top, and Bates the athletic trainer had to spend the evening in the bathroom, picking shards out of the guy's buttocks. But that was about it. In other pads in America, at some boomer bashes, marijuana, peyote, and mescaline were starting to be served alongside the Jack Daniels, but not at the bachelor apartment at 566 Commonwealth. Tony and his friends were too old-fashioned for that. Their tastes ran closer to the Rat Pack than the Rolling Stones. "We'd have a cocktail party," says Bates. "The idea was to collect as many phone numbers as possible. We weren't rock and roll imbeciles. But we had the chance to meet some of the greatest-looking women in Boston."

Tony usually collected the most and the best looking. He had charm. "When he walked into a room, the place lit up. He had presence," Athanas says. Often Tony liked to bring his dates to Bill and Donna Bates's home in Brookline and just hang around in a domestic setting. "That seemed to make him comfortable," says Bates. Tony would date four or five or six women at the same time, but he wasn't sloppy about it—he was a gentleman, which was part of his great attraction. Sometimes he just couldn't keep their names straight. Once Bates was in the Improper Bostonian when Tony arrived with a date. He took Bates aside and whispered, "When I go to the bathroom, ask her what her name is. I've forgotten."

"Anthony," Bates said. "You brought her in here."

"I know her address," Tony declared. "I don't know her name."

On the road Tony's favorite running mate was Mike Ryan. They would put on their Ban-lon shirts, buttoned all the way up, and sport jackets and check out the in spots in the American League circuit, from Whiskey A-Go-Go on Sunset Boulevard in Los Angeles to parties at the

Stew-Zoo in New York. It was just like the old days in Bradenton, only more so. Tony would walk into a club, and within ten minutes he'd be surrounded by pretty women. He continued to shock and impress his teammates with his audacity. "We'd be sitting in a restaurant and if he saw a girl he liked, he'd send over a note on a folded-up piece of paper," Petrocelli says. "If they threw the note away, he'd just laugh."

It wasn't always easy to have fun with Dick Williams right there in the same hotel. During one off-day in Anaheim, California, Tony and Ryan had all the makings of a party squirreled away in their room—a transistor radio, a six-pack of beer, and two stewardesses—when kindly but decidedly un-hip third-base coach Eddie Popowski checked in while making his rounds. Under Pop's watchful eye, Tony and Ryan escorted the women to the elevator but slipped them the word to wait down in the lobby. After an appropriate amount of time had passed, the boys retrieved the girls and resumed the party. The phone rang. "I want you in my room right now," barked Dick Williams. Ryan and Tony reported to the manager's suite and found Williams, Popowski, and pitching coach Sal Maglie awaiting them. "It was like facing the judge and jury," says Ryan. But the young, happy ballplayers were hardly penitent.

"We're trying to win a pennant here," Williams said.

"It's an off-day—" Ryan began.

"And you, Ryan—you're getting married after the season," Williams continued.

"What does that have to do with right now?" asked Ryan.

"Ryan," a nearly exasperated Williams sighed, "I don't know where you're coming from."

"I come from Haverhill, Massachusetts," Ryan said, and Tony burst out laughing.

"You," Williams said, "are going to see Tom Yawkey about this."

"I'll see Tom Yawkey any time you want," snapped Tony.

Williams threw the pair out of his suite. They went to the lobby, found the stewardesses again, and restarted the party.

Tony loved dinner and dancing and pretty women, but more than ever he hated it when the newspapers referred to him as a playboy. He thought "playboy" made him sound frivolous and unserious about his work—as if he were rolling out of a nightclub and going straight to the ballpark, still wearing a tall silk hat and tails. He was dead serious about sleep. Although he would stay out late, he nearly always got his cherished twelve hours of blissful snoozing. And he was dead serious about staying in shape. Bates noticed the calluses and bloody blisters on Tony's hands from extra batting practice and hours of swinging weighted bats in the apartment. He constantly squeezed a hand grip. Riding in a car, he would simulate his swing, rolling his wrists, repeating a batter's mantra, "Top hand. Top hand." Says Bates: "He was in excellent shape. He ran, he worked out. He was a great physical specimen. He was truly in baseball shape twelve months a year."

When Bates telephoned 566 Commonwealth, he could tell when Tony had played a good game or the Red Sox had won. Tony would hear Bates's voice and say exuberantly, "My . . . my . . . my . . . *my man!*" He said that a lot in the summer of '67. On July 23, Tony smacked the one hundredth home run of his career. At twenty-two years, six months, and sixteen days, he was the second-youngest player in baseball history to reach one hundred (Hall of Famer Mel Ott hit his one hundredth with the New York Giants when he was twenty-two years, four months, and ten days old). Babe Ruth had nine home runs when he was twenty-two. Lou Gehrig had twenty-two. Ted Williams had fifty-four. Yastrzemski had only notched his one hundredth home run on May 16, three months before his twenty-eighth birthday.

Going into August, Tony (with sixty-three fewer at-bats) was a respectable second behind Yastrzemski on the Sox's list of heroes. Tony was hitting .303, Yaz .322. Yaz had twenty-six home runs, Tony nineteen. Yaz had seventy-five runs batted in, Tony had sixty-one. He was the second-hottest player on the hottest team in Boston in twenty-one years. His phone constantly rang: Long-lost relatives called to score tickets. At restaurants breathless fans stopped by the table to request an autograph or just to babble. Tony tried hard not to be annoyed. "I can't be rude," he said. "These people are interested. I know how it is when nobody's interested and this way is better."

As September approached, excitement doubled and redoubled around Boston. The cool, crisp afternoons at Fenway promised to be packed with excitement. The players could feel it. Every move, every hit, every pitch, every catch would be pressed into memory forever. Restaurants in Kenmore Square brazenly announced they were accepting World Series reservations. Tony was again the kid who had everything, the car and the bachelor pad and the girls . . . and a shot at the brightest center stage in baseball, the World Series. It was a magical, sweet spot in time to be twenty-two years old, handsome, healthy, a hometown kid playing right field for the Boston Red Sox. "We were in the prime of our lives," Ryan says, "and on top of the world."

~9~

A Deafening Sound, a Sickening Sound

In the summer of 1967, Chip Penney, ten, and his brother Wayne, nine, residents of Framingham and fans of the Red Sox, were treated to a hitch at the Ted Williams Baseball Camp in Lakeville, Massachusetts. The session ended with graduation ceremonies on Thursday, August 17, and that night the boys' father, Ed Penney, Tony Conigliaro's rock 'n' roll business partner, hung around for a bull session with the Splendid Splinter himself. Ted had watched the contending Red Sox the previous night on television, and naturally had plenty of opinions about them. "The Red Sox made me believe that it is not impossible that they could win the pennant this year," Williams declared. He pontificated on Yastrzemski and George Scott, and then on Tony.

"Tony is crowding the plate," Williams said. "He's much too close. Tell him to back off. It's serious time now. The pitchers are going to get serious."

Penney mentioned he would attend the Red Sox-Angels game the next night at Fenway Park. "Tell Tony what I said," Williams ordered. And as Penney and his sons were leaving the camp, Williams shouted across the dark baseball diamond, "Don't forget to tell Tony what I told you."

The next night was a clear and pleasant Friday evening. The Red Sox were in fourth place, three and one-half games behind the first-place Minnesota Twins. Crowds had started to gather in the afternoon in the narrow streets around Fenway Park, the way they do when frenzied fans just can't wait to get to the game. The Red Sox were in a pennant race, and the excitement and tension spread across the city, with Kenmore Square at a festive, boisterous ground zero. The stands were filled with

31,027 exuberant fans who reveled in their team's first stretch run in a generation. Penney, who had a seat with the Conigliaro family, rapped on the clubhouse door before the game and a guard summoned Tony. "I told him exactly what Ted Williams had told me," recalls Penney.

Tony laughed. He was in another slump; his single in a ten-inning loss to the Detroit Tigers the night before had broken an oh-for-twenty slide. No pitcher throws at a struggling hitter—why shake him from the slumber? "No one is going to take me seriously," scoffed Tony. In fact, his remedy for the hitting drought was just the opposite—he would crowd in tighter than ever. As far as Tony was concerned, this was exactly the wrong time to back off. "He told me he was going to get closer," Billy Conigliaro recalls. "We were all apprehensive about that."

Billy, whose season in the Carolina League had ended early when he tore a hamstring, was at the game with Sal, Teresa, and Richie, fifteen, seated in their usual seats in section fourteen on the first-base side. Gary Bell, a right-handed pitcher who had joined the Red Sox from the Cleveland Indians during the season, started for Boston. Jack Hamilton, a six-foot, two-hundred-pound righty, started for the Angels. Hamilton, twenty-eight, had come up to the big leagues with the Philadelphia Phillies, then pitched for the Tigers and Mets before California picked him up from New York on June 10. On this Friday night in the middle of a pennant race, Hamilton and the Red Sox sparred in an ongoing psychological game. During a Boston loss in Anaheim the previous weekend, Red Sox second baseman Mike Andrews had complained that Hamilton was throwing spitballs. Now, at Fenway, manager Dick Williams again agitated over Hamilton, demanding that home-plate umpire Bill Valentine instruct him to wipe his fingers each time before he threw the ball.

When Tony stepped to the plate for his first at-bat in the second inning, the crowd noted his slump and booed heartily. Tony cracked a curveball for a base hit. In the fourth inning, the game was scoreless. Bell hadn't allowed a hit. Scott led off the Red Sox fourth with a base hit to center but tried for a double and was thrown out at second by Angels centerfielder Jose Cardenal. The crowd was stirred by the hit, Scott's mad dash, and the play at second, and a culprit in the left-field grandstand was moved to heave a smoke bomb onto the outfield grass. A gray cloud billowed over the field and time out was called. Grounds crewmen raced across the lawn and doused the smoke bomb with a fire extinguisher.

Hamilton left the mound for a respite in the visitors dugout. The grounds crew scooped up the smoke bomb in a bucket and play resumed. Reggie Smith lined out to center field. Tony, who batted sixth, stepped up. "He had told me he was going to look for a slider outside and nail it," remembers Scott. Recalls Red Sox third-base coach Bobby Doerr: "Tony was kind of leaning—he was leaning way too much to the outside of the plate." There were still wisps of smoke over the outfield. "It was kind of eerie," Richie Conigliaro says. "You almost felt something was going to happen."

Tony's mind flickered with a thought: "Did the delay stiffen Hamilton's arm?" as Hamilton unleashed the first pitch. It was a high, inside fastball. "A fastball that got away," Hamilton remembers. The ball buzzed toward Tony's head. He was very close to the plate—some contended the bill of his hat poked into the strike zone. Later, Hamilton and others said they thought Tony froze, as if he didn't see the ball. But Tony was never one to wildly duck out of the way of an inside pitch. He liked to flick his head back and let the ball whoosh past closely—it was a way to demonstrate an utter lack of fear to the pitcher. Tony nudged back his head, but the ball tailed in on him. It seemed to follow his head, bearing toward his face, as he moved. When the ball was four feet away, Tony knew he was going to be hit, the way a motorist knows the car is about to crash. He jerked his head back. His batting helmet—like almost everyone in the big leagues at the time, he wore one without an earflap—flipped off. He heard the ball hiss as it cut through the air and felt it wallop squarely at ninety miles per hour into his left eye and cheekbone just below his temple. It was not a glancing blow; the ball plopped onto home plate after it hit him.

"As soon as it crunched into me, it felt as if the ball would go in my head and come out the other side," Tony recalled.

Buck Rodgers, the Angels catcher, was crouched a foot away when the ball hit. "It sounded like a pumpkin, like taking a bat to a pumpkin," he says.

Bobby Knoop was playing second base for the Angels and heard "a very sick sound."

George Scott was in the Red Sox dugout and recalls, "It sounded like a shot. Like a popgun."

Mike Ryan was also on the Sox bench and was startled by "a whack, a sickening sound. I'd seen guys get hit in the neck, between the eyes, but this was different. The ball hit and it was almost like it stuck there."

Carl Yastrzemski was on the top step of the dugout, caught up in the scoreless game, rooting for a hit. "It was a deafening sound, a sickening sound," he says.

Red Sox pitcher Dave Morehead was stretched out on the steps on the far end of the dugout, keeping a pitching chart, as part of his duties as the next day's starter. "I used to love to watch him hit. There was always a chance he could hit one. Then there was a thud," he says.

George Thomas was warming up a pitcher in the Red Sox bullpen and heard the players on the bullpen bench exhale a horrified moan, as if they had witnessed something devastating. "We all stood up to look over the fence to see if Tony was moving his head," he remembers.

As the ball crashed into him, Tony had ducked toward the catcher, then pirouetted clockwise and sprawled head first toward the third-base line, face down, his head resting on his arms. Valentine stood over him, immediately saw the severity of the beaning, and waved frantically to the Red Sox bench for medical help. Concerned players from both teams clambered out of the dugouts and streaked to the plate. The crowd instantly fell completely silent, as if someone had turned off the volume. "You could hear nothing but breathing," remembers Fred Zurawel, who was seated in the right-field grandstand with his fourteen-year-old son, Gregory. "That's all you heard as everyone stood up to see the outcome. It was a tough thing to watch." From their box seats, Sal and Teresa looked on in stunned silence. "I was numb," says Teresa. Billy waited for his brother to get up and brush himself off, the way he always did when he had been plunked. This time, he didn't get up.

Tony, who did not lose consciousness, began to flail on the ground in agony. His eyes were clenched shut. His head was filled with a deafening whistle. The throbbing pain made him sick to his stomach. He could feel his mouth fill with fluid and he was afraid he would no longer be able to breathe. He started praying, begging: "God, please, please don't let me die right here in the dirt at home plate at Fenway Park."

A barely conscious Conigliaro is loaded onto a stretcher while members of the Red Sox crowd around, no one exactly sure what to say at the moment. (UPI/Corbis-Bettmann)

Rico Petrocelli, who was on deck, was the first teammate to reach him. He knelt near his friend's head and tried to soothe him. "Take it easy, Tony, you're going to be all right," he said. Petrocelli struggled hard to be convincing. Tony's eye was swelling and blackening. "It was just blown up in that spot, like you would blow up a balloon," Petrocelli remembers. It made him nauseous to look at it. Other teammates arrived on the scene and were also horrified. "At least for me, running out on the field, it took a couple of seconds to gather yourself," Yastrzemski says. "I almost didn't want to look." Scott was certain the blow had completely knocked out Tony's eye. Rodgers saw blood oozing out of Tony's ear, mouth, and nose, and turned away. Hamilton, visibly concerned, started in from the mound, but Rodgers blocked his path. "Get out of here, get away," Rodgers told him. "Jack, you don't want to see this."* Red Sox trainer Buddy LeRoux told Tony to stay still. Someone handed Mike Ryan an ice pack and he held it to Tony's face. He noticed there was an indentation, an actual dent, where the ball had hit. Doerr ambled in from the third-base coach's box. He had seen a lot of baseball and had seen a lot of batters get hit, but nothing like this. "You had to wonder if he would make it through the night," he says. Lonborg hurried a stretcher onto the field and Tony was carried off into the clubhouse. "Tony and I had our disagreements," Dick Williams would recall. "But at this moment, I actually prayed."

Tony was placed on a table in the trainer's room. He was awake, but groggy, and pleaded for something to dull the pain. Red Sox team physician Dr. Thomas M. Tierney checked his vital signs. Tony heard cleats scrape on the concrete floor as teammates ducked in to see him. "Roomie, hey, Roomie," said Ryan, but Tony could only moan. Ryan knew Tony was as tough as nails, but now he was worried. "He's really hurting," he thought. Richie cried in a corner, out of the way so Tony wouldn't hear. Sal stood and watched, stone silent as the sound of the approaching ambulance siren grew louder. Rick Williams, the ten-year-old son of the manager, sat and watched. He would never forget the discoloration in Tony's face and the scary air of deep concern in the quiet,

---

*Not all the Angels were so compassionate. Outfielder Jay Johnstone, caught up in the heat of battle, remembers wishing they would hurry up and remove Tony from the field so the game could continue.

crowded room. Even at ten Rick had noticed Tony seemed so much younger and more spirited than the other players. And here he was, on a stretcher, battered and moaning and apparently in grave danger.

Sal and Dr. Tierney rode with Tony in the fifteen-minute ambulance ride from Fenway Park to Sancta Maria Hospital across the Charles River in Cambridge. Every turn and jerk on the trip jolted Tony with pain. With Massachusetts General and several other distinguished hospitals nearby, relatively small Sancta Maria struck the family as an odd choice. It just happened to be where Red Sox players always went when they were injured. To Red Sox fans, it was a chilling reminder: Thirteen years earlier, another local hero from the North Shore, Harry Agganis of Lynn, was in his second season with the Red Sox when he was hospitalized at Sancta Maria with pneumonia and died of a pulmonary embolism at age twenty-five.

After he was x-rayed and examined by neurosurgeons, who were grateful to find no further internal bleeding, Tony was moved upstairs to a bed. He was given codeine, which left him woozy but still in considerable pain. Fluids oozed out of his mouth onto his pillow. Tony had suffered a fractured left cheekbone, scalp contusions, a dislocated jaw, and a severely bruised left eye. Sal was badly shaken when doctors determined that if the ball had struck two inches higher—on the temple—Tony would have been killed.

Sal, Teresa, Billy, and Richie were allowed to enter the room for a short visit. Teresa held Tony's hand, and no one said much. Then the family was ushered out and Tony was left alone, in the dark. He couldn't open his left eye at all. He could only open his right eye slightly. He was terrified by thoughts of dying. He wrote in *Seeing It Through,* "I wanted to have someone around to hold onto, but no one was there now. I was never so alone in my whole life." Every fifteen minutes, the nun-nurses checked his pulse and blood pressure and assured him he would be all right. Tony thought that was the kind of thing they said to everybody, even people who were about to die.

It was a long night for everyone associated with Tony. Dick O'Connell, the Red Sox general manager, spoke with Dr. Tierney before going to bed. "I'll only call you if something goes wrong," Tierney said. In the wee hours, O'Connell's phone jostled him awake. He answered, heard a voice say, "This is Tom," and felt a chill: He was sure his young

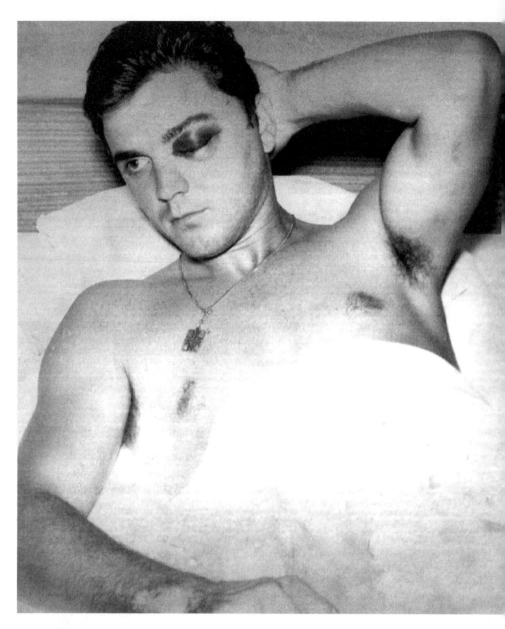

This was a sight that would haunt baseball fans for years. A day after being beaned by California Angels pitcher Jack Hamilton, Tony lies in a Sancta Maria Hospital bed, beginning his long road to recovery. (UPI/Corbis-Bettmann)

outfielder was gone and Tom Tierney was calling with the tragic news. "This is Tom Yawkey," the voice said, and O'Connell resumed normal breathing and gave the owner an update on Tony's condition.

On Saturday morning Tony awoke groggy and felt someone holding his hand. It was Yawkey, and Tony was moved by his visit. But he didn't feel much better. His left eye was still completely shut, he could barely see blurred images with his right eye, and his mouth was still badly swollen, so it hurt to talk or eat anything other than soup and frappés through a straw.

Besides family and patrician baseball owners, visitors were barred. Hamilton came to the hospital but was turned away. As Tony's roommate, Mike Ryan figured he was as good as family, but he was turned away as well. Undeterred, he went around the back of the old building, leaped to catch the fire escape ladder, pulled it down, and climbed to Tony's floor. A nun tried to stop him at the door, but Ryan politely talked his way past her and shouldered in.

"Hey, Roomie, come on out. I've got the babes and some beer waiting downstairs in the car," Ryan said.

"Hiya, Roomie," said Tony, but otherwise he wasn't up for banter.

He just wanted to rest, but the world wanted to reach out to him. A huge basket of fruit from his teammates was delivered to the room. Telegrams and flowers from friends and strangers followed. When the family came later in the day, Sal thought the jungle of floral arrangements made the place look like a funeral home. Red Sox team photographer Jerry Buckley was granted entry at noon, and he made photographs of Tony to distribute to the press. The image of the handsome young man with an ugly black welt over his left eye, a slight stubble of beard, sitting up in a hospital bed, Saint Christopher's medal on his bare chest, ran in newspapers across the country.

When it was clear Tony was out of danger, the reaction to his injury turned to mundane issues. Once he knew he wasn't going to expire in the middle of the night in a lonely hospital room, Tony's thoughts turned to baseball. He wanted to know who had won the game in which he was nearly killed.* And as he listened to the games on the radio (the television light bothered his eyes), he wanted to know when he could return to play and rejoin the fun. No one could say for sure—Tierney told him there was no permanent eye damage, but he would probably miss four weeks, maybe eight, which meant he would miss the rest of the season. Tony thought that was nuts, that he could be back in action in ten days or two weeks at the most, as soon as the swelling in his left eye subsided.

The Red Sox, meanwhile, had to address the loss of their second-best player in the middle of a tight pennant race. They were worried. "When we found out he was all right, but was going to miss the season, there was a lull," Yastrzemski recalls. "It was almost like, 'There goes our pennant chances.' You thought that way because you don't lose that caliber of a player in a pennant race with four teams going for a pennant." O'Connell, Williams, and player personnel director Haywood Sullivan considered Jim King, a lefty hitter with the Indians, and the aging defensive specialist Jim Landis, who had recently been released by the Tigers. Williams also thought of moving Joe Foy, Elston Howard, or even George Scott to the outfield.

Then there was the matter of passing judgment on Hamilton. At first Williams hinted the tragic pitch was a spitball, which would have brought the sanctimonious Great Aunt down hard on Hamilton. Even if he didn't mean to hit Tony, and even if dozens of pitchers around the league regularly served spitballs, Hamilton would have been pilloried for allowing an accident to happen on an illegal pitch. But then Williams and just about everyone else agreed Tony was beaned by a fastball that got away (in *Seeing It Through,* though, Tony said he thought it was a spitter). And the Great Aunt went easy on Hamilton, who had shown proper remorse immediately after the game and tried to visit the hospital the next day. He also did not have the reputation as a head-hunter. He was known to plunk a batter now and then—he had drilled Tony Horton in the minor leagues the previous season—but those were mostly the result of wildness. Hamilton did not always know where his fastball was going.

*The Red Sox did, 3-2; Tony had started the winning rally when he was hit. Jose Tartabull ran for him, and Tartabull and Petrocelli scored on Rico's triple and Jim Fregosi's throwing error.

No one accused Hamilton of purposely hitting Tony; it wouldn't make sense. The game was scoreless at the time and pitchers rarely put a man on base in a pitcher's duel. Furthermore, Tony was in a slump and didn't hit Hamilton particularly well: Pitchers plunk batters on hot streaks in general or on hot streaks against their pitches. At worst, Hamilton had tried to come inside to move Tony off the plate and set him up for an outside pitch, which was a perfectly legitimate baseball tactic.

It was simply a terrible accident, with no one to blame. But even in cases of arbitrary horror, people do what they can to distance themselves from culpability. Hamilton and Rodgers said Tony "froze," that maybe he lost sight of the ball, which of course deflected blame away from the person who threw the ball. Tony, meanwhile, wasn't going to take the rap for nearly getting himself killed. Immediately after he was hit, and for the rest of his life, he vehemently denied he froze. "I definitely made a move to get out of the way of the ball," he wrote in *Seeing It Through*.*

Tony improved each day in the hospital. The vision in his good eye came around. The headaches backed off. His mouth felt well enough to add pizza to his diet. Dr. Tierney thought his patient's spirits good enough to give him a mirror to get a look at the wound: Tony was initially sickened, then intrigued to examine closely and pick out the imprint from the stitches on the ball. On Thursday morning, August 25, Tony blinked in the bright sunlight on the hospital steps on his way home. His injured eye was still black and swollen, but far less grotesque. "My vision is blurred in my left eye, but the doctors told me there is no permanent damage," he told the press. He said his teeth still felt numb, the notion that Hamilton had hit him on purpose was "ridiculous," and he was taking a one-week vacation.

Sal toted home two large mail sacks, filled with get-well letters and postcards. During his six-day hospital stay, Tony had received ten thousand pieces of mail. Significantly, none of the mail, none of the phone calls, and none of the visits were from Dick Williams. Tony hadn't

---

*Oddly, as the long-range consequence of the injury became clear, the urge to purge even a wisp of guilt got stronger. After Tony's death, and after every obituary pointed to the beaning as the beginning of the end for the tragic figure, Hamilton and Rodgers both remembered the pitch coming on an oh-two count—the least likely count to hit a batter on purpose.

Accompanied by his father, Sal, and Sister Marie Leonard, Tony leaves the hospital for the first time after the beaning. The two sacks of mail are indicative of the large outpouring of support that came Conigliaro's way. (Boston Herald archives photo)

heard a peep from his manager since the beaning, which deeply angered and hurt him and completely poisoned his perspective on Williams for the rest of his life. In his autobiography Williams lamely explained his gross insensitivity: "We were all very upset by the beaning and tried almost immediately to visit Conigliaro in the hospital. But team owner Tom Yawkey said no. And not just in the beginning. Every time I tried to visit Conigliaro, Yawkey said no. He allowed only himself that privilege"—as if Yawkey monitored Williams's movements, mail, and telephone calls.

As a flight attendant—or "stewardess" in those days—Julie Markakis got to do a lot of traveling herself. She eventually met and for a while dated another baseball player, Ken "Hawk" Harrelson. Small world: Harrelson ended up being Tony C's replacement in right field for the Red Sox after Tony was beaned in August 1967. (Photo courtesy of Julie Markakis)

The day after Tony went home to Swampscott, the Red Sox signed Ken "Hawk" Harrelson to play right field in his absence. Harrelson was twenty-five, flamboyant, and outspoken. He became available after he criticized nutty Kansas City Athletics owner Charlie Finley for firing manager Alvin Dark, and Finley retaliated by releasing him. The world was too strange that summer. Harrelson had also recently become friendly with, and was about to start a romance with, an Eastern Air Lines flight attendant he had met in New York—Julie Markakis.

Tony fully intended to return to the Red Sox before the end of the season. Watching the team on television—something he had never done regularly before in his life—was eating at him. "I'd like to charge right through the screen and pick up a bat," he said. Also, for the first time in his life, he felt helpless. He had reached the big leagues by working hard, by pushing himself, by riding an incredible will to succeed. Now he was out of the big leagues, and he couldn't do a thing about it until he could see out of his left eye.

Tony and a friend, a round, Runyonesque nightclub manager named Jerry Maffeo, got away to Grossinger's, a resort in the Catskill Mountains there. Maffeo could always make Tony laugh, and he pulled out all his tricks on the long drive there. Eight years older than Tony, he told stories about growing up in the Italian-American North End of Boston, about taking baths in the kitchen sink, and how the neighborhood chooches had names like "Spinny Moe" and "Crap-in-the-Kisser" and "Billy Bong" and "Busy-Boops." And that did it: Tony had to pull the car off the road. "He was laughing so hard he was crying," Maffeo recalls. When they got to Grossinger's, they took a suite together and worked out a signal: If either of them had a girl in the room, he would place a chair upside down outside the door as a do-not-disturb sign. "I learned that from a dance teacher in the White Mountains," Maffeo says. "With Tony, every time I went to the room, the chair was upside down. How many times could this kid do it? He was always with a different girl, each one better than the last one. He had a nice, sincere way about him. Girls just took to him. They wanted to mother him."

Still, when he wasn't putting the chair in the hall or leading the Simon Says contest in the lounge ("He was the star. He loved it," says Maffeo), Tony tested the eye. He brought a handful of Ping-Pong balls and a broomstick to the room and had Maffeo pitch to him. Tony couldn't hit them. He saw double images and knocked over drinking glasses when he reached for them. The injury was playing havoc with his depth perception. Maffeo remembers introducing Tony to a friend who had lost an eye in the Pacific in World War II. The man took out a quarter and asked Tony to catch it. The man flipped the coin. Tony reached and grabbed air. "I know," said the one-eyed man.

When he got home Tony went to Dr. I. Francis Gregory in Cambridge for his first thorough eye examination since the beaning.

Previously, there had been too much swelling for an accurate evaluation. Tony couldn't see much of the wall chart. Since he was in the hospital, the eye had actually gotten worse. Then Gregory looked into the eye and said, "This is not good, my boy," and Tony could feel panic tighten his throat.

Gregory said the injury had caused a cyst to form on the macula lutea, the area of the retina responsible for direct, central vision. Tony asked if it would ever heal. Gregory said he didn't know and suggested they visit the retina expert, Dr. Charles Regan, of Retina Associates in Boston the next day.

Tony later said he was "scared to death," but as usual he masked it. Dr. Regan, erudite and no-nonsense, remembers that the young baseball player was "a pretty cocky character—difficult to handle. He was temperamental. The arrogance of youth. But we had a crusty old nurse who sat him down and handled him like a mother. She had him eating out of her hand." Regan did an examination and agreed that Tony had a blind spot from a cyst on the macula, which had formed during the massive swelling. He said it was a common development after a direct blow to the eye. He also said people who suffer the injury almost always healed well enough to resume perfectly normal lives—but not many of them were required to pick out the stitches on a baseball spinning at ninety miles per hour. Tony forced himself to ask, "Will I ever be able to see well enough to play ball again?" Regan said he didn't know, it was too soon to tell, and to come back in a week.

Tony went home to Swampscott and worried. He couldn't help checking the eye, hoping each time that somehow, some way, it would get better and he could tell the doctors they were all wrong. One day he sat in the living room with Richie and suddenly said, "Let's go see how I can see the ball." Richie fetched a couple of gloves and the brothers went into the yard and played catch. To Tony, the big leagues, Fenway Park, and the pennant race never seemed so far away. Never. "He was closing his injured eye and catching the ball," remembers Richie. "When he opened his eye, he wouldn't catch it."

Regan's next exam revealed no improvement. Tony was still unwilling just to sit around and wait while the pennant race rushed ahead without him. The following Monday, on September 11, he showed up in the early afternoon at mostly empty Fenway Park and had Billy pitch to him. He wore a helmet with an earflap and needed to compose himself for a moment when he realized he was back at home plate, the exact spot where he had nearly been killed. For the first time in his entire life, he was not overflowing with confidence while trying to hit a baseball. He took about twelve swings, without a solid hit and with many complete misses. "Not good, not good at all," Tony told reporters who happened to be at the ballpark. "I couldn't tell where the pitches were. I can see the ball, but I can't judge its location. Pitches come across a foot away from where I think they are. Inside pitches look outside. I can't kid myself." Then he turned to Billy and said, "I'm going to try it again. Get out there and throw hard." This time, he hit a couple to the wall in left. He was adjusting to his skewed depth perception and guessing where the ball was. "That was better," he said. "But I know I'm not ready."

Three days later Regan examined him again and gave him the verdict: It would be dangerous to play baseball again in 1967. Tony went to his apartment at 566 Commonwealth Avenue. The Red Sox were playing an important weekend series against the Baltimore Orioles. Boston, Detroit, and Minnesota were tied for first place and Chicago was a half-game back. It was a grand pennant race, a national story, the brightest spotlight in Boston sports since 1946 . . . and Tony was two blocks away, watching from a tenth-floor balcony. At night Fenway Park glowed like a green jewel. Tony could hear the thunder of the crowd roll across the darkened rooftops. He could even see Harrelson, a small figure in a bright, white uniform, dart in and out of view in Tony's old position in right field. It had all come so easily to him: He had worked hard and was immediately rewarded with a dizzying ride to the big leagues. Now, one pitch had changed everything. He was offstage—just another average nobody spectator. For the first time, now that it was gone, he appreciated what he had had. He didn't care about beauty queens or owning a slick nightclub or getting a faster car. He wanted to play baseball, to be with his teammates, to rejoin the party that was raging downstairs while he sat alone, upstairs in the dark. Tony looked at the tiny, white figure in right field and cried.

He visited the clubhouse before a game and saw his old teammates doing their old routines, was greeted by Ryan and Petrocelli, exchanged hand-slaps with Scott, and felt his face tighten when Dick

Williams emerged from his corner office, strolled over, and shook his hand. Williams didn't say a word about not visiting or calling Tony since the beaning, and as far as Tony was concerned, that was the thoughtless manager's last chance. He had to get out of the clubhouse and get away from the ballpark. He had to get away from Williams. And he had to get away from the terrible feeling of being an outsider. A baseball team is a tightly closed group—a true clubhouse—with the world divided into members and nonmembers. Tony now was a nonmember. When the Red Sox posed for the official World Series team photo, for use in case they won the pennant, Tony wore a uniform and sat with his hands on his knees in the front row. But he was the twenty-sixth man on a twenty-five-man team. He might as well have been a batboy.

Tony's immediate sorrow was missing the fabulous pennant race, but he was also secretly fearful for his career. The doctors could throw sophisticated tests and Latin terminology at him, but none of them could say for sure if the eye would ever clear up. Tony, of course, kept testing himself, the way a kid with a skinned knee picks at the scab. When the team was at home, he suited up and shagged flies before games—but found he had to let fly balls drop in front of him because he couldn't gauge their flight. When the team was on the road, he went to Fenway and had a batboy, Keith Rosenfeld, pitch to him—and found he couldn't even hit the offerings of a 120-pound teenager. Whenever people asked how the eye was doing—and everyone asked—Tony would tell them, "Fine. Just fine."

Going into the final weekend of the season, the American League title was still undecided among Minnesota, Detroit, Boston, and the White Sox. Chicago lost Friday night and was eliminated. So it came down to the Red Sox and Twins, who would play a two-game series at Fenway, and the Tigers, who were playing the Angels. O'Connell secured special permission from the commissioner's office for Tony to sit on the bench in uniform. Tony roamed the dugout. He cheered, conferred with Yastrzemski about pitchers, and felt better to be with his teammates, but he still felt like an outsider. The Red Sox won Saturday and won again Sunday on a three-run homer by Yastrzemski, whose fabulous Triple Crown season elevated him to the top of the baseball ziggurat with Hank Aaron, Frank Robinson, Al Kaline, and Willie Mays. The victory ignited a riotous celebration. Fans poured out of the bleachers, grandstand, and box seats and covered the infield with a mob of squirming, dancing, jumping humanity. Lonborg, the winning pitcher, was carried off the field. Frenzied celebrants ripped pieces off the left-field scoreboard, pulled up swatches of the hallowed turf, climbed the screen behind home plate, and pounded on the dugout. On Lansdowne Street, which runs behind the left-field wall, on Brookline Avenue and Kenmore Square, people paraded and danced and screamed. It was called Boston's greatest street demonstration of joy since the autumn night John F. Kennedy won the 1960 presidential election.

The Red Sox, meanwhile, retired to their clubhouse and sat on their celebration. The pennant was Boston's only if Detroit lost the second game of its doubleheader against the Angels, and they listened to the game on the radio. Detroit trailed in the ninth and when Dick McAuliffe hit into a double play to end it, the Red Sox clubhouse exploded with pent-up partying. Players threw one another into the showers. Champagne sprayed across the room. Schlitz beer poured from brown bottles. Shaving cream squirted in every direction. Players hugged and hollered and danced. They had been one-hundred-to-one shots to win the pennant. Now they were going to the World Series. Yastrzemski, the ultimate hero, deliriously paraded through the celebration with a glob of shaving cream on his head and an unlit cigar clenched in his teeth. And Tony, who had hollered gleefully with his teammates, suddenly sat before his locker and cried.

Ryan, standing nearby, stopped cheering and put his arm around Tony. "What's wrong, Roomie?"

"It's nothing," Tony said. "Just what the hell did I do? What did I contribute?"

"You helped," Ryan reassured him. "You know that. Come on, that's nothing to cry about. Damn it, we're champs."

Tony shook his head as tears poured down his cheeks. Tom Yawkey sat next to him, put his arms around him, and said, "Tony, you helped. You were a part of it. Those games you won for us in the early part of the season, well, they're just as important as today's game."

Tony just kept crying. He felt like an interloper, as if he were one of the yahoos outside pounding on the dugout who somehow found his way into the clubhouse. He also felt terribly cheated. For three years he had drudged through terrible, tedious seasons with the

Red Sox. Now, the Impossible Dream had come true, and he was out of it, all because of one lousy pitch. This wasn't supposed to happen, not to him. He was the Child of Destiny—the newspapers actually called him that, over and over again. His career, his story—"Local Teen Reaches Red Sox"—had always been something to savor, something to marvel at. Now people felt sorry for him, and he felt sorry for himself. That wasn't unusual—he had felt sorry for himself when Billy Herman benched him and the fans booed him—but to show it, right there in the Red Sox clubhouse, was rare and startling. He was hurting. Rico had never seen his friend so down. Neither had Ryan, the man who could always make Tony laugh.

"Come on, Roomie, I've got two outside," Ryan urged. "Let's go. The city's ours tonight."

"No," thought Tony. "The city is yours tonight." He exited the rocking, happy clubhouse, left the ballpark, shouldered through the narrow, mobbed streets, and made his way to Sonny's, a club in Kenmore Square, where his pal and roommate, Tony Athanas, waited. Tony was still sad and grieving, but somewhere on the walk between the Red Sox clubhouse and the bar, he became his old self. He tucked his trouble deep inside. "When I saw him," said Athanas, "he was thrilled."

The Red Sox played the Cardinals in the World Series, and Tony was again granted permission to wear a uniform and sit on the bench. And it was torture. Tony lived for the spotlight, craved clutch situations, and dreamed of being the hero, and here was the World Series, where heroic legends are pressed into history forever. And he was just a spectator with a swell seat. Tony tried to get involved. He cheered and clapped for his teammates and issued individual pep talks before games, and his teammates looked at him and nodded, but it was all a little pathetic. "He was completely lost," Ryan reflects. "It was hurting him inside. It was killing him. Here was a guy who dreams of the limelight and there was the World Series and he's on the bench and can't do anything."

The Red Sox lost the Series in seven games. Harrelson batted .077 and Tartabull .154 as Tony's replacements in right field. For the Red Sox, a franchise haunted by what-might-have-beens, there was one more: What might have been had Tony Conigliaro played in the 1967 World Series? "There's no doubt, I've said it a million times, if Tony had been in that lineup, we would have won," Scott says. "He was one of those guys. Reggie Jackson was a big-game player. Tony was that kind of player." Notes Yastrzemski, "I'd like to have seen the outcome of the World Series with his bat in there."

What might have been—at age twenty-two, unable to hit pitches thrown by the Red Sox batboy, Tony did not want to even think about it.

~10~

HEY, TONY, HOW'S THE EYE?

IF TONY CONIGLIARO HEARD IT ONCE, HE HEARD IT A BILLION TIMES, EVERYWHERE HE WENT. People no longer said hello. They said, "Hey, Tony, how's the eye?"

He heard it from teammates in the clubhouse and from school kids on the street.

"Hey, Tony, how's the eye?"

He heard it from old guys in the pizza joint and from young women in the nightclub.

"Hey, Tony, how's the eye?"

He heard it from traffic cops in Kenmore Square and from Orlando Cepeda on the field before Game One of the World Series.

"Hey, Tony, how's the eye?"

His eye was terrible, but Tony always gave a thumbs-up or made an OK circle with his thumb and forefinger or just muttered, "Great. It's great." To Tony, it was just another well-meaning, if inane, greeting, and after a while it became Muzak to his everyday life and he really didn't even hear it.

Then he went to Vietnam.

The trip was arranged by the commissioner's office a few weeks after the World Series. The war had become a bloody sinkhole and peace protests were spreading, so America's bedrock institutions, such as Major League Baseball, Bob Hope, and *Playboy* magazine, were needed more than ever to boost troop morale. At first, Tony was reluctant. He didn't see what good a Boston Red Sox outfielder could do for grunts in a combat zone. They needed showgirls, not ballplayers. But Tony had always respected and admired war veterans. His grandfather, Antonio Conigliaro, had served in World War I, Uncle Vinnie was wounded in the Pacific in World War II, his friend, Bill Bates, had been wounded in Korea, and his best pal, Freddie Atkinson, had been killed in Vietnam. Tony thought they were heroes. So he joined Yankees legend Joe DiMaggio, Cincinnati Reds star Pete Rose, and former Yankees second baseman and Korean War combat pilot Jerry Coleman on a fifteen-day tour.

Tony got a taste of the most chilling experience of his generation. He made the twenty-nine-and-one-half-hour flight from Boston to Southeast Asia and felt the weirdness of riding a commercial jet into a war zone, including the roller-coaster descent into Saigon in order to avoid ground fire. He was hit in the face by the stink and ninety-degree heat. He shook hands with the commander of U.S. forces, Gen. William Westmoreland. He rode in Huey helicopter gunships over thick jungles and brown rivers and saw orange explosions amid the greenery and the wink of enemy fire in the distance. Down below, Americans around his own age fought and died and wondered what for, and what the hell was going on back home. Tony was not into geopolitics, but he knew a thankless task when he saw it. "I won't say the antiwar demonstrations are hurting the guys' morale," he later told Tim Horgan of the *Boston Herald*. "But they aren't helping it any, either."

Tony slept in tents and lay awake at night, listening to the crump of artillery. He went to Da Nang, Khe Sanh, Dong Ha, Cua Viet, and Con Thien. He saw soldiers younger than he, with faces blackened with camouflage paint and toting M-16s, grenades, and rocket launchers, saddle up and troop off into the jungle at night. He saw helicopters unload body bags as if they were sacks of mail. "It was just stunned silence," Coleman remembers. "We saw it all."

And everywhere he went, Tony heard it. "Hey, Tony, how's the eye?" asked a private stretched out on a hospital table in Da Nang, his thigh ripped open by shrapnel.

From a marine about to head into the bush at Phu Bai: "Hey, Tony, how's the eye?"

From a GI in an intensive care unit in a hospital, sitting in a wheelchair, a scar from his neck to his navel, burns on his hands and arms, a portion of his skull blown off: "Tony, come here," and when Tony approached and bent over close enough to smell antiseptic, the man said, "How's your eye?"

It's November 1967 and Tony joins a USO entourage headed to Vietnam and Thailand to entertain the troops. Note fellow baseball star Pete Rose among those preparing to fly out of Travis Air Force Base in California. (UPI/Corbis-Bettmann)

Tony returned home with a captured Viet Cong flag to hang on the wall at 566 Commonwealth Avenue, and a better attitude. He would not feel sorry for himself and question the unfairness of having his life changed by one pitch. Not after what he had seen in Vietnam. "I had only an eye injury from a baseball game," Tony wrote in *Seeing It Through,* "and even if I never played again, what did that add up to compared to these kids who were losing their lives and coming home with broken bodies."

So, how *was* the eye? Regan examined Tony on November 17 and said it had stabilized. The doctor told Tony that, basically, the rest was up to him. He had two problems to deal with. He had a small, blurry spot when he looked straight ahead with his left eye. This was caused by scar tissue on the macula. He also had warped depth perception, the result of his newly uneven vision: The right eye was 20-10, but now the left was 20-50. It was a matter of Tony's adjusting to the blurry spot and his brain's getting used to the altered signals coming from his eyes. Regan said that practice—using the eyes—would help the adjustment, just as an injured arm or leg is rehabilitated after an injury. Whether Tony could ever adjust well enough to play major-league baseball was anyone's guess.

Tony was grateful to get back to work. He constantly tested the eye—closing the right to check the view from the left. Now he was cleared to test it in a batting cage. On November 29, he went to the Dillon Field House at Harvard University and batted against Red Sox right-hander Darrell Brandon, who was working out back and shoulder ailments. Brandon threw him thirty-seven pitches. Tony missed only one of them and to untrained observers appeared to smack the others with authority. "I feel terrific," Tony commented afterward, but then he went upstairs, showered, and confided in Red Sox trainer Buddy LeRoux, "I don't know where the hell the ball is. I don't know if I can make it this year." It would not be the last time Tony fibbed about his eye and not the last time wishful-thinking onlookers were gladly misled.

Through the winter Tony worked out three times a week at Harvard without much progress. For the first time in his life, he was not fun to be around. When Sal wanted to hold a baseball in front of Tony's face

*Conigliaro arrives at Retina Associates for another eye test in early April 1968. It's unsure what Tony was trying to illustrate with his fingers, although that could have meant how close he thought he was to being able to make a comeback. (*Boston Herald *archives photo)*

and move it around to test his vision, Tony snapped at his father and told him to go away. When Billy stopped by the apartment with a date to watch television, Tony embarrassed his brother by telling him to find somewhere else to watch TV. Tony, the kid who was always trying something new, was mostly sitting around the house and the apartment. He needed distractions and needed to stop obsessing about the eye and baseball. At last, after the holidays, he went on a hunting expedition to New Mexico for Curt Gowdy's television show *The American Sportsman.* In late January 1968, with Ed Penney's help, he made his first appearance on *The Merv Griffin Show.* And he starting singing engagements at a club called O'Dee's in Cambridge.

O'Dee's was large and smoky, with a long bar and small tables and a loud juke box blaring "Soul Man" and "The Letter" and "Groovin' " and "Don't Sleep in the Subway." The cover charge was a dollar, coats were checked for a quarter, and the place was usually crammed with swinging sixties youths, young men in tight slacks and turtlenecks, young women in pantsuits or miniskirts, most of them looking for free love. The juke box would be turned off at nine o'clock and Tony would sing, often accompanied by a petite blonde singer named Cheryl Ann Parker and the All Night Workers band. Wearing a formal dinner jacket and black tie, using a hand-held mike, Tony belted out songs like "Can't Take My Eyes off You" and "Testify," and many young women in the audience would swoon, even if, in the words of a *Boston Globe* reviewer, "his main trouble is that his singing is average, very average." His banter between songs was worse. Many used the break between songs to order beers at the bar. "I had a good voice," Tony offered years later, "but I was as mobile as a mannequin onstage." In the first week of February he happily ditched the diversions, loaded his convertible, and drove with Billy to Florida. Tony knew a big test was ahead. "It wasn't a matter of if I could do it," he recalled later. "It was a matter of I must do it."

Tony started by hitting against pitching machines. As usual, he was tireless—he swung at about three hundred balls a day. He was also annoyed. The batting cages were just a few feet away from the Red Sox's cinder-block clubhouse at Chain o' Lakes Park, and just about anybody could press against the chain-link fencing and watch. For once, Tony didn't want to be onstage—not until he got it perfect. Sal, Uncle Vinnie, neighbors from Swampscott, and the press scrutinized every swing, and they were all wishful thinkers. "The kid looks good," somebody would say, and Tony would quietly bristle. He could see well enough to time and hit straight pitches from a machine, but his left eye still wasn't right. Even people who should have known better were overly optimistic. Dick Williams watched him hit on the first day, looked satisfied, and said, "You're doing all right."

After a few days, Tony was ready for a living, breathing pitcher. Veteran left-hander Dick Ellsworth—a one-time twenty-game winner with the Cubs now with the Red Sox—was summoned to the mound.

Wearing a specially designed temple and cheekbone protector attached to his batting helmet, Tony gets in some swings at Harvard University in January 1968. (AP/Wide World Photos)

While with the Phillies the previous spring, Ellsworth had pitched against a healthy Tony. This time he saw a completely different batter. For one thing, Tony stood about six inches farther off the plate. "He was somewhat tentative," remembers Ellsworth. "But I don't think it took him long to shake that and he went to the task at hand. You could tell that he sensed he had a battle ahead of him."

Part of Tony's battle was mental. Every beaned batter must struggle with the awful memory when he steps to the plate. As Sal observed, "You get hit over the head with a sledgehammer and you don't forget about it in a hurry." One of Tony's greatest assets had been his utter fearlessness, and he had to revive it. He had to force himself to crowd in close and stick his face right back where it was the night Hamilton's fastball crashed into it. But there were huge differences now. For one, Tony's vision was impaired. He had to stand tough against fastballs that he couldn't quite see. For another, in the Darwinian world of major-league baseball, pitchers would test his nerve with extra ruthlessness. They would throw at him.

On the eve of his debut in the exhibition season, Tony was asked about head-hunting pitchers. Lonborg had said, "It wouldn't surprise me if Tony got knocked down Opening Day." Tony shot back, "The next time a pitcher throws at me deliberately I am going to the mound with a bat in my hands. I'm not going to let some pitcher kill me. If I think they're throwing at me, I'm heading for the mound, and I'm not going out there with my bare hands." The Red Sox opened the preseason against the White Sox, and Tony's audacious challenge was posted in the Chicago locker room. Eddie Stanky's pitchers naturally took the dare. Tommy John hurled a pitch eighteen inches above Tony's head. Don McMahon, a Sox teammate the previous summer, sailed a high and tight pitch that sent Tony sprawling in the dirt.

For the first two weeks of the exhibition season, Tony batted moderately well. During a batting practice session against teammate Gary Bell, Tony hit mostly line drives, and Williams said, "What am I worrying about? Tony's back on the beam." As far as the wishful thinkers were concerned, the eye was all right. And when Tony's hitting started to deteriorate, they all chalked it up to a slump. After all, once an eye is all right, it doesn't go bad again. Besides, Tony didn't complain about his eyesight.

But the eye was getting worse, and a terrible panic churned in him. In a game against the Cardinals he doubled against Steve Carlton but was shaken as he trotted off the field for a pinch runner. He hadn't seen the ball—he had merely guessed. If it had been a knockdown, it would have hit him in the head. Tony rarely revealed self-doubt to anybody, but he started to confide in his closest friends on the team. In the third week of March, Tony was sitting in the dugout next to Ken Harrelson and said, "Hawk, do you see that light pole over there by third base?" Harrelson said he did. "Well, I can't see that light on top of it," said Tony. Harrelson simply didn't believe him—he knew Tony was prone to exaggerate. That night the Hawk took his friend to dinner, and Tony brought it up again. "Hawk, I can't see out of my left eye," he said. "If this keeps up, I'll never play again."

A few days later Tony was rooming with Petrocelli on an exhibition road trip to Atlanta. In their quarters they talked hitting and Tony confessed, "Rico, I can't see the ball right. Something's wrong with my eye." Later, Tony telephoned home from the room and talked to Sal, and Rico could hear his friend cry.

Tony never told Williams, which made matters worse. Although Williams was innately insensitive, it was impossible for him to indulge a problem he didn't know about. At the start of camp Williams had told Tony, "You're on your own this spring, Tony. You can do anything you want. I won't push you. When you're ready to play in a game, just let me know. Everything's up to you this spring." But now Williams thought the eye was all right and Tony was just being a nuisance about a slump. When a pitcher didn't arrive as scheduled to throw him extra batting practice, Tony complained and Williams fumed. When Tony took more than his allotted swings in the cage one day, Williams grumbled to him and Tony fumed. Pressure brought out the worst in both of them. Tony needed more coddling than ever, and Williams more than ever was incapable of giving it to him. Tony was in the greatest stress of his life and needed handling with care. Williams was under stress, too—his second-best hitter, Tony, was questionable, and his best pitcher, Lonborg, was out with a knee injury suffered on a ski slope. "I was the one who had to put up with things like Conigliaro's comeback from eye trouble," Williams wrote in his autobiography. "Yes, it was a brave and impressive effort he made, but Conigliaro soured everyone by expecting all of us to treat him like a superstar."

Tony's hitting worsened. He no longer even made contact. "Lately, he wasn't even fouling the pitches off," noted Red Sox outfielder Reggie Smith. "He was missing pitches by a foot." Everyone had a theory: It was glare from the bright Florida sunshine; pitchers were always ahead of the hitters in the spring. One theory rattled Tony to his bones: He was slumping because he was gun-shy. They said he was afraid of getting beaned. "Every official in the Red Sox camp denies it," *Herald* columnist Tim Horgan wrote, "but my own and a dozen other sets of eyeballs insist that Tony is 'bailing out' at the plate. He's sticking his left foot into the bucket toward third base instead of stepping into the ball as he previously did. As a result he can't cover the outside corner."

Before a Saturday game against the Yankees, Tony was hit in the shin during a round of pepper and his worry deepened. If he couldn't see the ball playing pepper, how could he see a ninety-mile-per-hour fastball? Tony said he had a sore throat and asked out of the lineup. Williams, showing a knack for doing precisely the wrong thing, penciled him in anyway. Tony struck out four times and felt tears come to his eyes as he stood in right field. "We were talking in the outfield and he told me about his eye," Yastrzemski said. "And when he did, I believed him because he was missing the pitches by more each day."

That night Petrocelli saw his pal's deep anxiety. "He was really down," Petrocelli recalls. "The frustration. He was so frustrated. He couldn't see the ball." Rico suggested they go to Christy's, the restaurant next door to the team quarters at the Haven Hotel, and get a drink. Tony said no. Rico persisted and Tony gave in. He wasn't good company. Christy's was crowded on Saturday nights, with writers, players, and fans from up north elbowing back and forth. Somebody ordered a beer for Tony and it sat, barely sipped, on the bar in front of him. Petrocelli studied Tony, sitting quietly amid the loud talk and clanking glasses, and saw him, Rico said, "in deep thought. Frustrated. Angry a little bit. You could see his mind churning. Part of him was worried that his career was over. Another part was thinking that he had to get back, somehow. It was his identity. He had to get back."

The next morning Tony telephoned LeRoux at the Red Sox clubhouse and said he still had a sore throat and wanted to ask Williams for permission to skip the game against the Twins in Orlando. Tony heard LeRoux turn to Williams and relay the message and heard Williams retort loudly, "If he'd spend more time out of those barrooms he'd be a pretty good ballplayer." In his autobiography, Williams justified his rough treatment with a supremely unfair rationale: "The guy loved to play. But he also loved to go catting around at night. It continued to make me worry that he was hampering his comeback. After seeing him at bars more often than at batting cages, I finally decided, he plays like one of the boys, he'll be treated like one of the boys."

Tony's fear, frustration, and deep resentment of Williams finally bubbled over.

"Buddy, put that guy on the phone. I want to talk to him," Tony hollered. "I'm going to come down there and kill him. Get him on the phone."

"I don't want to talk to him," he heard Williams say in the background.

"*Buddy, put that bastard on the phone!*" Tony exploded. "Buddy, I'm coming down and I'm going to beat the shit out of him."

"Stay in your room," LeRoux ordered. "I'll be right over."

LeRoux made the short drive from the ballpark to the hotel in time to catch Tony getting dressed. LeRoux told the kid to calm down and offered him something to soothe his throat. "But, Buddy, it's not the throat," Tony said. "Don't you understand? I can't see." LeRoux looked at Tony for a moment and said, "We ought to tell someone."

General manager Dick O'Connell was informed. He suggested Tony return to Boston for a checkup at Retina Associates. Tony agreed; he had to attend an Army Reserve meeting back home that week and could use it as cover for the trip.

Tony played on Monday against the Braves and struck out in his last at-bat without having seen the ball. On Tuesday he played against the Washington Senators in Pompano Beach. He struck out in his first two at-bats. In his third at-bat, he stepped to the plate against left-hander Frank Bertaina and prayed to God to let him just get his bat on the ball, just a piece of it. He made a cross with his bat on home plate. He swung at the first pitch, a change-up outside, and missed. He took a ball high. He took a waist-high fastball right down the middle for a called strike—he didn't see the ball. He swung at a fastball outside and missed it by a foot. His prayers did no good. He had struck out for the eighth time in ten at-bats. For the spring, he had struck out twenty-two times in sixty-six at-bats with zero home runs and a .125 average.

He dropped his helmet at home plate. He dropped his bat at home plate. He ran into the empty clubhouse, picked up a chair, and threw it against a wall. He ripped clothes out of lockers and flung them in the air. He tipped over stools, threw shoes, and vented the fear he had tried to bottle up. He screamed as loudly as he could, "My whole career is gone." Remembers Rico: "It hurt to see him that way. To me, it was his way of saying, 'I can't believe this.' "

Tony dressed for New England spring weather—white turtleneck, peach sweater-coat, cranberry slacks—and flew from Miami to Boston on a Northeast Yellowbird and arrived at Logan Airport just after nine o'clock. The Great Aunt, now beside herself with worry for the kid, waited for him. Tony told the press he had a reserves meeting and an eye appointment because he was bothered by the Florida glare and mysterious headaches. But he continued to encourage wishful thinkers, saying, "I still feel I'm going to be okay and be ready for the opening game in Detroit next Tuesday."

Tony had a pizza dinner at his old hangout, the Ritz in Revere. After midnight he drove a girlfriend, Donna Chaves, home to nearby Somerville. He was in a funk, distracted, as he motored back to Swampscott, when a carful of teenagers ran a stop sign and T-boned Tony's car. His legs bruised and his head ringing from a smack against the windshield, Tony was taken by ambulance to Somerville Hospital. He was released and got a ride from Somerville police to the apartment in Kenmore Square, where he spent the rest of the night throwing up and wondering what he had done to deserve so much trouble.

Sal was eating breakfast at 7:30 A.M. when he heard about the accident on the radio. He waited several anxious hours expecting to hear from his son—Tony and Athanas had a brand-new phone number and hadn't yet given it to Sal. Tony went home to spend Wednesday in Swampscott. He rested his bumps and bruises and prayed over and over that the eye exam the next day at Retina Associates would somehow turn out all right.

At eleven on Thursday morning Tony reported to Dr. Regan's office, where he was paraded from the eye chart to the slit lamp to the double-lens microscope. Regan told Tony they wanted to analyze the results and asked him to come back in an hour or so. Tony could tell by the look on the faces of the medical people that he would not be getting good news.

Before they went to the parking lot, Sal took Tony aside, unfolded a copy of that day's *Herald Traveler,* and put his finger on a quote from Dick Williams. "I don't think there's anything the matter with Tony's vision despite what he said when he got to Boston last night." The headline read: "Dick Doubts Tony's Tale." Sal wanted Tony to see the story before the newspapermen huddled outside Retina Associates asked him about it. "The words ate into my flesh," Tony wrote in *Seeing It Through.* "Oh, I hated him at that moment."

Tony and Sal went outside. Newspapermen gathered around and Tony told them there was no news yet, that there were more tests scheduled for the afternoon. Someone mentioned Dick Williams's astonishing comment, and Tony said, "I thought Dick was a baseball manager and not an eye doctor."

Later, Sal and Tony returned as requested and sat in an office with Dr. Regan. "I don't want to be cruel, and there's no way of telling you this in a nice way, but it's not safe for you to play ball anymore," he said. Regan explained that the cyst on Tony's macula had burst while he was in Florida, essentially leaving a hole at the center of Tony's vision in his left eye. The blurry blind spot, plus his poor—nearly nonexistent—depth perception resulting from 20-10 vision in one eye and 20-300 (legally blind) vision in the other made it impossible for Tony to properly see and judge a pitched baseball. Regan also said Tony risked a detached retina if he continued strenuous exercise. And that was that. Tony was twenty-three years and three months old, and it was all over.

Tony tried not to cry in front of Sal. Sal tried not to cry in front of Tony. Sal, the father who had always been there for his sons, welled with frustration. He would do anything for Tony. Now, there was nothing he could do for him. Finally, Sal said to Regan, "Could you take my eye out and put it in him?"

Sal and Tony walked through the parking lot and were surrounded by newspapermen again. "All right, fellows," Tony said, "let's make it fast, huh? I really don't know too much. They're going to let me know later." But the newsmen looked at Sal, shaking his head and fighting back tears, and they knew. Someone brought up Dick Williams again. "If he doesn't say he's sorry, then he's not a man," Tony said. "I didn't come here for kicks."

Someone asked Tony when he expected to rejoin the Red Sox. Now Tony was gulping and fighting back tears. "I don't know," he said. "Maybe tomorrow, maybe the next day . . . " Sal tugged at his son's jacket and they walked together to the car. On the drive to Swampscott, which took them past the hill where they used to live in East Boston, where Tony played stickball, and through Revere, where Tony used to run out of the house first thing in the morning and play all day in Ambrose Park, Tony looked out the window in silence. All he ever really wanted to do was play and play and play, and now he could never play again. When they got home, Tony bounded up the steps to his room and could hear Sal tell Teresa, "He's all through."

Later in the afternoon the Red Sox issued an official press release announcing that Tony's "baseball future at this time is very doubtful." Baseball fans across New England sat at their dinner tables with the terrible news. In Winter Haven the Red Sox clattered into the clubhouse, in uniform, sweaty and tired from their exhibition game in Clearwater, and were told Tony's baseball days were done. Yastrzemski, too stunned to comment, plopped onto a stool in front of his locker and said, "Terrible . . . terrible." Others pulled off their uniforms in silence, or spoke quietly, respecting the death of a colleague's career as they would any other death. Later, some lingered near their cars in the parking lot to talk about it. "Just awful," reflected Norm Siebern, a veteran thirty-four-year-old first baseman finishing his career with the Red Sox. "His future is unlimited and he had been so great." Catcher Gene Oliver, thirty-three and also at the end of a long career, mourned, "What a shame. How old is Tony? Only twenty-three? What a future he had going for him." Oliver walked away, shaking his head.

Williams, at last, said all the right things. "I feel so sorry for the kid," he told the newsmen. "I think of the future he had. I feel very sorry for his fate. It took a lot of guts on his part to stay in and bat when he wasn't seeing the pitches well."

Back in Swampscott, Tony stayed in his room, crying in his bed. That night there was a feeling of dread everywhere, as the radio and television crackled with news of the assassination of Martin Luther King Jr.

Joe Tauro, a family friend and lawyer, came to the house and helped Tony draft a luckiest-man-on-the-face-of-the-earth statement for the press, thanking his friends and family and teammates. Just like Tony, even though the doctors told him his playing days were through, he ended the statement by saying, "And I want all these friends to know that I'm not going to quit and that somehow, some way, there will be good days again."

On Friday the Red Sox broke camp and flew to Washington for an exhibition series with the Senators. O'Connell announced that Tony would be placed on the emergency disabled list, which would allow him a fifth year in the major-league pension plan. He was twenty-three and people were thinking about his pension. Yastrzemski, who was more like Tony than many realized, knew exactly what Tony was thinking about. "He'll try again. I'm sure of it," Yaz predicted. "It may not be for a month or two, it may take a year, but I'm convinced in my own mind that he'll try again. I never saw a player with greater determination. Baseball is his life and knowing him as I know, he'll try."

Baseball fans everywhere pulled for him. In the age of Vietnam and dead Kennedys, there were already too much dashed hope and wasted youth in the news section of the morning paper. People didn't need to see more tragedy in the sports section. Many New Englanders felt as if they had grown up with Tony, and to see him down and out at twenty-three made them old before their time. Immediately after Tony retired, cards, letters, packages, phone calls, and gifts began to pour into the Conigliaro home in Swampscott—some from South America and Africa. Mass cards, novenas, Bibles, and miraculous medals arrived by the dozens. A woman Tony had met in the Catskills sent a Jewish blessing. Someone sent a vial of holy water from Lourdes. Others mailed secular cures, including ointments, salves, and magic potions. People wrote and offered Tony their eyes.

Sal winced each time he saw the mailbags brimming with false hopes. After a lifetime of encouraging his son to chase his wildest dreams, he discouraged Tony from sitting around now, and for the next forty years, chasing a miracle. "He won't get his vision back again," he told Clif Keane of the *Boston Globe*. "Of course, he hopes for miracles. But it doesn't look that way. So he can't be thinking about playing baseball again."

~11~

HE WASN'T A TERRIBLE PITCHER

LIKE MILLIONS OF TWENTY-SOMETHINGS ACROSS AMERICA, TONY CONIGLIARO
SPENT THE SPRING AND SUMMER OF '68 WONDERING WHAT HE WAS GOING TO DO
WITH HIS LIFE. He was still collecting a $55,000-a-year salary from the Red
Sox, but money was never really a problem—remember, he was cruising
in his father's white Eldorado convertible while still in high school. He
needed to do something with all that restless energy. Since Little League
he had been relentlessly driven toward a single goal. Now there was
nothing to shoot for.

The atmosphere around the Conigliaro home, usually bubbling
with happy, loud sons and people over for dinner, was gloomy and grieving. Teresa cried when she watched television and saw old clips of Tony
in action. His first home run, the one on Opening Day at Fenway in 1964,
was especially hard to relive. Tony sat around the house in silence, rarely
emerging from his room. In mid-April, Sal told Tim Horgan of the *Herald:*
"Every morning I wake up and start to plan my day and then I think of
Tony and it ruins everything. And when I look at him, when I look at this
great, big, strong, powerful kid and I look at his eyes and they seem to be
all right, I say to myself it can't be true. But it is true and we've just got
to get used to it, that's all."

Tony got plenty of offers. Some of them seemed wildly inappro-
priate for a folk hero. A company offered him $35,000 a year to sell ency-
clopedias door-to-door. A brewery wanted him to tour liquor stores to sell
its beer. Another company wanted him to sell mutual funds. Other jobs
were fine but more suited for washed-up players in their thirties and forties—there was talk the Red Sox might let him join the guys with beer

bellies, sun hats, and clipboards and drag himself through the back roads of America as a scout. It was painful to imagine his doing that. He was only twenty-three. "It took a little while to get over it. He was just a baby," remembers Uncle Vinnie Martelli. "It killed me."

The only career option with a remote attraction was sportscasting, which would keep him near the game and in the limelight. The three network affiliates in Boston were interested in Tony. During the World Series the previous fall, Tony had discussed broadcasting with Sandy Koufax, who had turned to television at age thirty-one when arm trouble ended his brilliant career with the Dodgers. But first Tony was more interested in something else on Koufax's résumé: pitching.

Immediately after his retirement, Tony desperately searched his mind for anything to keep alive his baseball career. He entertained, then disposed of, thoughts of coming back as a left-handed batter, which would have allowed him to use his uninjured right eye to initially pick up the spin on the ball. But the more he thought about it, the more he liked the idea of pitching. He had a strong arm. Pitchers don't need a lot of depth perception. He had pitched in high school and in the American Legion. One day Tony and Richie were in the yard playing catch, and suddenly Tony said, "Pitchers don't bat anyway." He went to the garage, brought out rakes, shovels, and a measuring tape, and began to dig up the lawn to fashion a pitcher's mound.

"Dad's going to kill us, tearing up the grass," Richie observed as he dug in.

"We'll just fill it back in and plant seed later," replied Tony.

After marking off sixty feet, six inches, the brothers scratched out a home plate, Richie squatted like a catcher, and Tony started hurling. Accustomed to the high school pitchers he faced at Swampscott, Richie was impressed. He could also see some of the gloom lift from Tony. "He had no question he was going to be able to do it," Richie says. "He really believed he was going to play. That's quite a difference from thinking he was never going to play again." Tony's doctors, however, read in the newspapers about his high hopes to pitch and sent out a rocket to him: no strenuous physical activity until the danger of a detached retina passes. The eye would be reassessed in June. In the meantime Tony had to sit around, wait, and continue to plan for a life without playing baseball.

Penney booked him on *The Merv Griffin Show* and *The Tonight Show* with Johnny Carson, which were nice distractions but hardly career moves. "He still loves to sing," Penney said. "But he knows he has no real future as a singer. He's a realist. He knows he wouldn't have cut any records or sung on any TV shows if he hadn't played baseball." He continued to appear at O'Dee's, but even that wasn't as much fun anymore. Cruel, drunken patrons who wouldn't have dreamed of heckling a star rightfielder for the Red Sox felt free to taunt a washed-up ballplayer. "He can't sing any better than he can see," a beer-soaked boor cried out one night, and Tony foolishly stopped in midsong to try to pick out his tormentor.

The world was cruel to average nobodies but crueler perhaps to stars who had lost their credentials. At a nightclub in Kenmore Square, a man who was a casual acquaintance and envious of Tony's girlfriend, Donna Chaves, approached Tony Athanas and demanded, "Tell Tony to stay away from Donna or I'll take his good eye out with a meathook."* Tony also noticed that a lot of his friends didn't come around as much as formerly, or weren't so eager to rush up to him at a restaurant, or weren't so quick to return telephone calls. It had been something Tony worried about, that people liked him only because he was a famous ballplayer. "He realized that a lot of people who he thought were friends really weren't friends," Athanas says. "A lot of them disappeared. He paid attention to that." Less hurtful, but still disheartening, were the business snubs. A deal had been arranged for Tony to model a raincoat in a national magazine, but the company pulled the offer when his baseball career appeared to be over. A hair tonic commercial also fell through. During spring training MacGregor sporting goods had sent him a fancy complimentary golf bag. When the doctors said he was finished, MacGregor called and asked him to send the bag back.

Tony's ego was battered, and baseball wasn't there to heal it. He missed the competition and fame and the chance every night to be a

---

*The man later appeared at a party at the apartment at 566 Commonwealth, produced a handgun, and fired a round into the air from the balcony, apparently to show Tony he meant business. Tony went to Jerry Maffeo, told him what had happened, and asked Jerry to help him make sure it didn't happen anymore. Maffeo contacted mobster friends from the North End, who contacted the man with the gun and made it clear any further harassment of Tony would be a health hazard. The man never bothered Tony again.

hero. When he came onstage at O'Dee's, the announcer would say, "And now, here's Tony Conigliaro . . ." and it sounded too much like the public address announcer at Fenway Park, where the baseball season pushed on without him. Tony craved the baseball life, but he couldn't bear to attend games. When the team was on the road, he went to the ballpark to leave notes in the lockers of his friends. "It was happy and sad to get those notes," says Petrocelli. "It was nice to know Tony was thinking of you. It was sad because he wasn't able to be there with us."

When Tony stayed at the apartment at 566 Commonwealth, the crowd noises and the glow of the ballpark across the dark rooftops made him crazy. He could still see Harrelson darting in and out of view in right field. The Hawk was having a great season—he finished with thirty-five home runs—and even replaced Tony's charisma with his own brand of flamboyance, which included a shaggy haircut, cowboy hats, and Nehru jackets. Tony finally suggested to Athanas that they get a smaller apartment on a lower floor. "He told me he wanted to do it to save a little money," Athanas says. "But I think he really wanted to move to an apartment where you couldn't see the ballpark."

In early May, Tony visited the clubhouse and, among other things, he urged his teammates—especially Yastrzemski—to switch to batting helmets with an earflap. Second baseman Mike Andrews was the only Red Sox regular who wore one. "If I'd been wearing an earflap helmet that night last August," Tony said, "I'd have been back in the lineup in a few days." Tony also wrote a letter to baseball commissioner William Eckert (nicknamed "William Inert" by his critics), prodding him to make the extraprotective helmets mandatory "as fast as possible."* Later in the season at Fenway, in an irony of setting and teams involved, California Angels third baseman Paul Schaal, batting without an earflap on his helmet, was hit in the head and badly hurt by a Jose Santiago pitch. Yastrzemski began to wear an earflap.

The beaning was never far from Tony's thoughts, but it wasn't something he talked about. He never complained. But it was clearly traumatic for him—not so much the pain and injury, but the consequences.

---

*Baseball decided to ease in the extra protection. Earflaps were ruled mandatory in Class A and rookie leagues in 1970, in Double-A in 1972, in Triple-A in 1973, and in the major leagues in 1974. A grandfather provision allowed players already in the big leagues to wear the old, half-shell helmets.

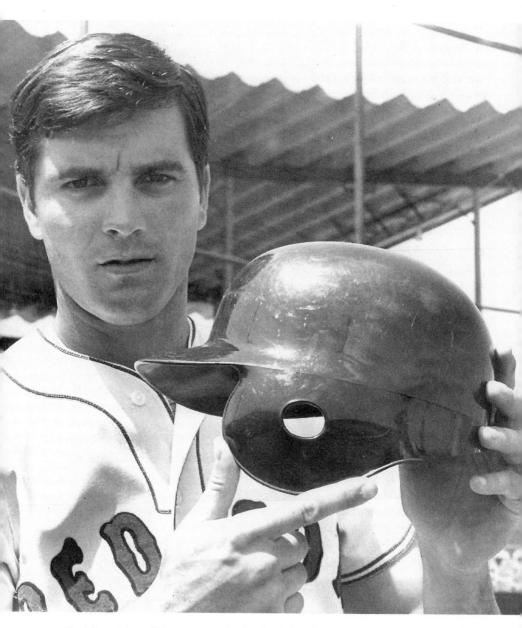

*Conigliaro shows off the new protective batting helmet he was now wearing, complete with newly designed earflap. (*Boston Herald *archives photo)*

He couldn't believe one pitch could cause so much misery. Hamilton, a decent man deeply sorrowful to see Tony out of baseball, tried several times to get in touch with him, but Tony would have none of it. Hamilton finally went to Ken Harrelson, who took Hamilton to see Tony's friend, Jerry Maffeo, to arrange a meeting. "He felt so bad," Maffeo recalls. "He wanted to meet Tony and tell him he didn't mean it. He swore to God he wasn't throwing at him. He wanted to shake hands with Tony. I told him I'd take care of it." But when Maffeo brought up the subject, Tony declared, "Jerry, just leave the issue the way it is."

On a Friday afternoon, May 24, Tony went to the ballpark to see Tom Yawkey, his first meeting with the patriarchal owner since the wild pennant celebration in the clubhouse on October 1.

"You don't ever have to worry about a job," Yawkey said during their one-hour, forty-five-minute conversation. "If it ever comes that you need work, we'll take care of you."

Tony thanked Yawkey for his kindness.

"What type of work do you think you'd be interested in?" Yawkey said.

"Mr. Yawkey, my future is set for the next ten years," Tony said. "I'm going to be a pitcher with the Red Sox."

On June 20, Tony submitted to the long-awaited checkup at Retina Associates, praying that this time the visit to the red brick building would bring good news. When the tests were over, Regan said the eye had stabilized, the retina would not detach, and his sight had improved from 20-300 to 20-100. Then the doctor uttered the magic words, "I can see no reason why you can't begin working out again." That was all Tony ever wanted—the go-ahead to resume battling back. "We were afraid that the area would have deteriorated so badly that there would be a real hole in the retina," Regan told the newspapers. "This has not occurred. It has healed, so that now there is only a small defect in the center of his vision. We thought it would be a bigger defect than it is. In other words, he is not as bad as he was. If he can learn to coordinate his left eye with his right—and this can be done with practice, by using the eye—then anything can happen." That night Tony ate dinner at his parents' home in Swampscott, took a nap, showered, put on a cherry-colored sport shirt and rust-colored slacks, plopped into an easy chair, and said, "It's like beginning all over again."

Tony told himself that his ticket back to baseball was pitching, but in the back of his mind, he craved to hit again. He constantly tested himself. Tony and Jerry Maffeo were walking down the street in Swampscott one day when they came across a gang of Little League-aged boys playing baseball. Tony walked onto the field, picked up a bat, and said to one of them, "Come on, pitch to me." The wide-eyed kid struck him out. Tony made a joke out of it, but he concentrated his energy more than ever on pitching.

He wasn't a terrible pitcher. Tony had a decent curveball and a so-so fastball. When the Red Sox were in town, he went out to the bullpen before games and was tutored by pitching coach Darrell Johnson, who diplomatically reported to the press, "There are loads of things he doesn't even know about pitching, but certainly the fact he's a major leaguer will help. It's premature right now to say how he'll do." He simply did not have major-league stuff. If it were anyone else, the whole notion would have been preposterous, but this was Tony. No one who knew him and his will to succeed would count him out. "To me, he looked pretty good," Petrocelli says. "I could see his enthusiasm coming back. I thought, 'This guy is something. He just might do it. If anyone could do it, he could.' "

Fans, meanwhile, were charmed to see Tony drudge out to the bullpen to grind out a new career. He was obviously desperate to play for the Red Sox. A lot of guys would have cashed their check and played golf. "There's only one way of looking at it," Tony told a television reporter. "I want to be up here, one way or the other. I'm not giving up on the hitting. But if I can't make it as a hitter, I know I can make it as a pitcher." The Red Sox were eager to oblige their fallen hero and on the surface encouraged him to pursue pitching. But the Boston brass really wanted him to hit. They told Tony to go ahead, sure, pitch all you want, and don't even think about playing outfield again, but . . . take a few cuts in the cage now and then, just to keep your hand in it.

He had been such a sweet hitter and no one wanted to think it was really, really over. On Wednesday afternoon, August 14, in the late afternoon lull between a split-admission doubleheader, Tony stepped into

Intent on making his baseball comeback one way or another, Tony spent part of 1968 working on a conversion to pitcher. Here he is warming up in the bullpen at Fenway Park. (Boston Herald *archives photo*)

the cage at Fenway for batting practice. The ballpark was empty, except for ushers and a few white-uniformed vendors draped across seats. Pigeons flapped after scraps in the aisles. But when word passed that Tony was hitting, a small crowd gathered on the field. Newsmen traipsed down from the rooftop press room. Hawk Harrelson, Rico Petrocelli, and Sparky Lyle put down their sandwiches and playing cards in the clubhouse and came out to stand behind the cage. Tom Yawkey appeared. Darrell Johnson pitched and Tony—wearing a sweatshirt and uniform pants—hit for about ten minutes. On his final swing, he launched the ball into a high arc over the left-field wall, where it clanged into a light tower. Afterward, Tony said he had a slow bat and talked about his plans to pitch, but the only thing anybody could think about as they walked away was that ball rattling into the distant girders.

In the off-season Tony reported to the Red Sox's Instructional League team in Sarasota. Upon arrival he informed manager Billy Gardner—a former Red Sox infielder and coach, then managing Boston's minor-league club in Pittsfield, Massachusetts—that he was there to learn to pitch, and nothing else—he didn't want to think about hitting. Gardner agreed. Amid the hopeful young players dreaming of the major leagues, Tony the former All-Star went to work. He impressed everyone. "He was dedicated," remembers Gardner. "He worked. When you get a guy who had been in the majors, you expect trouble. But Tony was perfect. He was on time; he did everything. He worked with the kids. He even took me out to dinner."

The young players looked up to him and listened eagerly when he talked late into the night about hitting. They were also taken by his hard work. One day when it was raining hard, young outfielder Dennis Gilbert reported to camp and found the place deserted because of the lousy weather. Then he heard the rhythmic *thwack* of a baseball hitting concrete. Gilbert followed the sound and came across Tony throwing a ball against a wall. "He was the only other one besides me foolish enough to work out in the rain," Gilbert recalls. "The guy was a machine. He would work from early in the morning till late in the day. He was there on a mission."

After about a week Gardner suggested Tony take a little batting practice, as pitchers, in those days before the designated hitter, still had to step to the plate. Tony hadn't batted since the summer sessions at

Fenway. Later, he said he reluctantly picked out a bat and helmet and feared getting hit—a huge admission for him. He took a couple of pitches without swinging and noticed he could see the spin on the ball almost as well as before the beaning. He felt his confidence seep back, dug in, and hit a few solid line drives. Gardner was enthusiastic, but Tony downplayed the hits—it was only batting practice—and insisted he wanted to be a pitcher. Gardner agreed again but induced Tony to promise to take batting practice every day. "The Red Sox wanted to get him back in action, back into a routine, and maybe he'd get the urge to come back," says Gardner.

Tony's hitting improved with each batting practice. He was hitting curves. He was hitting the ball harder. He even hit a couple over the fence. He felt the tug of hitting. Gardner remembers Tony's watching the ball sail in the distance and saying, "Look at that! I'm back in style." But he resisted getting seduced by it. When Gardner came right out and advised Tony to give up pitching to come back as an outfielder, he refused. Memories of the spring—the anguish and embarrassment when he couldn't see—were too fresh. Pitching was his safe backup. During one batting practice Red Sox scouts Sam Mele and Frank Malzone came around and were impressed. Sal and Uncle Vinnie visited. They were also encouraged to see Tony sting the ball. But whenever anybody complimented his hitting, Tony changed the subject and talked about pitching.

On November 4, Tony got his first start as a pitcher against the Philadelphia Phillies in Sarasota. It rained hard in the morning, soaking the Red Sox's park, so the game was moved across town to the White Sox's Allyn Field. About twenty-four fans, including Uncle Vinnie and Sal, paid fifty cents each to watch the game. They were outnumbered by baseball coaches and scouts. Tony was scheduled to pitch three innings. Gardner also penciled him in at leadoff, so he would likely get at least two at-bats.

Tony threw his first pitch in the dirt; he had, in fact, wanted it well out of the strike zone. "All I could think of was my first pitch as a pro being walloped nine miles over the fence," he said, always mindful of appearances. "And I didn't want that distinction." The next pitch was also in the dirt, and he told himself, "Hey, you better start getting going." The leadoff man popped up, and Tony retired the next five batters in a row, striking out one and allowing only a soft fly to center out of the infield.

To start the third inning, his old teammate and roommate, Mike Ryan, who had been traded to Philadelphia the previous winter, stepped up and the moment was too much for both of them. Ryan kept one foot out of the batter's box, giggling and trying to catch Tony's eye. Tony turned and faced center field so no one in the stands could see him laugh. Ryan stepped in, looked out at Tony on the mound, and felt a surge of sadness push out the irony. Tony had been so good, young, dashing, and swashbuckling, oozing ability and ambition out of every pore. And here he was struggling desperately to hang on as a pitcher. "How're you doing, Roomie," Ryan said to himself as he hefted his bat. "It's not supposed to be this way." Years later Ryan recalls he didn't want to get a hit. "I wanted to strike out," he says. "I didn't want to do anything to discourage him." But his competitive juices took over, and he cracked Tony's first pitch, a curveball, on a line drive to left field. The ball landed ten feet foul and was the hardest hit against Tony all day. Then Ryan grounded out to third. "How the hell did you ever get me out?" Ryan called as he ran off the field and passed the mound. "There's been a few guys who've got you out," responded Tony, and they both laughed.

In his three innings Tony allowed two hits and three walks and took the loss when mental errors by his young teammates allowed three runs to score. Afterward, Tony talked about bending his knee and pivoting and keeping his eye on the batter during his delivery. Others wanted to talk about his hitting: He lined out hard to shortstop in his first at-bat and walked on five pitches in his second. Gardner was as impressed by the walk—Tony could judge the strike zone again—as the line out. Tony told the newspapers he wasn't ruling out coming back as a hitter, but was "concentrating 80 percent on pitching, 20 percent on batting."

That ratio began to change the morning after his forty-pitch performance, when Tony awoke with an aching sore arm. In his next start against the Twins in Saint Petersburg, he was shelled for fifteen runs. Some of the rockets whizzing past his ear reminded him that pitchers, too, can get hit in the head with baseballs. His record dropped to 0-3 when he allowed three runs in six innings to the Cardinals. At the Red Sox's request, he had started playing the outfield on days he wasn't pitching. During a game in Dunedin against the Tigers, Tony doubled off the wall and singled sharply through the middle of the infield. Dick O'Connell and Dick Williams were in the stands, and after the game the hinting and cajoling ended.

"Tony, you look great," O'Connell declared. "We think you can make it back next year."

"I hear you've been doing great down here," Williams remarked with a smile. "Keep up the good work. I want you back in Winter Haven this spring to play right field for me and bat cleanup."

"Now we're going to get out of here," O'Connell announced. "It's too cold and we've seen enough."

And that was that. Tony was through with pitching. He was coming back to fulfill his destiny as a hitter.

When he returned to Swampscott, he found the house cheery and full of life again. "Now the laughing was back," Tony recalled in *Seeing It Through*. But there was one more hurdle: The Red Sox made an appointment for an exam at Retina Associates. Sal took off from work and drove Tony into Boston, and again he looked at the charts and followed the white lights and felt Dr. Regan's breath on his cheek as the ophthalmologist peered through an instrument into his left eye. Finally, the doctor leaned back and gave him good news. The eye was dramatically improved. The tissues on the inner rim of the hole in the macula had sealed down smoothly. There was no scar tissue. There was only a small pigmentation problem. Most of his depth perception was recovered. The left eye was 20-20, and that sealed it for the wishful thinkers—20-20 was perfect vision, right? They didn't want to hear that Tony's vision in his left eye used to be 20-10 and that regaining "most" of his depth perception meant he had lost some of his depth perception and that bright sunlight still made it hard for him to see the ball. Tony was coming back, and that was that.

After all he had been through in the previous eighteen months, Tony gave himself a vacation. He went to Hawaii but stopped en route in Las Vegas for four days to take in a few shows at Caesars Palace. He saw Frank Sinatra, Shirley Bassey, Jose Feliciano, and Buddy Hackett. During his comedy routine, Hackett—wearing a Nehru jacket and love beads—squeaked out that Tony was in the audience and asked him to take a bow. The spotlights crisscrossed onto Tony and he got up and the crowd clapped heartily. Standing in the bright lights, soaking up the applause, Tony didn't care much whether his eye was 20-20 or 20-10, either. He was back where he belonged.

~12~

THE POOR KID COULDN'T SEE

IN THE SPRING OF 1969 TONY CONIGLIARO TOTED HIS HOPES AND FEARS TO PRE-
SEASON CAMP. Again he could feel everyone scrutinizing him. His comeback was the big story of spring training, and people stood around, arms
folded, looking closely for clues. Everybody wanted to know: Was the eye
all right? Or wasn't it? Everybody had an opinion. Truth is, the poor kid
couldn't see.

At the start of camp Tony stood far off the plate and to bridge the
extra distance used a thirty-six-inch bat instead of the old thirty-four-and-
a-half-inch stick. Seeing this, people were sure his vision must be haywire.

"He didn't look good in early batting practices," Red Sox pitcher
Jerry Stephenson said. "Everyone hits then, but Tony was missing the
ball. He stood back away from the plate and he couldn't get his bat on
anything outside."

Carl Yastrzemski studied his colleague and decided that Tony's
eye was all right. "Last year he swung at everything. He couldn't see the
ball well to check his swing," Yaz explained. "He missed all the time. I
looked at him in batting practice this spring and noticed he could check
himself again. It was so obvious. And that told me he could see."

Tony gradually moved closer to the plate, finally hugging it as
cozily as he had done before Jack Hamilton's fastball hit him in the
head—the kid was all right. But he struck out thirteen times in his first
fifty exhibition at-bats—the kid couldn't see. Which was it? Tony said he
could see just fine, then offered an explanation that hinted that he couldn't.
"The only times I couldn't see the ball were when the backgrounds were
real bad," he noted. "A year ago I couldn't see the ball at all. You know,

they talk about the troubles of hitters and they talk about lowering the mound and making the plate smaller and getting a livelier ball and shortening the strike zone. Well, the single most important thing they could do to help hitters would be to make all hitting backgrounds the same. Some backgrounds are ridiculous."

His teammates wondered if his spirit would wobble if he were beaned again or if a pitch were to come dangerously close. "Any pitcher who throws at Tony deliberately better be prepared for one hell of a fight on the field," Ken Harrelson warned. In the third exhibition game, against the Twins, a rookie pitcher sailed a ball inside and knocked Tony on his back in the dirt. The Red Sox surged to the top step of the dugout and watched intently.

"We wondered if he would back up from the plate," Rico Petrocelli recalls. Tony slapped the dust from his uniform and stepped right back to where he had originally taken his stance.

Tony knew exactly what he, and the people gawking at him, needed—a monstrous, breathtaking home run. Throughout his life, home runs had been his identity, the secret to his success, and the perfect cure-all. Home runs at Noyes Park had lifted his embarrassment over being the new kid in the neighborhood and a poor student at school. During the American Legion trip to Newburgh, hitting a few balls over the fence had shut up the loudmouth New Yorkers. When he was with Wellsville, a home run in Jamestown had redeemed his back-to-back, three-base errors. A home run in Scottsdale had elicited sacks of fan mail and sped his ticket to the major leagues. A home run on Opening Day at Fenway Park instantly turned him from local boy to local hero. Home runs had helped him wriggle out of touchy spots with ticked-off managers. Home runs had always soothed the Great Aunt whenever she got testy over the kid's brassiness. Now he needed a home run to smother doubts about his damaged eye. There was nothing ambiguous, no room for interpretation, in a 420-foot blast.

By the last week of March he still hadn't hit one. His kid brother Billy, making a strong bid to join Tony on the Red Sox, smashed a pinch-hit home run against the Cardinals, and the irony of it struck Tony that night when he heard on the radio: "Tony Conigliaro is off to a great start in his comeback. Today he hit a home run against Saint Louis as Boston . . ."

On March 25, in Fort Myers, Tony struck out twice. The next day he was hitless again and badly misplayed a fly ball in right field. That night Sal implored a reporter in Winter Haven, "Stick with the kid. You wrote a couple of weeks ago that he is going to make it big and you were right. I know Tony hasn't looked good the last day or two, but he told me he's seeing the ball as well as he ever did, and I believe him."

On Thursday, March 27, the Red Sox traveled to Tampa for an exhibition game against the Cincinnati Reds. Before he left the clubhouse for the field, Tony stashed a set of rosary beads—a gift that had arrived in fan mail—in his back pocket. Maybe it would take divine intervention for him to hit his first home run.

Nature, at least, was not cooperating. Members of the Boston traveling contingent loitered around the batting cage and noted that the wind was blowing in hard from left field. "Look at that wind," Harrelson said. "There will be no home runs to left field today." For Tony, there had been too many days without home runs. During batting practice Larry Claflin of the *Record* watched Tony hit and thought the kid looked glum, and that wasn't like him.

In the first inning Tony lashed a hard single to drive in a run. That wasn't what he was looking for. In the third inning he stepped in against Mel Queen. The Reds right-hander threw a fastball at the knees. Tony attacked it with his sweeping, slashing swing and smashed the ball high into the air toward left field, smack-dab into the teeth of the wind.

Tony scrambled out of the batter's box, eyes fixed on the ball as it fought the gusts. "Please, let it clear the fence," he thought. In the Red Sox dugout Tony's teammates spilled off the bench and onto the steps, stared into the air in left, and grunted encouragement through clenched teeth, like touts rooting a racehorse down the stretch. Up in the press box the newspapermen fell silent amid their papers and scorecards and coffee cups and watched the ball, hoping the wind would not knock it down, because even the hardened Great Aunt was sick of seeing Tony Conigliaro get knocked down.

As he ran up the first-base line, Tony shouted, "*Go! Go! Get the hell out of here!*" The ball seemed to momentarily sit still in the breeze. Cincinnati leftfielder Alex Johnson backpedaled to the fence, then swiveled and followed the ball with his eyes as it sailed over his head, far over the wall. The newspapermen in the press box pounded their tables with glee. The

Boston dugout erupted with joy, as if it had been a World Series home run. Tony smiled broadly as he rounded third. He could practically feel the accumulated tension drain away. The ball cleared the fence and cleared Tony's mind of the beaning, the endless trips to doctors, the strangers asking about his eye, the agony of the spring of '68, the summer nights on the balcony as the Red Sox played without him, the desperate pitching in his backyard, the uncertain winter, the spring without a home run. Now he had a home run, his first since August 8, 1967, ten days before the pitch hit him in the head and toppled him into a strange, blurry world.

Now, he touched the plate, and finally he was home. When he undressed after the game, he stuck his hand into his back pocket and felt the rosary. "I was impressed," he remembered. And at last everything was all right. "I was able to sleep," Tony wrote in his autobiography. "My personality changed. I laughed a lot more."

After the game in Tampa, Tony rode back to Winter Haven in a car with Harrelson and Yastrzemski. "Tony, have you ever felt so good?" Harrelson asked. Tony smiled.

"I got an idea," said the always exuberant Hawk. "I'll buy the champagne and we'll do some celebrating tonight in Winter Haven."

Tony twisted around to face Harrelson in the back seat. "Okay, Hawk," he said, "but just this once. If we drink champagne every time I hit a home run this season, we'll be two drunken bums at the end of the year."

In the next week he hit three more homers to lead the team in the preseason with four. Tony Conigliaro was back.

On the night of April 7, Tony went to bed in his room in the Statler Hilton in Baltimore but couldn't find peace in sleep. He dozed fitfully, awoke suddenly, and drifted back to sleep. He had crazy dreams: He was singing on *The Merv Griffin Show*; he was trying to hit inside sliders from Baltimore Orioles pitcher Dave McNally; he approached a nightclub table to say hello to Jimmy Durante, and Durante suddenly disappeared. Finally, Tony gave up. He sat up in his room in the dark and watched the sky get light around the edges and the sun rise over the city.

The Red Sox and Tony were opening the season that afternoon against the Orioles at Memorial Stadium. Tony hadn't played in a major-league game in twenty months. He looked at his brother Billy, who had made the team as an outfielder, breathing deeply, snoozing soundly, in the next bed. Billy was twenty-one. Tony was twenty-four, but sometimes he felt a thousand years older.

Tony and Billy ordered breakfast at the hotel coffee shop with a writer from *Sport* magazine, but Tony barely touched his bananas and strawberries. There is always a pleasant, nervous excitement in the buildup to Opening Day—Joe DiMaggio once compared it to the feeling a child gets on the way to a birthday party—but Tony had extra butterflies. The morning was warm, and as they waited on the sidewalk outside the hotel for the team bus, Tony and Billy and the rest of the Red Sox admired the coatless office girls hurrying by in the sunshine. On the ride to the ballpark Tony opened a window and silently watched the buildings and sidewalks slide past.

When they reached the visitors' clubhouse at Memorial Stadium, Tony and Bill were greeted by an oversized horseshoe of flowers—it was from the gang at O'Dee's. Tony took off his street clothes and carefully went through the ritual of pulling on his gray Boston road uniform. Reggie Smith sat beside Tony and confided, "I'd like to hit one out first time at-bat." Tony pulled his black belt through the loops in his uniform pants and replied absently, "You can do it, Reggie. You're my kind of hitter." Smith grunted and went out to the field.

Tony followed, his spikes scraping on the concrete floor of the tunnel leading to the dugout. He checked the cardboard lineup card posted on the dugout wall and noted "Conigliaro, T." marked in the fifth slot. Someone noticed Tony carried a clean, new glove and asked, "Where's your old glove?" Tony said, "Last spring I gave all my old gloves away. I didn't think I'd need one anymore."

Tony took batting practice, jogged in the outfield, and shagged fly balls, while the crowd trickled into the stands. A brisk wind snapped the outfield flag, positioned at half-staff in honor of former president Dwight Eisenhower, who had died March 28. A young girl called to Tony from the seats that she and her friends had brought a banner reading, "Welcome back, Tony C," but that stadium security wouldn't allow her to string it up. "Christ, that wouldn't have hurt

Tony and younger brother Billy pose as Red Sox teammates in spring training, 1970. By the time Billy joined the Bosox, Tony already was an established star who ran in off-the-field circles separate from his brother. (UPI/Corbis-Bettmann)

anyone," Tony thought as he loitered on the outfield lawn. "Wouldn't have hurt anyone at all."

The batting cage was folded down, the grounds crew swept and freshened the infield, the national anthem played, and Maryland governor Marvin Mandell threw out the first ball. McNally, a lefty who had won twenty-two games with a 1.95 earned run average the year before, started the game by walking Reggie Smith. Mike Andrews singled. Yastrzemski doubled. Harrelson fouled out behind home plate, and Tony strode to the batter's box. The crowd clapped politely, then applauded louder and louder as if the significance of the moment was dawning on them. Tony took ball one, then ball two. The third pitch was a fastball at the knees and the umpire hollered, "Strike!" Tony cried, "No, it was inside." The umpire shook his head and mandated, "No, it's a strike." Then Tony realized he was crowding the plate again—he was back where he belonged—so balls over the plate seemed inside. Tony fouled off two pitches. McNally followed with an inside slider, the pitch in Tony's dreams, and he swung and missed it for strike three. "I was nervous," Tony admitted afterward. "But the next time I went to the plate, I felt like I was boss."

In the third inning Tony walked. In the fifth inning he roped a single to center. In the eighth inning he lifted a soft fly to left field. By the tenth inning, with the score tied at 2, the stadium lights had been turned on because daylight was fading in the late spring afternoon. Harrelson led off with a grounder to Frank Robinson, who had been shifted to first base in the later innings. Robinson botched the toss to pitcher Pete Richert covering first. With Harrelson on base, Tony stepped in and peered at third-base coach Eddie Popowski, who flashed the sign to bunt. Tony squared his bat at the first pitch and missed. He stared again at Popowski—now the bunt was off.

Tony swung at a pitch and missed. "Settle down," he told himself. He backed away from an inside pitch. He took another pitch that was barely low—the umpire nearly shot his right arm up to signal strike three—and the count was 2-2. Richert looked in for the sign from catcher Andy Etchebarren and threw a fastball, chest high and over the plate. Tony crushed it to deep left-center field. Orioles centerfielder Paul Blair angled back to the wall, then turned and watched the ball bounce on a grassy hill beyond the fence.

"I ran the bases as if I was floating," Tony recalled. As he rounded third, he paused with Popowski, who was practically doing a jig, and said, "Oh, Pop. Oh, Pop!" As he reached home plate, he slapped hands with George Scott. "What do you think of that, Boomer?" Tony exulted. Harrelson hugged him and kept an arm looped around his neck as they pranced to the dugout. Many Red Sox had bubbled up the steps and onto the dirt to hug Tony and pound on his back. Billy joined the celebration but half-wondered why such a fuss—Tony always did that sort of thing.

"You did kind of expect it because of his great determination and aggressiveness," Yastrzemski says. "He probably willed a home run."

Dick Williams kissed him on the cheek. Rico Petrocelli embraced his friend.

Number 25 follows the flight of yet another home-run ball headed over the left-field wall. (Boston Herald *archives photo*)

"When that ball went out, chills went all though my body," Rico says. "It was exhilarating. It was incredible. To see that ball go out—it was a miracle. The smile on his face, I'll never forget."

Back home in Swampscott, Richie Conigliaro was playing in a high school baseball game when someone ran onto the field and hollered, "Tony just a hit a home run to win the game!"* At the Triangle Tool and Die Company in Lynn, Sal leaped out of his chair as the knot of office workers, who were gathered around a small television, shouted and exchanged hugs. At the Conigliaro home in Swampscott, Teresa was watching the game on television alone—she preferred it that way, because it allowed her to pray silently. Soon after the ball cleared the fence, the phone rang. It was a friend, excitedly offering congratulations. As soon as she hung up, the phone rang again. It would keep ringing into the night.

In the clubhouse after the game Tony opened telegrams and talked to a swarm of reporters. Someone brought him a cold beer. "I guess it will taste good," he laughed. "What a difference a year makes. A year ago I was listening sickly to the team playing in Detroit. I knew I was all done, and I was sick." Still sweating, wrists taped, the antiglare black paint caked under his eyes, Harrelson looked on and murmured, "Only Tony could have done it." Yastrzemski sat at his locker and repeated, "Fabulous . . . fabulous . . . fabulous . . ." Dick Williams sipped a beer in his office and said, "It's his guts. Tony has as much guts as any player I have ever seen," then added, incredibly, "He was that way when I roomed with him back in 1964, and he hasn't changed a bit."

Tony went out to dinner that night with Billy and Mike Andrews, ate a steak, returned to the hotel at 10:30, picked up a sandwich at a snack shop across the street and snacked in his room, and telephoned his parents. "I was tired, exhausted," he recalled. "I think it was more emotional than physical." He went to bed and slept peacefully, without a nightmare.

*The home run, in fact, did *not* win the game. Baltimore tied the game at 4-4 in the bottom of the tenth. In the twelfth Tony walked and scored the winning run on Dalton Jones's sacrifice fly.

Dark moments from the past could find him when he was awake, though. Two days after the opener in Baltimore, the Red Sox visited Cleveland to play the Indians. In the thirteenth inning, Tony stepped to the plate with a runner on first base, looked out at the mound, and saw the bogeyman: Jack Hamilton, who had been traded from the Angels to the Indians in the off-season. Tony decided he would edge a little closer to the plate than usual, because he wanted to show the world he wasn't afraid of Hamilton or any other ghosts from August 18, 1967. But then he looked down at Popowski in the third-base coach's box. Pop was flashing the *bunt* sign, and Tony felt like screaming. A bunt? He wanted to do something majestic against Hamilton, not something practical. Still, Tony dutifully bunted and moved the runner over. When Tony batted again in the fifteenth inning, Hamilton was still pitching. Tony leaned over the plate and lashed a deep line drive that Lee Maye tracked down and caught in left field.

After the Red Sox won, 2-1, in sixteen innings, the newspapermen asked Tony about facing Hamilton. "That's all forgotten and over with as far as I'm concerned," Tony lied. "He's just another pitcher to me." Said Hamilton, "Tony was just one more hitter to me. What happened is all in the past. But I'm very happy to see him back, very pleased for his sake." * In *Seeing It Through* Tony tried to explain his essentially irrational anger toward Hamilton. "I know it was an accident," he wrote, "but I honestly don't know if I have ever really forgiven him for it." It was a terrible mischance, but Tony, by human nature, especially among twenty-four-year-old humans, felt obliged to blame somebody.

On Sunday night, April 13, the Red Sox arrived in Boston on the eve of their home opener at Fenway Park, which for Tony was the greatest symbol of all he had lost. He would not truly believe he was back until he played in Fenway. The old greeting committee awaited the team flight at Logan: Sal, Teresa, Richie, Uncle Vinnie, and Aunt Phyllis. Tony watched Sal's face as he emerged with Billy from the jetway and wondered what his father was thinking as he greeted two sons playing for the Red Sox. Everybody caravaned up to Swampscott to the Conigliaro home, which was loud and joyous again, just like old times. Teresa whipped up a little

*In the spring of 1997 Hamilton had no recollection of pitching to Tony in 1969, lending credence to his contention at the time that Tony was just another hitter.

something to eat—gnocchi, veal Parmesan, chicken cacciatore, chicken soup, artichokes in olive oil, stuffed peppers, and stuffed shells. Neighbors dropped by. Before Tony went to bed around 1:00 A.M., he told his father, "Tomorrow is going to be the biggest day of my life."

Tony and Billy left the house early to drive down Route 1-A, past the old neighborhood in East Boston, across the Tobin Bridge, and out Storrow Drive to get to Fenway for the afternoon game. In the Red Sox clubhouse, the radio blared ("ABC" by the Jackson Five and "Let It Be" by the Beatles were hottest that week). Tony found his locker near Billy's and George Scott's. "I see they put all the Italians together," Tony commented to the Boomer. A pile of telegrams and letters—at least 150 of them—awaited him, including a letter from a nun in Rome, who said she was praying for Tony to get the game-winning hit that day. Tony pulled on his bright white home uniform with "Red Sox" in red Old English lettering across the chest, a one-hundredth-anniversary-of-baseball patch on the left sleeve, and a red number 25 on the back. He yanked open the heavy metal clubhouse door, walked down a flight of steps, clomped along the damp, badly lit concrete tunnel, and emerged at last in the bright midday sunshine in the Red Sox dugout. He mounted the dugout steps and tossed his glove onto the fresh green lawn. Finally, he was back where he belonged. Instead of watching from the balcony at 566 Commonwealth, he would again be the white figure in right field (Harrelson played first, and the Boomer had moved to third).

Tony jogged in the outfield, took batting practice, and was so excited and nervous that he felt short of breath. When it was time for infield practice, he was sick to his stomach and went to the trainer's room to stretch out and try to calm his nerves. He eventually returned to the dugout and saw the stands teeming with 35,341 squirming, buzzing, laughing, talking, shouting onlookers. Ken Coleman, the radio voice of the Red Sox, then introduced both teams over the public address system. He named the Orioles and they trotted out of the visitors dugout one by one to stand on the third-base chalk line. Coleman introduced the Red Sox, first Dick Williams, then the coaches, then the players in numerical order, starting with number 2, Mike Andrews. When he got to number 24, pitcher Juan Pizarro trotted out of the dugout and stood on the first-base line. Then Coleman continued, "Number 25 . . ." and the crowd jumped to its feet, its collective roar drowning out Coleman. Tony jogged out, took his place in formation, and doffed his cap to every corner of the ball-park. "I got goose pimples when I heard the applause and then I felt like crying," Tony said. "I wanted to cry so much I had to fight to hold it in."

Tony came up to bat against Mike Cuellar in the first inning, with Yastrzemski on second and Harrelson on first. The crowd again jumped to its feet and hollered and clapped and whistled. The ovation grew louder. Cuellar stood on the mound and held the ball; he wasn't going to end Tony's moment, and he wasn't going to try to concentrate amid all that racket. "Maybe you better step out and let them get it out of their systems," home-plate umpire John Rice suggested. So Tony placed a foot outside the batter's box and tried not to cry. A plane droned overhead. It was trailing a banner that read "Welcome back."

Tony stepped in and knew exactly what he wanted to do. Cuellar knew, too, and threw him a screwball outside the strike zone. Tony swung hard and missed by a foot. "I was nervous," he would admit. "Well, not so much nervous as anxious. I wanted to do something for the fans so much that I was swinging at bad pitches."

Tony swung and missed another screwball. He took a ball outside, then lined a Cuellar fastball to right field, where Frank Robinson made the catch with ease.

The Red Sox were ahead, 2-0, when Tony came to the plate in the third inning, with Yastrzemski at third. The crowd cheered again, but not as much out of sentiment for the kid's valiant comeback as now they wanted him to get the run home. Tony swung at and missed two pitches, then hit a grounder to shortstop Mark Belanger, who threw home and trapped Yaz in a rundown while Tony alertly scampered all the way to second. Scott followed with a single and Tony scored. So far his gala return had included a fly out, a fielder's choice, and a run scored—solid, helpful baseball, but hardly the mythic feats he had envisioned for the occasion.

In the fourth Tony came to bat with the table nicely set for a legendary moment. The game was tied, 3-3, and the bases were loaded, with one out. Mike Adamson, a twenty-one-year-old right-hander, was on the mound for the Orioles. His first pitch whistled under Tony's chin. The crowd gasped as Tony jerked his head out of the way. It was not a purposeful pitch—no one brushes back a hitter with the bases loaded. The next pitch was a fastball, and Tony pounced on it, determined to launch the ball into the brilliant blue sky, way over the green fence in right and into the storybook pages. He swung mightily—and barely topped the ball, trickling it onto the grass up the third-base line. "I was going for the downs on that pitch," Tony confessed. "I wasn't up there looking for a base hit. I wanted a home run." But he still ran as hard as he could down the first-base line as Baltimore's Brooks Robinson, "the Vacuum Cleaner," one of the greatest third basemen in baseball history, raced in, scooped the ball, and fired to first. Tony's cleats hit the bag an instant before the ball whacked into first baseman Boog Powell's glove. Andrews scored from third. "I hit the ball fifteen feet," Tony said. "But I'll take eighty more like it because my only goals this season are to play well defensively and get clutch hits to help this team win." The Red Sox won, 5-3, so technically, Tony's dribbler was the game-winning hit, and the Great Aunt was happy to give him a hero's treatment for it. So were the fans. Somewhere, a nun was jumping up and down. In 1969 it was getting harder to tell the good guys from the bad guys—Dr. Spock was marching with the longhairs, cops were beating up college kids in the streets, and *Easy Rider* was motoring its way through theaters. Tony's courageous comeback was good and nice and simple, as unmuddled as a John Wayne western. Larry Claflin wrote in his column in the *Sunday Advertiser*:

> ·Before this season ends Tony will wreck many a pitcher and beat many a rival manager with hits. But his opponents are rooting for him almost as hard as his teammates and friends are. Why? Because, in a world marked by too many unhappy events in our lifetime, we all recognize that Tony's comeback is something good for all of us.
>
> There is no attempt on my part to equate Tony's comeback with the far more important things of life, such as a boy coming home safely from Vietnam. But such is the nature of the American people, that a comeback by a kid from Swampscott warms the heart of a whole nation. Many is the boy in Vietnam at this moment who is forgetting his own troubles and cheering the comeback of Tony C. . . .
>
> Maybe Tony's comeback is not important. I prefer to think otherwise. I would rather think that a nation torn by an unpopular war and confronted by its own guilt complex needs

something to cheer for. Tony has provided that for every baseball fan in the country.

Tony was back. Amid fractious times, everybody—fascist pigs, pinko college kids, wide-eyed teeny boppers, tie-dyed hippies—could cheer together. In the top of the seventh inning of his Fenway return, Tony took his position in right field when a young, shaggy-haired man with baggy trousers and an untucked, blue sports shirt darted out of the grandstand and shook Tony's hand.

"It's nice to have you back, Tony," the young man said. "You're the only reason I'm here today."

"You won't be here much longer, kid," Tony said, as stadium cops hurried across the grass toward them.

~13~

Not as Perfect as Before

Tony was back, and he was like a man returning to his old neighborhood, settling scores, stumbling across ancient demons, embracing long-lost friends, and rediscovering former delights. The old days lurked everywhere.

Before the season Tony and Athanas had moved out of 566 Commonwealth Avenue and rented an apartment on Mason Terrace in Brookline, a bedroom community nudged into the western outskirts of Boston. They lived on the second floor, and Hawk Harrelson lived on the first floor. One day early in the season Tony was walking down the hallway and coming toward him was Julie Markakis, who had dropped by to see the Hawk. Tony and Julie chatted, and Tony invited her up to his apartment to talk some more. Once inside Tony's pad, Julie felt her shoes sink into the shaggy, Greek goatskin carpets. She admired the driftwood coffee table, grass-cloth wallpaper, and bamboo bar with a thatched-hut roof. Looking around, she spotted the buffalo head—a souvenir of the African safari—mounted on the wall. (Tony liked to tell visitors the rest of the buffalo was on the other side of the wall, in the bedroom.)

At one point Tony turned serious and told his high school sweetheart that she could do better than date the flamboyant Harrelson, with his orange-tinted sunglasses, psychedelic jackets, love beads, and peace signs. "He told me that out of honest concern," Julie says. "He thought I deserved the best. He didn't approve of my relationship with the Hawk." It was an awkward moment between the former lovers, one when they realized nothing was the same. Finally, Julie stood and told Tony she had

166

to go, that Harrelson would be coming home soon, and she didn't want to have to explain why she was upstairs in Tony's apartment.

Tony was back, but nothing was the same. He had changed, and not just in his mod wardrobe, slightly shaggier haircut, and boss sideburns that crept close to the bottom of his earlobes. His twenty months as an average nobody had dampened his brashness. For twenty months he had known what it is like to be an outsider. For the first time he knew what it is like to be a fan, to watch big-league baseball and desperately wish to be out there in the sunshine playing on the green grass. He just wanted to play.

"I think he appreciated being in baseball again, rather than thinking baseball was lucky to have him," Petrocelli recalls.

This was not 1967 all over again. Sure, he hit a home run on Opening Day, and people smiled and agreed Tony C had returned, as if nothing had ever happened. But Tony was reminded what had happened every time he stepped to the plate.

His left eye was not all right. The Boston press and the suffering legions of Red Sox Nation liked the simple pleasure of Tony's comeback story, and they weren't going to let the facts get in the way. Tony's return was heralded as a blessing from God—Dr. Tierney, the Red Sox team physician, said, "Somebody must have made a novena for that fellow." The press loved it. No one wanted to read the fine print in a miracle.

On April 15 the *Record* ran a long story about Tony's comeback, and the headline was "Somebody Up There Likes Tony Conigliaro." It wasn't until the third-from-last paragraph that general manager Dick O'Connell was quoted as saying, "Tony's eye—let's be honest about things—is not as perfect as before, but he has normal vision. Using both eyes to focus on an object, his eyes are almost as perfect." No one, except perhaps a few linguists, saw the irony in the phrase, "not as perfect as before."

After the Red Sox played the Detroit Tigers in a game featured on NBC's *Saturday Game of the Week*—the only regular-season national baseball telecasts in those days—Angels manager Bill Rigney, who greatly admired Tony, said he watched the game on the tube and thought, "Conigliaro is not quite as ready as we had been led to believe. He's bailing out and that's something he never did before." Tony bristled. Of all people, this was the manager of the Angels, the team that nearly killed him! He assured everyone there was nothing wrong with his eye.

In fact, Rigney had been dead right. Tony struggled to pick up the spin on curveballs. When a pitch headed straight for him and he couldn't see the rotation of the ball, which told him it would curve back in toward the plate, it was too much to ask him not to flinch and pull away. The problem was worse in bright daylight. In 1969 day games were still a large part of the major-league scene. Boston played eighty-six of 162 games during the day that year, as opposed to forty-five of 162 in 1997. Word quickly spread among American League pitchers that Tony Conigliaro was struggling with curveballs. Before long he was being fed a steady diet of them.

After a Sunday afternoon game against the Tigers on May 4 at Fenway Park, Tony's frustration burst into headlines. He struck out four times during an eleven-inning Boston victory. Afterward he complained to the press that fans wearing white shirts in the bleacher seats produced a bright hitting background that obscured the ball. "I couldn't see a curveball out there all afternoon," Tony fumed as the writers scribbled. "The glare that comes off the shirts of those fans in the left-hand corner of the center-field seats produces a glare that makes it impossible for me to pick up breaking balls. It's dangerous, real dangerous. Somebody's going to get killed one of these sunny days. They should do something about it." He went on to suggest, preposterously, that fans wearing white shirts in the offending sections be issued green or blue vests to put on during the game.

As it is today, the hitting background at Fenway was an obstacle, especially during day games featuring left-handed pitchers. When asked why he had had no complaints in previous seasons, Tony retorted that Fenway Park attendance was so poor in those days, no one—white-shirted or otherwise—sat out there. Andrews and Petrocelli backed up Tony's complaint, but the fact remained that not everybody was striking out the way Tony was. No one brought up the subject of his vision.

The Red Sox brass thought he was merely being a pain in the butt. Big-league baseball is an unsentimental world, and Tony's status as the heroic comeback kid only went so far. "How long has this ballpark been built?" team vice president Haywood Sullivan drawled with a scowl when informed of Tony's comments. "And how long has Tony been playing here? That's all I've got to say about it."

The Red Sox embarked on a West Coast trip, the first stop being Seattle to play the expansion Pilots. Then came Anaheim, where Tony hit a home run and glared into the Angels dugout at Rigney as he rounded third. He hit well in Oakland, too. When the team returned from the trip, he was batting .304. In those pitching-dominant days, that was good enough to be ranked tenth in the league.

Back at Fenway Tony discovered that the Red Sox had decided, after all, to address the glare problem in center field. Not wanting to be responsible for getting their heroic gladiator beaned again, but also not wanting to flush away nine hundred paying customers, the Sox brain trust compromised. They gave that section of the ballpark a cutesy nickname, "Conig's Corner," and posted a sign that read: "Dear Patron, please do not sit in green seat section unless you are wearing dark-colored clothing. Conig thanks you. Management thanks you."

Fans entering the center-field seats were also issued cards stating, "You are now an official member of Conig's Corner. The Red Sox and Tony C appreciate your cooperation in helping to provide a good hitting background."

Tony was not happy. He did not appreciate having his name attached to the affair. He was the one who had spoken up, but the improved hitting background benefited every hitter in the league.

Then, just as the team publicly accommodated him by installing an unprecedented dress code for ticket holders, he was swallowed up by a terrible slump with the worst possible timing. During a horrendous weekend series at Fenway against Seattle, he had one hit, a scratch single in the ninth inning of the Sunday game, in thirteen at-bats. Overall for the homestand he had struck out twelve times in nineteen at-bats. He was frustrated and stricken by severe headaches. "I've been getting these headaches ever since I was beaned," he complained Sunday as he wobbled around the clubhouse clutching both hands to the back of his head. "I get them when I'm overtired. The mental strain makes me tired. It's the pressure."

This clearly was not the cocky, brash Tony Conigliaro of days gone by. Williams, still mindful of how ogreish he had come across in the papers the previous spring when Tony's eye went bad, was extrasolicitous of his young slugger. After the Sunday game Williams made sure there were plenty of reporters around to witness his generosity when he approached Tony in the clubhouse and asked if he wanted a few days off.

"No," Tony replied. "I sat it out for a year and a half. That was long enough."

Williams said he was going to drop Tony from cleanup to sixth in the order.

"If you want to, but—" Tony began.

"It'll take the pressure off," interrupted Williams.

"I suppose," Tony said.

Tony told the reporters he was "under a lot of tension," that he was aiming at the ball instead of snapping at it, that he was in fact bailing out on curveballs, but "it's not my eyes. I'm seeing the ball all right."

Plenty of people believed him about the eyes, because they saw another more titillating explanation for the slump: actress Mamie Van Doren. Merv Griffin had introduced them in New York in late April, and they had one date, dinner at Bachelors III, the restaurant-nightspot owned by the hip Joe Namath, quarterback of the New York Jets. Tony and Mamie went out again when the Red Sox were in Anaheim during the West Coast trip. Then the newspapermen got hold of the story and made mischief. The Great Aunt, still stubbornly prudish, couldn't resist clucking her tongue over the young slugger and the blonde bombshell. Tony was twenty-four. Mamie was thirty-six. Her film credits included *High School Confidential* (costarring Jan Sterling), *Las Vegas Hillbillies* (costarring Ferlin Husky and Jayne Mansfield), *The Navy vs. the Night Monsters* (costarring Bobby Van), and *Three Nuts in Search of a Bolt* (costarring Tommy Noonan). She had been romantically involved with Angels pitcher and legendary hell-raiser Bo Belinsky, and she had been briefly married to a minor-league pitcher named Lee Meyer. All this led Ray Fitzgerald of the *Globe* to point out that Tony marked "the first time she's dated an athlete who plays every day, if you'll pardon the expression."

Tony reported that he liked Mamie, and that during their date in Anaheim they had talked about hitting. "If she was 150, I'd go out with her if she looked the way she does," Tony told reporters. "She has a beautiful face and a beautiful body. For someone thirty-six years old, she is solid all over." The middle-aged writers interviewing Tony gulped, looked at each other, looked back at Tony, and one of them said, "I am *not* going to ask you the next question."

Many Red Sox fans didn't see anything funny about it. In the summer of '69, as Pilots pitcher Jim Bouton scribbled in a notebook the stuff that would become the tell-all tome *Ball Four*, the general public was still incredibly naive about their all-American heroes playing big-league

In 1960, nearly a decade before she dated Tony, movie actress Mamie Van Doren was just another Hollywood sex symbol looking very Marilyn Monroe-esque. This publicity photo shows Van Doren posing in two fad styles of the day, the "new" sack style and the more familiar form fit. (Boston Herald archives photo)

baseball. Tony's fan mail took a troubling turn. "How an innocent boy like you can get involved with somebody like her I don't know. I don't like the idea of your marrying her," wrote a seventy-five-year-old woman. "I decided to marry you, after seeing you play against the Indians," a twenty-one-year-old woman wrote from Cleveland. "Now you are going to marry a thirty-six-year-old woman. I'm fractured and think I might kill myself." Of course, once his slump settled in, fans began to shout from the stands, "Mamie's too much for you."

Even people who should have known better joined the chorus. "I would hope that l'affaire Van Doren is not worrying him too much," Claflin wrote. "Mamie is nice, but she is a bit old for him, wouldn't you say?" The headline over the column read "All Kinds of Curves Troubling Tony C". His storybook comeback year was turning to tatters. He was striking out, and people were making him out to be some sort of pervert because he dated a sexy blonde.

Dating a movie star, even a grade-B movie star who had appeared in *Playboy*, should have been fun for a young baseball star still sowing his oats, but a lot of the summer of '69 wasn't as much fun as it seemed. Tony and Billy were on the same major-league team. The Great Aunt, even the more sophisticated *Sports Illustrated*, thought it was a heartwarming tale, two brothers playing baseball together, just like when they were kids. In reality the arrangement wasn't that much of a warm fuzzy, precisely because it was just like it had been when they were kids: Tony and Billy usually went their separate ways. Of course, just like when they were kids, Billy didn't have much choice. Except for Opening Day in Baltimore, Tony roomed by himself. He preferred to do a lot of things by himself. Billy remembers hanging around the Biltmore on a trip to New York and seeing Tony striding across the lobby toward the door.

"Where are you going?" Billy asked.

"I got a date," Tony answered.

"Oh," said Billy, who felt a little lost as he watched his brother brush by, push out the door, and disappear into the streets of the Big Apple.

Billy recalls that he was "kind of shocked at the beginning. You'd think he would have said, 'Come on, let's go out.' But he did his own thing. I usually went out to dinner with Rico and other guys on the team."

The Red Sox were no longer the tightly knit, adorable bunch of scrappy underdogs they had been in 1967. They weren't terrible—they would finish 87-75, but they could not contend with the powerful Orioles, who would win 109 games. Team morale was low and Dick Williams's act was wearing thin. Bad karma had begun to set in on April 19, when Williams engineered a trade that sent the popular Harrelson, Pizarro, and Dick Ellsworth to the White Sox for catcher Joe Azcue and pitchers Sonny Siebert and Vicente Romo. Tired of sitting on the bench, Azcue jumped the club in Minneapolis in June and demanded to be traded. Romo later disappeared in Chicago: Police were brought in on the search until he finally turned up three days later in the company of a waitress from a Mexican restaurant. No one was happy. Fuming at Williams's mistreatment, George Scott told friends how much fun it had been to play for Frank Robinson in winter ball. Former "can't-miss" prospect Joe Lahoud griped about not playing.

Tony showed flashes of his old self but also struggled through terrible slumps, especially at Fenway Park. The home fans began to boo the hometown kid. They unleashed extracruel taunts against Tony, who just a couple of months earlier, in Claflin's words, had warmed "the heart of a whole nation" with his comeback. Now fans hollered, "Go home, blind man" and "Get Lahoud in there" and "We want Billy." During the home opener, their cheers had moved Tony to tears. Now the extrasensitive Tony heard every heckler and was wounded. In *Seeing It Through* he remembered standing at the plate, saying to himself, "If you knew the truth, you wouldn't boo. I'm trying very hard and I need your help. You all think my eye is perfect again, just like before. Well, you're wrong." It was part his own fault: They thought the eye was perfect again because that's what he had been telling them.

Williams, who had kissed the comeback kid on the cheek after the home run on Opening Day, and Tony barely spoke to one another. During a pitching change in a game against Oakland, Tony was chatting with Reggie Smith in the outfield, when, suddenly, Lahoud appeared at his side. "I'm in for you," he said. Tony was embarrassed and stunned as he trotted into the dugout. He fumed as he sought out Williams, who turned his back on him. Eventually, Tony deduced that he was removed as part of a double-switch: Lahoud batted in the pitcher's spot and the new pitcher batted in Tony's spot. But he wondered why Williams wouldn't tell him that.

Their relationship took another blow after a game against the Senators in late June. The Red Sox blew a three-run lead in the ninth when (1) Tony misjudged a fly ball, (2) a pitcher picked up a sacrifice bunt and threw it into right field, and (3) the catcher threw a double-play relay over the first baseman's head. Afterward, a simmering Williams mentioned, over and over, only one of the three botches to the press. "He quit on that ball," he said of Tony's misplay. "He cost us the game."

On a hot and muggy July 4, the Red Sox, losers of seven straight, played the second game of a doubleheader against the Washington Senators—managed by Ted Williams—at Fenway Park. Tony had already struck out three times and hit into two double plays on that day when he came to bat with the bases loaded in the seventh inning of the nightcap. Tony took the first two pitches for balls, then swung and missed a high slider. The fans booed. He swung and missed another pitch that was shoulder high. The boos and catcalls intensified. However, Tony slashed the next pitch past leftfielder Frank Howard, who teetered after the ball, for a bases-clearing double. As he stood on second base, Tony surveyed the crowd cheering and clapping, and he was sickened. "You front-running sons of bitches!" he yelled. "You front-running sons of bitches!" He turned to the second-base umpire and said, "Boy, they boo you when you're down, but get a hit when they want one and they're with you all over again. What kind of people are they?" The umpire replied, "They're front-running sons of bitches."

After the All-Star break the Red Sox fell hopelessly out of contention. Tony spent the long, hot summer trying to reestablish his stardom. For two weeks in mid-July he was platooned with the lefty-hitting Lahoud, then he surged to win back his full-time job. On July 20 he was warming up in right field before the start of the eighth inning against the Orioles when the gravelly voice of public address announcer Sherm Feller announced that man had just landed on the moon. On July 24 in Seattle Tony smashed a home run but wrenched his back on the swing and remained hunched over at the plate. Trainer Buddy LeRoux and Dick Williams rushed out. Tony told them he couldn't move. Williams asked the umpire if he could insert a pinch-runner to trot out Tony's homer. The umpire said yes, but the pinch-runner would get credit for the homer.

"Wait a minute," Tony interjected, "I'll make it around," and he circled the bases hunched over like Groucho Marx.

There wasn't much else historic or comical about the Red Sox as the season dragged on. Around Fenway Park it was most definitely not the summer of love. On August 1 Williams fined Yastrzemski five hundred dollars because the manager thought Yaz had loafed running out a ground ball. Hard liquor was banned on team charter flights after a Red Sox player made an obscene gesture toward a stewardess on a trip from the West Coast. On August 10, Billy, who had been demoted to the Red Sox's Triple-A minor-league team in Louisville, blasted Williams in a story in the *Sunday Advertiser,* saying he thought Williams was a dishonest manager and he didn't want to play for the Red Sox as long as Williams was in charge. Newsmen went to Tom Yawkey for a comment on Billy's outburst. The Red Sox owner—the same man who had held Tony's hand in Sancta Maria hospital the morning after he was hit, the man who told Tony he would always have a job with the Red Sox—said, "It seems like it runs in the family." Not long afterward, after dinner at the family home in Swampscott, Tony turned to Sal and said, "I don't love it anymore. I hate every part of going to that ballpark every day."

It was a terrible feeling and a horrible admission for someone who had dedicated nearly his whole life to going to the ballpark every day. But the spasm of bitterness passed on Monday night, August 18. As woozy rockers picked up the pieces from the weekend concert and love-in in Woodstock, the Red Sox played the Twins at Fenway Park. In the eighth inning, with the Red Sox trailing, 6-3, Tony stepped up against Minnesota right-hander Bill Zepp with one out. Yastrzemski and Reggie Smith were on base. Tony smacked a home run into the left-field screen to tie the game. It was his first Fenway homer since June. The Red Sox won in the tenth. Tony, the hero of the game, felt a calmness wash over him when he thought back to where he had been exactly two years earlier: face down at home plate.

At noon on September 23 Williams was fired. That night against the Yankees, with Eddie Popowski serving as interim manager, Tony hit his twentieth home run of the season. "He told me that was a big goal for him," Tony Athanas remembers. "He wanted to hit twenty home runs to prove to himself and to Dick Williams that he could still play." He had led the team by batting .315 in September. Overall, with his twenty home runs, he batted .255 with eighty-two runs batted in while playing 141 games. Despite everything—the bleary eye, Mamie Van Doren, Dick Williams, fickle fans—Tony had come back, and no one could ever take that away from him.

"I knew it was an uphill fight, but I knew if anybody could do it, it would have been him," offers Yastrzemski, who then grants Tony the best compliment an ego-driven athlete can give to another: "He's the only guy who could have done it—him or me."

~14~

THE WORLD CHAMPIONSHIP OF KARATE

TONY CONIGLIARO WAS A HERO AGAIN, BUT HIS STORY HAD ACQUIRED A DIFFER-
ENT SPIN. He was no longer the precocious phenom, Ted Williams in
embryo, the teen dream, singing slugger with unlimited potential. Now
his story was bigger than baseball: He had crossed the line into human
interest. Now he was the man of the Inspirational Comeback, a profile in
courage, a character out of a John R. Tunis book. Tony won the Comeback
of the Year award. He won the prestigious Hutch Award for courage. Now,
Tony was the kind of ballplayer they made movies about. Monte Stratton
(*The Monte Stratton Story,* 1949, starring James Stewart and June Allyson)
overcame losing a leg to resume his pitching career. Grover Cleveland
Alexander (*The Winning Team,* 1952, starring Ronald Reagan and Doris Day)
overcame dizzy spells to become a World Series hero. Tony C overcame a
beaning and blurry vision to hit home runs again. Tony, undoubtedly,
would have been delighted to play himself on the big screen.

In the meantime, he wrote a book about himself. In the winter
of 1969–70 Tony collaborated with freelance sportswriter Jack Zanger to
produce *Seeing It Through* for Macmillan. It was an unusually frank first-
person account of Tony's life and career, with the attendant exaggera-
tions and faulty memories of an athlete talking about himself into a tape
recorder. He went extra hard on Dick Williams and out of his way to
stroke Carl Yastrzemski and Tom Yawkey—Tony knew he would be playing alongside Yaz and Yawkey would be signing his paychecks—when
the tome hit the stores the following summer. In the second-to-last paragraph of the book, Tony wrote, "There is no way of hiding from death.
Me, I want to live till I'm 104 and play five more years after that." Eerily,

Zanger died unexpectedly at age forty-three almost immediately after the manuscript was completed.*

Tony enjoyed his revived, if altered, celebrity status with extra enthusiasm. The phone was ringing again, and no one was calling to ask him to send back the free golf bag. He was a guest on *To Tell the Truth* and *The American Sportsman*. He continued to make singing appearances on *The Merv Griffin Show*. Tony Athanas remembers his roommate's coming home from the record store with a copy of "If I Had a Hammer," playing it over and over to copy down the lyrics, then playing it over and over to sing along. "He went and sang it on the show," Athanas says. "That's how he got ready to sing a song on television."

Tony was also the guest on an episode of *The Dating Game*. Three bachelorettes were hidden behind a screen while Tony asked them a series of insipid questions, such as "Bachelorette Number One, if you were a tree, what tree would you be?" Then Tony picked one to accompany him on a night on the town. Like every red-blooded male who had seen the show, Tony had concocted a plan to ensure that he would pick the best-looking young woman: Athanas would flash him a signal from the audience. But Athanas was late making his way from backstage to his seat, and Tony had to pick on his own. The mix-up was costly. Tony failed to select Dawn Wells, the actress who had portrayed the wholesome Mary Ann—the object of many male fantasies in the sixties—on the television comedy *Gilligan's Island*.

It was a minor setback for Tony, who didn't need a game show to land dates with celebrities, starlets, beauty queens, and pinup girls. He went out with, among many others, a Miss Massachusetts; Lana Wood, the sister of actress Natalie Wood and herself soon to appear in the James Bond flick *Diamonds Are Forever*; Sue Bernard, a *Playboy* Playmate of the Month; and a woman who was on the rebound from a fling with Elvis Presley. When he and Billy were featured in a *Boston Herald* series "Eligible Bachelors," Tony said of his taste in women: "I can't stand a girl who is possessive . . . who wants everything arranged by schedule. My whole life's a schedule—games, traveling. I don't like girls who talk about other

---

*All in all, the book was well received. Dick Williams was understandably peeved over his portrayal. Tony and Hawk Harrelson also had a mild falling-out over the inclusion of Julie Markakis in the book.

people, girls or guys." He said another pet peeve was women who dated one guy, then dated the guy's friend, that he and Athanas had an ironclad agreement to stay away from each other's girlfriends, past or present.* Tony also told the *Herald* he liked women who were attractive, outgoing, and casual, with long hair. "More or less the all-American, rather than sexy," Tony explained.

He didn't mention that he would cheerfully make an exception if the women were sexy enough—Mamie Van Doren was nobody's all-American—but it was true that he was turned off by tawdriness or even a hint of sloppiness. Bill Bates, then the Boston Patriots trainer and Tony's pal, recalls Tony's taking a date, a waitress from Bachelors III in New York, to watch Richie play football for Swampscott against rival Marblehead. "On a zero to ten, she was a twelve," Bates says. "She was beautiful. And I think she went to Columbia or something." In the third quarter of the game Tony leaned in close to Bates and whispered, "You've got to help me get rid of her."

"What? Why?" Bates wanted to know. "She's delightful."

"She has popcorn in her teeth," Tony said.

"Tony," Bates declared, "we're at a football game. We're eating popcorn. Of course she has popcorn in her teeth. Are you out of your mind? Buy her a toothbrush."

Besides dabbling with barmaids and game shows in the winter of 1969–70, Tony also got down to work. He had battled back, and he was an inspiration to thousands, but now he needed to resume his pursuit of greatness. Hitting twenty home runs was fine, but not for someone whose career goals included being better than Ted Williams. Tony knew that the Comeback of the Year award was a trophy nobody won two years in a row.

He also knew the Red Sox brass would quickly run low on sentiment for the gutsy kid. They had already turned a little snotty the previous summer when Tony complained about the white shirts and when Billy complained about Dick Williams.

Immediately after the season, new manager Eddie Kasko was asked to list which Red Sox players were untouchable in prospective winter trades: He did not mention Tony. During the American League play-offs

---

*Tony and Athanas also had a standing bet on which of them would marry first. The wager started at two hundred dollars, and escalated over the years into four figures.

between the Baltimore Orioles and Minnesota Twins, the scuttlebutt was that Tony would be dealt to the New York Mets for a pitcher, such as Jim McAndrew, Gary Gentry, or an unpolished twenty-two-year-old named Nolan Ryan.

Tony didn't like feeling expendable. He needed an edge. Hitting a baseball is mostly hand-eye coordination. Tony couldn't do much about the eye, so he needed to work on quickening his hands and sharpening his concentration. He decided to take up karate and in December went to see Kazumi Tabata at the Northeast Judo Club in nearby Somerville. Tabata, a master in the *shotokan* style of karate who had emigrated from Japan in 1967, was world class. He told Tony he did not offer individual lessons but relented when he saw the disappointment in Tony's face. "I

During his comeback from the beaning, Tony got more serious than ever about his conditioning. To help improve his hand-eye coordination, he took up karate with instructor Kazumi Tabata in Somerville, Massachusetts. Here he is practicing some sort of frontal kick. (Boston Herald archives photo)

would consider it if you follow what I say without objection for the next three months," Tabata decreed. Tony agreed. Tabata asked Tony to stand nearby and "try blocking my punches just like how you catch the ball." Without warning Tabata jabbed at Tony with closed fists. "I wanted to make sure to see his reflexes and the ability of the eye," Tabata remembers. "Tony avoided the punch without difficulties. He was indeed a professional baseball cleanup batter. He could be able to win the world championship of karate if he tried."

Tabata warned Tony, "My training is very hard. Come to me no matter what, otherwise you will not last three months." He looked hard at Tony, sizing him up. "Our eyes met and I saw the spark that would soon be a fire," Tabata says. He gave Tony a book about Zen. In the week before lessons began, as Tony read about the samurai, Tabata studied books about baseball.

Three times a week Tony reported to the *dojo* in Somerville for three-hour karate sessions that Tabata had modified for baseball training. He worked Tony harder than Dick Williams or the drill instructors at Fort Dix ever dared. The regimen included 100 deep knee bends; 100 push-ups; 100 front-side-reverse-back kicks with each foot; 100 lifts of a twenty-pound dumbbell with each arm; 250 punches with each hand on a padded block; 200 steps of running in place; squatting, kicking, and punching sequences; and 500 swings of a lead baseball bat. Tabata recalls that during the first session Tony was ready to telephone Amnesty International. "He was already rushing away into the bathroom. His suffering scream could be heard throughout the *dojo*," Tabata says. "I grabbed his hair and pulled him back inside the *dojo*. And then I trained him even harder, without mercy." After his second lesson Tony told Clif Keane of the *Globe*, "I never was so beat up in my life. I'm lame all over."

In February, just before the start of spring training, Tony reported for his final karate session and Tabata told him, "Tony, today is the last day. We'll do our last part of the training. If you can follow me, you will be qualified." The final exam required going nonstop for five hours. "Tony was out of breath," Tabata said. "He almost fell down many times." At last Tabata hollered, "*Yame!*" and Tony put up his hands and crumpled to the floor, breathing heavily and collecting himself. Tabata congratulated him and said he would award him the *kyu* rank of karate. Tony stood, grasped Tabata's hands, and thanked him. "I sent him off to spring training with the celebration of his new beginning," Tabata says. The karate lessons stuck. Dennis Gilbert, the Red Sox minor leaguer who had met Tony in the Instructional League in 1968 and became a lifelong friend, recalls, "Tony could catch a fly—a housefly—in midair. That's how quick his hands got."

On the eve of the spring camp—at age twenty-five, it was his seventh season with the Red Sox—Tony told the press that in 1970 he wanted to "be a happy ballplayer, play nothing but good defense, and hit the damn ball all over the place." He switched from the thirty-one-ounce bat he had used during the 1969 season to a thirty-four-ounce bat to generate more power. And he hugged home plate more tightly than ever. He was more afraid of becoming an average ballplayer than he was of getting beaned.

On March 9 in the first exhibition game, he smacked a 450-foot home run to right-center field in Winter Haven against Houston Astros starter and former teammate Dan Osinski. Said Osinski, "Tony was leaning out over the plate farther than I've seen him since he was beaned. Maybe it was because he knew I wouldn't throw at him and maybe not." Home-plate umpire John Rice agreed Tony was back tight where he used to be and shed his impartiality for a moment to observe, "That's Tony's style and it's a good thing because a sound Conigliaro is good for baseball."

On March 14, Tony tumbled and cracked a rib while chasing a wind-blown double by the Mets' Bud Harrelson. He was out of the lineup for a week, then had an unremarkable spring. Kasko had planned to bat him cleanup to start the season, but George Scott—thriving without Dick Williams around to call him "Cement Head" and other pleasantries—hit well during the exhibition season. On Opening Day at Yankee Stadium, Scott batted fourth. Tony hit sixth.

On April 17, with the team languishing at 7-8, Kasko moved Tony to cleanup. Three weeks later he was still hitting only .259 with two home runs and a mere nine runs batted in. It's not as if Tony had forgotten his karate: During an April 29 game at Fenway, Red Sox right-hander Ray Culp drilled a pitch into Oakland Athletics slugger Reggie Jackson. Jackson ran to the mound to punish Culp, and both teams streamed from their dugouts and bullpens for a baseball brawl, which meant a lot of holding and tackling and hollering. Tony hurried in from right field, and amid the swirl of humanity, sat down on first base to remove his cleats.

"T. C., what are you doing?" George Scott demanded.

"These are considered lethal weapons now," Tony said, showing the Boomer his Tabata-trained feet.

Then, as if the adrenaline from his return to the beloved cleanup spot kicked in, Tony erupted. On May 9 in Oakland the game was tied at 3-3 in the ninth and Yastrzemski was on first, when Tony broke an oh-for-twelve streak with a home run deep into the left-field seats. The next night he clanged a home run high off the left-field foul pole against Athletics reliever Rollie Fingers. On May 12 in Anaheim he homered against Angels knuckleballer Eddie Fisher. The next night he blasted two home runs against the Angels.

On May 16 against the Indians at Fenway Park, Tony tied the game at 2-2 with a two-run homer in the sixth inning. In the eighth Yastrzemski crushed a ball against Cleveland righty Dennis Higgins to the right of the center-field flagpole, over the rear wall of the center-field grandstand, onto Lansdowne Street—an estimated five-hundred-foot wallop. Tony stepped to the plate, shocked by the immensity of Yaz's blast. He also thought, "What can I ever do to top that?" At last Tony was back, competing with Yaz on equal terms, superstar-to-superstar. Tony was no longer the poignant comeback kid in the shadow of Yaz's healthy heroics. After the Indians game Tony was hitting .288 with eight homers and twenty runs batted in. Yaz was hitting .307 with nine homers and twenty-two RBIs. He was the old Tony, craving the chance to bat with runners on base. Yastrzemski hit more home runs and compiled a higher batting average, but in the summer of 1970 nobody on the Red Sox would drive home more runs.

"Every time somebody was in scoring position, it seemed he knocked them in," Petrocelli says. "He was back and better than normal. He was better than he was prior to the beaning. More so than ever, he was a clutch hitter."

Kasko recalls, "He was very conscious of center stage. He liked to be up there with the bases loaded and the game on the line. And I'll tell you, there weren't too many others I'd rather see up there. Him or Yaz."

On May 19 at Fenway, with the game tied and the bases loaded in the ninth, Tony singled against reliever Fred Lasher to beat the Tigers.

It was the bright, flashy kind of moment in the arena he lived for—getting the big hit in the ninth—but he also had an underrated knack for playing solid, helpful baseball. During a May 24 doubleheader against the Orioles, the Red Sox clung to a 1-0 lead in the bottom of the ninth with a runner on second when Baltimore first baseman Boog Powell slashed a single to right. Tony fielded the ball on one hop and roped a one-hop throw to home plate, where catcher Gerry Moses lunged and tagged out Terry Crowley trying to score. In the nightcap Tony walked in the ninth to start a game-winning rally.

On May 25 Tony hit two home runs against the Senators at Fenway Park. The second was clearly foul, and Tony had stopped halfway up the first-base line when third-base umpire George Maloney ruled it fair. Tony circled the bases repressing an impish smile while the Red Sox bench convulsed in laughter. The next night he smashed a two-run home run over the left-field screen, his ninth homer in sixteen games. "He doesn't look like a guy who has any eye problems when he's hitting," Washington manager Ted Williams observed.

His outfield play, however, had been sending a different message. In Milwaukee a fly ball went over his head. In Anaheim he misplayed a line drive. In Baltimore he raced in to chase a fly ball by Brooks Robinson, stopped, then raced backward as the ball dropped onto the lawn behind him. Even on balls he caught, he was breaking late and lunging at the last instant. On May 27 against the Senators, Tony misjudged a fly ball by Bernie Allen, who legged out a triple. Tony pulled a groin muscle chasing the ball and was startled by the chorus of boos from the Fenway stands. He couldn't believe it: He was white hot at the plate but got heckled over a botched fly ball. Then general manager Dick O'Connell and Kasko huddled with team physician Dr. Thomas Tierney. They decided Tony should have an eye exam. Tony's sensitive side was rubbed raw: He angrily refused to have the eyes checked.

"It's always something with me," he ranted. "If the team isn't doing well, then have Tony's eye checked. I've had enough of it." He offered a laundry list of excuses and reasons for the botched fly balls and added, "I'm good and tired of having people check my eyesight. I'll be imagining things all my life. My eyes are 20-20. There is no reason for the slightest concern."

This was humbug. He was hitting home runs like the old Tony and driving in runs like the old Tony, and it was all remarkable, because he couldn't see. His left eye was getting worse and he struggled more than ever on bright days. He never owned up to Kasko or the press, but sometimes his anxiety surfaced around his teammates. "He kept mentioning it," Yastrzemski says. "He complained a lot about it. But what kept carrying him was that tremendous competitiveness. He wouldn't give in."

More than ever Tony was a thinking man's hitter. "He worked a lot mentally," Kasko says. "He went out of his way to find out about pitchers, and he stored that stuff away in his head." Tony had been reading Zen in the off-season, and he was certain hard work and concentration could beat lousy eyesight. One rainy day in May, Tony asked clubhouse man Don Fitzpatrick, a fixture at Fenway since the forties, about Ted Williams's work habits. "He worked like a madman," Fitzpatrick told Tony. "He was always honing his bats, strengthening his wrists, perfecting his swing." Tony fetched a weighted bat, stood in front of a mirror to analyze his technique, and took 150 swings.

One Friday night after a game, Tony approached Kasko, who constantly encouraged his charges to take as much extra batting practice as they could stomach. "I'd like to take some extra hitting," Tony proclaimed as the last stragglers left the clubhouse.

"Sure," Kasko replied. "Why don't you come in early tomorrow and we'll arrange it."

"No, I meant right now," Tony declared.

Kasko was silent for a moment, then explained, "Tony, we'd have to put the lights on. That would involve a lot of extra expense. It just isn't possible—"

"Aww," interrupted Tony, breaking into a smile, "I was only kidding."

Remembers Kasko: "He said he was only kidding, but I'm not so sure. If I had said okay and went out to turn on the lights, I'm sure he would have gone out there with me and hit."

The seeds of the Fred Lasher Incident were planted on the Fourth of July at Fenway. Lasher, the sidearming right-hander freshly traded from the Tigers to the Indians, entered the game to start the seventh inning.

Less than two months earlier Tony had beaten Lasher and the Tigers with a ninth-inning bases-loaded single. This time around, Tony was the first batter in the seventh, and Lasher decked him with a pitch. Tony got up and smashed a home run. After the game Lasher said, "Tell Tony Conigliaro he better be a little careful the next time he faces me. The next time he just may get a little jammed." And as if that weren't enough, Lasher added, "And you can also tell him his home run was no great accomplishment. That pitch was so fat and down the gut even I could have hit it out."

Billy read the quotes in the newspaper and asked his brother, "What are you going to do if he throws at you?"

"I'm going to go out to the mound," said Tony.

On July 12 the Red Sox and Indians played a Sunday afternoon doubleheader in Cleveland. In the nightcap Lasher was granted the first and only start of his major-league career. Tony stepped to bat in the first inning and Lasher's first pitch plunked him in the left forearm.

"The way to get him out was to pitch him in, on the hands," Lasher recalls. "Wouldn't you know, I hit him. But it was unintentional. He figured it was intentional."

Tony had been hit seven times since the beaning that nearly killed him and had never charged the pitcher. This time he dashed to the mound, let out a small yell, and karate-kicked Lasher on the left thigh and hacked him in the face with a left-handed karate chop. "I think he was trying to kick me in the nuts," Lasher says.

Cleveland catcher Ray Fosse, hot on Tony's heels between home plate and the mound, tackled Tony to the ground as the entire roster from both teams converged on the infield. Duke Sims of the Indians arrived from left field and tussled with Red Sox catcher Gerry Moses. Billy appeared and made a running leap onto Sims. George Scott, who had trouble hitting Lasher's pitches, reached into the scrum and tried to hit Lasher with a fist. Yastrzemski hollered and gestured at Cleveland manager Alvin Dark. Mike Andrews and Sparky Lyle worked the crowd, jawing with Indians. The scene quieted quickly, as baseball dustups often do. Umpire Hank Soar gestured that Tony was ejected from the game, but Lasher was allowed to stay. This blew Tony's fuse again, and teammate Reggie Smith had to grab him in a bear hug and cart him off the field.

Having been beaned and now somewhat of an expert in the martial arts, Conigliaro was no one to be messed with. Red Sox teammate Reggie Smith restrains Tony from going after Indians pitcher Fred Lasher after Lasher hit Tony with a pitch. (AP/Wide World Photos)

"When I got hit, there was no question in my mind it was deliberate," Tony maintained. "And I don't want any more broken bones in my hands or arms. I'm having too good a season."

"After going through what he did, I could see where he would react the way he reacted," reflects Lasher, looking back with twenty-seven years' perspective.

Billy replaced Tony in right field. He led off the second inning, and Lasher was still in the game. The crowd booed. Some people tensed: Would Lasher dare drill Tony's brother, just to make it a complete set? Billy had other worries. He knew Tony was in the clubhouse, watching the game on television. When the count ran to 1-2, Billy thought, "If I strike out, Tony will never talk to me again." Lasher threw a curveball. Billy clobbered it into the upper deck of spacious Municipal Stadium. When he checked in with his brother in the clubhouse afterward, Billy recalls, "Tony was jumping up and down." It was one of Billy's favorite moments in the big leagues.

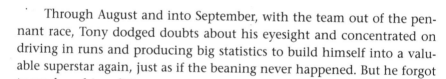

Through August and into September, with the team out of the pennant race, Tony dodged doubts about his eyesight and concentrated on driving in runs and producing big statistics to build himself into a valuable superstar again, just as if the beaning never happened. But he forgot to work on his politics.

As usual in the summer of 1970, baseball reflected American society. In the months after Kent State, student strikes, and the Beatles' breakup, this meant there was disorder, confusion, conflict, chaos, and ridiculous sideburns. Baseball fans wondered where all the clean-cut heroes had gone. In Detroit Denny McLain, the thirty-one-game winner of 1968, mixed with gamblers, carried a gun on road trips, and doused a couple of baseball writers with buckets of ice water. Outfielder Curt Flood was traded from the Cardinals to the Phillies, challenged baseball's reserve system, and spent the summer painting portraits in Denmark. Salaries spiraled out of sight. Incredibly, ten players in the majors, including Yastrzemski, topped one hundred thousand dollars a year. Bouton's book *Ball Four* portrayed baseball players as peeping Toms and drunken boors.

And in Boston the Red Sox drifted into apathy and anarchy. Dick Williams was gone. With the tough homeroom teacher out of the picture, the Red Sox treated the summer of 1970 like study hall. They were not a cohesive bunch; the battle of Cleveland was a rare moment of solidarity. There was no quest for the pennant to pull them together; for the first time since 1966, the team was not in the race from the beginning, as the mighty Orioles again ran away with the American League East. Kasko wasn't going to rally them under one flag, either. He was a pleasant, bespectacled organization man; after the despotic Williams, the players were happy to have a manager they could walk all over.

In the absence of leadership, the Red Sox congealed into tribes. Like the nation as a whole, the Red Sox were divided and choosing up sides. Yaz and Reggie Smith were the leaders of the most powerful clan; Tony was the leader of the other; and relations between the two Red Sox stars frosted over. Yaz had grown accustomed to unchallenged stardom while Tony was out of baseball in 1968 and preoccupied with battling his way back in 1969. Now Tony kept pace with Yaz in home runs and exceeded him in runs batted in. Tony was a rival again. "There were cliques," Billy says. "It was supposed to be a team."

Tony and others on the team thought Yastrzemski was accorded special treatment, that he trod Fenway Park with royal privileges, and that he operated under his own set of rules. It started at the top: Everyone knew Tom Yawkey, lifelong star worshiper, adored Yaz. Billy remembers Kasko's issuing orders for everybody on the team to be out on the field before the game at a certain time or risk a fine. Although the rest of the team reported for duty as ordered, Yastrzemski and Reggie Smith wandered out of the clubhouse long after the deadline, and no one said a word to them.

With no big issues to address, such as a pennant race, the resentments often grew out of incredible pettiness. Clubhouse man Fitzpatrick was seen as Yaz's personal valet. When Yaz wanted a sandwich, he got it. When Yaz needed a pair of sanitary socks, he got two pair. The rest of the Red Sox could fend for themselves. It became a running joke on the team that if you wanted your spikes polished, you had to give them to Yaz, who would get Fitzy to do them for you. Tony would shake his head with a can-you-believe-this look on his face. He didn't think anybody should get special treatment, except, perhaps, Tony. "Tony thought Carl was getting treated a little better in the clubhouse," Petrocelli says. "Tony got a little angry about that. Tony wanted to be the best. He wanted to be treated like a superstar. It was his hometown. He was a star. He felt he should have been the guy, the man. He didn't like it, but he didn't show it in a weaselly way. He wasn't a troublemaker. He was perplexed. He couldn't understand what was going on with Yaz."

It was typical of the Red Sox as a churlish, quirky institution that the team could be shredded over socks and sandwiches. Recalls Billy, "When Tony hit a home run, you had to wonder, 'Is Yaz going to shake his hand?' 'Is Reggie Smith going to shake his hand?' There was so much tension in that clubhouse."

As silly as it was, the tribal tension more seriously threatened Tony's future with the Red Sox than the beaning or Mamie Van Doren ever did. In 1970 he had his best year in the major leagues, at least at the plate: Playing 146 games with one good eye, he batted .266, with thirty-six home runs (fourth in the league) and 116 runs batted in (second in the league). But the Red Sox finished 87-75, in third place, twenty-one games behind Baltimore. The team would have to make changes, and Tony was uneasy. He could visualize Yaz sitting across the desk from Mr. Yawkey.

On Friday, October 9, the day before the start of the World Series between the Orioles and the Big Red Machine Cincinnati Reds, Tony played a round of golf in California. When he came off the course into the clubhouse, somebody called to him, "Heard about the trade?"

Tony's stomach dropped and he felt empty. It didn't seem possible the Red Sox would actually go ahead and—

"Denny McLain was traded to the Senators," the man explained.

"Oh," Tony said, and he relaxed, if only for a moment.

~15~

SHOCKED BY THE TRADE

On Sunday night, October 11, 1970, Tony Conigliaro flew into Logan Airport from a speaking engagement in Connecticut. As usual Sal was waiting for him as he stepped off the plane. Tony looked at his father's face and knew something was wrong. It was the same tight, mournful look Sal had worn when he told Tony that his grandfather was dead.

"What's up?" Tony nervously inquired.

"Tony, you've been traded."

Staggered, Tony blurted out, "You're kidding. It's impossible." Then he asked where he had been sent. And like every ballplayer shipped away in a deal, he wanted to know for whom he had been traded. That was a cold, blunt measure of what his own team thought he was worth. Sal ticked off the details: Tony, catcher Gerry Moses, and reliever Ray Jarvis had been packaged off to the California Angels for closer Ken Tatum, outfielder Jarvis Tatum, and second baseman Doug Griffin. Like everyone else, Tony was momentarily confused by the number of people named Jarvis and Tatum in the deal, but the essence of the transaction seared him. They had dumped him on the Angels, the team that had nearly killed him. And Tony C, the slugging local hero, the next DiMaggio, the next Ted Williams, the comeback kid, the man whose courage had a nation rooting for him, was shipped out for a relief pitcher who had recorded seventeen saves in 1970.

"*Impossible!*" Tony cried. "How many years do you get out of a relief pitcher? How long do they last?"

Tony and Sal started to walk through the terminal. Reporters and photographers, who had been alerted to the trade and Tony's expected arrival at the airport, swarmed close. Uncharacteristically, Tony shooed them away and ordered them to not make any photos. He wasn't in the mood.

In the car Tony tried to be philosophical. Just a couple of years earlier, he was out of baseball and getting offers to sell encyclopedias door-to-door. "I'm still alive," he told himself. "And I'm still a major leaguer." Sal and Tony met Tony Athanas at Santarpio's restaurant in East Boston, but Tony's effort to stay upbeat faded over pizza. "It was a sad night," Athanas remembers.

Nearly twenty-seven years later, no one claims responsibility for the trade that jettisoned Boston's folk hero. The Sunday deal had been hatched in the previous two days at the World Series in Cincinnati, during meetings between Red Sox General Manager Dick O'Connell and Angels General Manager Dick Walsh. O'Connell remembers that the impetus to move Tony came from manager Eddie Kasko, who wanted to remove the tension between the superstars in his clubhouse, and who also thought the Conigliaro brothers would prosper if they were separated. "Kasko is a do-gooder," O'Connell explains. "He thought he might help them by splitting them up. And at the time, we thought Billy was going to be a better ballplayer." Billy scoffs at the compliment. "Tony had thirty-six home runs and 116 RBIs," he says. "Who's going to be a better ballplayer than that?"

Kasko denies he was behind the trade. He remembers that O'Connell asked him at the end of the season what the team needed, and Kasko replied he needed a top reliever. The Red Sox had blown a lot of games in the late innings in 1970. "We needed a horse," Kasko says. "We needed a closer. And Tatum's name was out there."*

Billy is sure his brother was traded because the Red Sox knew his left eye was going bad. Tony had met with Kasko and player personnel director Haywood Sullivan in September, at which time he had asked to be shifted to left field, because the glare in right bothered his eye, but they turned him down. The Sox wanted to unload him while his stock was high. Billy also thinks Yastrzemski, somehow, was party to it.

There is likely some truth in all the theories. The Red Sox wanted to fix their balkanized clubhouse, and they weren't going to ditch Yastrzemski.

---

*This was a historic miscalculation by the Red Sox, who already had Sparky Lyle in their bullpen. Lyle was traded to the Yankees two years later and thrived as a closer on two pennant winners in New York. He won the Cy Young Award in 1977.

After Conig's Corner and those botched fly balls in right field, they were skittish about Tony's longevity. Trying to determine the mover and shaker behind a baseball deal is often like trying to find which rooster fertilized the egg. What is certain is that none of the suspects—O'Connell, Kasko, Yastrzemski, or owner Tom Yawkey—were against throwing Tony overboard.

Many of Tony's teammates, especially the members of his clubhouse tribe, were astonished. "Shocked. Shocked," Petrocelli recalls. "Most of the guys couldn't believe it. He had such a good year. Why would you want to trade a guy after having such a good year?" George Scott says, "I didn't like the trade." The man who lockered on the opposite side of the clubhouse, Yastrzemski, remembers: "You just hoped it was the best thing for him. Maybe going somewhere else might do something

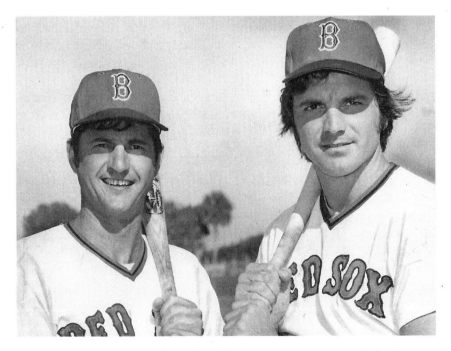

*Several years after Tony was traded to the California Angels in a move some believed was at least in part engineered by teammate Carl Yastrzemski, they ended up together again, albeit briefly, when Conigliaro attempted one last comeback with the Bosox in 1975. (*Boston Herald *archives photo)*

for him." He didn't explain what kind of boost a man who had hit thirty-six home runs needed.

Tony battled to prop up his ego, but he was deeply wounded. He thrived on acceptance—he loved being wanted—and getting traded was total, humiliating rejection. It was like getting dumped by a girlfriend in front of fifty million people. From his home in Mississippi, Moses telephoned Tony shortly after the trade and could tell, saying, "For Tony, a hometown kid who had been through so much, I think it really hurt him badly." Richie remembers: "The trade was the worst day of his life. He reacted worse to that than he did to not playing in the World Series. He was devastated. He was hurt. He was promised by Tom Yawkey after he was almost killed that as long as he owned the team, he'd be a member of the Red Sox."

The day after the trade Tony flew to Reno, Nevada, to play in a celebrity golf tournament. "The golf course is a good place to think about things," he reasoned. When he finally made a statement to the press, he refused to criticize the Red Sox, but admitted: "I am confused by this trade. I don't understand it. I'm not going to do anything sneaky, though. No baloney. I'll report to the Angels. And I'm going to California with one thing in mind, to prove to Boston that it was a mistake." Then Tony asked, "Know anyone who needs an apartment? I just paid next year's rent on my Boston apartment."

It wasn't easy to be flip. He told a television interviewer who asked for his thoughts on the trade: "I have many thoughts, most of which I can't say in front of the camera. I don't want to go to California. But that's the way trades are. You don't have the chance to say anything." Months later the hurt was still fresh when Tony said, "I'm still shocked by the trade. I was born in Boston, almost died there, and expected to play all my career there."

During the winter Tony was able to sort through the gloom and find something about which he could be enthusiastic. If he had to leave his hometown, his friends, and his family, Tony was glad to go somewhere that had style and plenty of young women in summer clothing. He would have taken the bright lights of New York. He could be enchanted by the glitz of southern California. Anaheim was just a convertible ride away from Hollywood, whose glitter, fame, and beautiful people tickled Tony. He could see himself in pictures someday, or perhaps some sort of television action series. Tony liked fun, and in the early seventies southern California was an up-and-coming fun place, a happening place, and Tony C was a happening guy.

But Tony C and southern California just didn't happen. Bill Bates, Tony's friend from Boston, once said, "If anyone ever lived like Joe Btfsplk in *Li'l Abner* with the cloud over his head, it's Tony," and that was never more true then when Tony went west.

He was in the backyard of the movie industry, but that only meant another tantalizing might-have-been. Tony wangled a meeting with producer Al Ruddy, who was considering using unknowns in a new gangster movie *The Godfather.* He thought Tony, with his Italian-American good looks, might work in the role of Michael Corleone and gave him an audition. "He was attractive. He was Italian. And he wasn't afraid," remembers Ruddy. However, Michael was the last role to be cast. "We signed Brando, Bobby Duvall, Jimmy Caan," says Ruddy, and the idea of using a rookie actor to play Michael didn't seem to make sense any more. Ruddy turned to another Italian-American with liquidy brown eyes—Al Pacino. Richie remembers consoling Tony, telling him, "What do you want with this, anyway, some dud movie?'"

If Tony needed a hint about his destiny in California, there was a loud omen just before the start of spring training, when he traveled to Los Angeles for an appearance on *The Merv Griffin Show.* At about six in the morning on February 9, 1971, he was asleep in his hotel room on the twenty-second floor when his bed began to shake, the bureau dressers fell out and crashed to the floor, and the lamp hanging from the ceiling began to sway wildly. Wearing just a pair of shorts and a T-shirt, he bolted out the door and bounded down twenty-two flights to the street. "I ran down the stairs in about two seconds," he said. "I got my spring training in."

When guests were allowed back into the hotel, Tony hurried to his room, dressed in any old thing, gathered his clothes in a ball, and was stuffing them into a suitcase when another tremor vibrated the walls. He grabbed a cab for the airport and took the first flight to Boston. When he arrived—wearing blue jeans, mismatched shoes, a sweatshirt, and no underwear—he learned that he had just lived through the San Fernando Valley earthquake, 6.6 on the Richter scale, and sixty-five people had been killed. Tony had planned to report to spring training early but decided, "I'll be right here in Boston until February 22."

Upon returning to California, Tony took a five-hundred-dollar-a-month duplex in ritzy Newport Beach and planned to live it up. The bachelor digs, spread over two stories, had two bedrooms, three bathrooms, a living room, and a balcony overlooking a bay. Tony brought the goatskin rug from Brookline and spread it out in front of the fireplace. Then he found out his next-door neighbor was the curvaceous movie actress Raquel Welch. The newspaper boys winked and nudged each other in print about the sex kitten and the dashing slugger sharing a fence. However, says Richie, "He told me he ran into her once and she looked the other way."

None of it—stuck-up stars, the movies, earthquakes—would have mattered if Tony's baseball life had prospered, but the most severe letdown about California was the Angels. It was the biggest mismatch in Tony's life since the Red Sox roomed him with Dick Williams.

Orange County was mellow about its baseball. Tony was used to the hardball intensity of Boston, where zealots deeply cared about the Red Sox, thought they could outmanage John McGraw, and liked to pass winter days recounting the starting nine for the 1912 Sox. At Anaheim Stadium fans cheered foul flies and thought tradition meant reminiscing about Steve Bilko's twenty-one homers way back in '61.

In Anaheim, says Tom Murphy, a right-handed starter for the Angels from 1968 until 1972, who later pitched parts of two seasons for the Red Sox, "Baseball is just another form of entertainment. It's like going to the opera or to the movies. Nobody knows who you are." And Tony liked to be famous.

Even the ballpark was unsuited for him. His right-handed power swing had been a dream matchup for left field at Fenway, but left field at Anaheim Stadium was 333 feet away, and in the night air, "The ball just didn't carry," Murphy says. "It took a cannon to get one out. Balls that were out at Fenway were caught in Anaheim."

Tony's new teammates were an odd collection and not an easy bunch for a new guy to be with. The Red Sox clubhouse had never been a warm, cuddly place, but to Tony it was home, and there was always Rico and the Boomer and baby brother Billy. The Angels had Alex Johnson, a surly, brooding outfielder who was openly proud of the fact that he seldom hustled, and Chico Ruiz, the infielder who in the course of the season would pull a gun on Johnson. Infielder Jim Fregosi, the team leader, was intense and wary of the new intense guy. It was a young team: None of the regular eight players was older than thirty.

The manager was Lefty Phillips, who chewed on unlit cigars, spoke out of the side of his mouth, and seemed older than his fifty-two years because of a variety of health problems, including asthma. One of Phillips's coaches was Pete Reiser, who should have understood Tony: He had been a star outfielder with Hall of Fame potential for the Brooklyn Dodgers in the 1940s until he injured himself eleven times running into outfield walls. Now he mostly barked at the Angels like a drill sergeant and threatened lazy players with a bat if they didn't shape up.

"It was the most different ballclub I had ever been on," catcher Gerry Moses remembers. At least Jack Hamilton was gone. But one of Tony's new teammates was Fred Lasher, who sought out Tony during spring training and told him he meant no harm during the beanball war the previous summer. Tony agreed there were no hard feelings, but Lasher was the least of his worries in Anaheim.

Tony was performing without a net. Friends, family, familiar faces, and his credentials as Local Legend were a continent away. Not many Californians had a copy of "Little Red Scooter" in their record collection. And he was under more pressure than ever. However, he was making big money—before the start of the season he had signed for eighty thousand dollars a year and conjured big expectations. The Angels had finished third the previous season, twelve games behind the first-place Minnesota Twins, and the addition of power-hitting Tony was supposed to catapult them into the pennant race. "He got a lot of notoriety," Moses says. "Tony was the guy that trade was made for. We were supposed to win that Western Division."

Tony reported for spring training in Palm Springs, California, and the sheer beauty of the place made him feel better about being away from home. He was issued uniform number 4, which he had sought in Boston at the end of his rookie season, but Roman Mejias had it, and was penciled in as cleanup hitter. "I'll tell you something, we may have made a steal in the deal that landed him," Phillips proclaimed. "I'm surprised he was available."

Tony put in long hours, just as he had in Boston. "From the first day of preseason camp, he has worked as hard as anyone," Phillips said. "Instead of taking a day off when he had reserve service commitments, he came out to the ballpark early to get in practice. Usually, he stayed late."

But his season in the sun unraveled quickly. Tony struggled in the spring, as he often did in Boston, but now, amid strangers in a strange place, a bad spring wasn't so easy to shake off. In the press box there was no Great Aunt pounding the table when he smacked an exhibition home run. On April 3, during the annual preseason series between the Angels and Dodgers, Tony telephoned the ballpark and without even asking for Phillips, told clubhouse attendant Roger Haley that he was sick and would stay home that night. Phillips was rightfully livid, but now Sal was too far away to straighten things out with his son's manager.

Tony slumped into the regular season, and the pressure was greater than ever. He was trying to show the Angels how good he was and the Red Sox how wrong they were. He was the new kid in the neighborhood. Just like when he was the new kid in East Boston, he needed to win everyone over with baseball heroics. But he was failing. After twenty games he was hitting .240. His left eye nettled him, just as it had in 1970, but somehow it seemed harder to handle in California. "He talked to me about it a lot," says Jerry Maffeo, Tony's pal back in Boston. "His eye bothered him in bright sunshine, and the sun was bright every day in California."

For inspiration, Tony kept a photo in his locker showing himself in the dirt, on his back, flailing from a knockdown pitch in 1969. "You look at that picture and it gives you incentive," he reflected. "I had to either get up or stay down and there wasn't much future in staying down."

Every day Tony telephoned his parents at home in Nahant, where they had moved the previous summer to a new house on the ocean. Sal traveled to Baltimore and New York when California visited the Orioles and Yankees. Tony needed the support. He wasn't hitting and he developed a string of pesky injuries, such as a bad leg and a pinched nerve in his neck. He underwent heat treatments, had cortisone shots, and popped muscle relaxants. In mid-May, he put himself in traction for an hour before every game. Instead of winning over his new teammates, he was turning them off. Some Angels started to grumble about the high-priced slugger who didn't play and who couldn't hit a lick when he did play. "He always seemed to be hurt," Murphy remembers. "He always had some malady or affliction—so much so that it caught the notice of his teammates."

The Angels didn't dislike Tony. They just didn't get a chance to know him. Tony was partly to blame. He kept to himself when the team was home and mixed mostly with Moses when the team was on the road. "It was difficult for Tony," Moses adds. "When he was with the Red Sox, Boston was his town. When he went to Los Angeles, I don't think they really understood Tony. I think if they had gotten the chance to be around him, they would have come to like him—like everybody else."

By Memorial Day he had hit only four home runs, the last on May 30 against Mel Stottlemyre at Yankee Stadium. "He was clearly having difficulty," Murphy recalls. "Something was obviously different with his hand-eye coordination. He was striking out a lot. He was not making contact. There were huge holes in his swing."

On June 4, the Angels traveled to Boston, and Tony entered the visitors' clubhouse at Fenway Park for the first time in his life. Even when he tried out for the team fresh out of high school, he had dressed in the Red Sox clubhouse. Now, it was a strange sensation to squeeze into his uniform in the tiny, cramped locker room and to walk onto the familiar lawn from the unfamiliar dugout on the left side of the diamond. It was also a strange sight for Red Sox fans: Tony in a road gray California getup, with an interlocking *CA* on his blue cap, and "Tony C" for his nameline across the back of his jersey. "It was very strange," says Billy, who was across the field in the Boston dugout, "seeing him in another uniform, playing against the home team. You thought things like that didn't happen."

Tony was not parading through his old haunts in triumph. He was batting just .242 with four homers and thirteen runs batted in. His new team was in fourth place, four games under .500, ten games behind first-place Oakland in the American League West. His old team was eleven games over .500, in first place in the American League East, and did not seem to miss him a bit. Billy, who was playing center field and batting .294 for first-place Boston, said of his brother: "I hope he does well, but I hope we win. It'll be all business on the field. We're in first place and we're going to stay there."

Tony, the old master dramatist, knew a heroic home run at Fenway Park would be a precious delight. "I've got a sort of funny feeling," he said before the game. "The adrenaline seems to be flowing a little quicker. And the bat that has felt heavy lately seems like a feather right now."

But in the summer of 1971 Tony found majestic moments hard to come by. In case anyone in Boston didn't know how bizarre Tony's new team was, Alex Johnson advertised it: He failed to run out a routine grounder in the first inning and was yanked from the game. In the bottom of the first, when Tony trotted out to his old spot in right field, the crowd of 31,376 granted him only a polite ripple of applause. When he stepped to the plate for his first at-bat, there was only a slightly above-average ovation. "That surprised me," Billy says.

To complete the dour atmosphere, in the second inning rain began to fall, and the teams had to vacate the field for thirteen minutes. Tony failed to get a hit in his first three times up. In the top of the ninth, with his team trailing, 10-1, Tony looped a single to left—his flair for drama was down to that. "It's been tough," Tony said after the game. "But I'm not giving up on myself."

Many of his teammates were giving up on him. When the Angels played the Washington Senators in Anaheim on June 11, Tony was out of the lineup again, because of a pinched nerve in his neck. He hadn't played at all during California's previous three home games against the Yankees. When he entered the clubhouse, he found a stretcher set up in front of his locker with his uniform spread out on it and a pair of crutches wrapped in Ace bandages forming a coat of arms. For extra hilarity, feminine napkins and blood red ketchup were added to the display.

This was almost too much for Tony. He had built his legend on great physical courage and incredible perseverance. He was nearly killed by a pitch but came back to play with a blurry eye and stood close to the plate when he couldn't quite see ninety-mile-per-hour fastballs whizzing near his face. Yet here were his teammates questioning his toughness. He looked at the hateful display and silently walked into the trainer's room. The next day he checked into Saint Joseph's hospital and spent four days in traction.

"Gentlemen, let me tell you one thing," Phillips said after newsmen got word of the stunt. "As long as the game of baseball will be played, there will be pranks. And that's all this was." Which was hogwash. The Angels were looking for more than laughs. "There was a message being sent there," Murphy says.

More than ever Tony wanted to show them all—the Red Sox, his tormenting teammates, the New England fans who were lukewarm toward him at Fenway—but he only stumbled further. In the middle of June a *Los Angeles Times* story quoted several anonymous Angels who thought Tony was a malingerer. In the third week of June in Milwaukee, Phillips took Tony aside and said, "I won't quit on you if you won't quit on yourself." During a plane ride Tony sat next to Moses and mentioned the practical joke, saying no one was going to accuse him of being a pussycat. Significantly, Tony began to spend more time with Alex Johnson, the ultimate outsider, who addressed many of his teammates with a familiar profanity that starts with "mother." Tony said, "I like Alex. I sympathize with him. I know there's something bothering Alex inwardly."

On Friday night, July 9, in the last series before the All-Star break, Tony's demons ganged up on him in Oakland. He was hitting .229 with four home runs. In the course of the season, he had more cortisone shots (twenty) than runs batted in (fifteen). He was getting headaches again, and his stomach was going sour. There, smirking out onto the field from the home dugout, managing the Athletics, was Dick Williams.

The fans came out to see Oakland's amazing rookie left-hander, Vida Blue. The game was a scoreless tie as it went into extra innings. "I remember Billy Cowan striking out five times," says Murphy. "Vida was *un-believable*. He just blew everybody away." When he stepped to the plate in the eleventh, Tony was already oh-for-six in the game, with three strike-outs. With a runner on first, Tony swung at strike three and the ball squirted away from the catcher. Tony ran to first base—even though, under the rules, with a man on first he was automatically out. Tony, incredibly, loudly argued the point with home-plate umpire Merle Anthony.

The game dragged on past midnight. Tony came to bat in the nineteenth after Ken Berry had singled. Ordered to bunt, Tony squared at the first two pitches and missed. With two strikes, the bunt sign was removed. Tony bunted again anyway, and missed. Anthony called him out. Tony became unglued.

He exploded at Anthony, and when the umpire walked away, Tony followed him around the field, shouting and gesturing wildly. Tony whipped the batting helmet off his head, flipped it in the air, swung his bat at it, and drove it sixty feet down the first-base line. First-base umpire George Maloney immediately threw Tony out of the game. Tony heaved his bat over Maloney's head and continued to shout. Phillips came out of the dugout, disgusted with Tony. The fans howled. The message board flashed, in what was meant to be a humorous touch, "Censored." Dick Williams's son, Rick, fifteen, watched the scene from the visitors' side of the field, and remembered back to when he was a batboy at Fenway Park and Tony was the fresh, youthful hero. "He was trying so hard," Rick says. "I thought about the night he got hit. It was so sad."

When the Athletics won, 1-0, on Angel Mangual's single in the twentieth inning at 1:05 in the morning, Tony was no longer in the clubhouse. Phillips told the newsmen gathered in his office, "He doesn't even know the rules of the game. He ran to first when he couldn't and then he got into a big argument. Then he tried his favorite play, bunting with two strikes, the one that never works. He does a lot of things on his own. You never know what he's going to do." Then Phillips declared, "The man belongs in an institution." The startled newsmen stopped scribbling in their pads, looked at each other, and looked at Phillips.

"Are you speaking for the record?" one of them asked.

"The man belongs in an institution," Phillips repeated.

In his room at the Edgewater Hotel, Tony began to think Phillips was right. He couldn't sleep. He twitched and his stomach was in knots. He felt frightened and alone. He couldn't take it anymore. At 5:00 A.M., Tony picked up the phone and woke up the beat writers who traveled with the Angels and told them to meet him downstairs. As the first light of dawn streaked into the lobby, Tony told the bleary-eyed newsmen he was quitting baseball.

"I almost lost my mind out there on the field tonight," Tony confessed. "I was doing things on the field and saying things on the bench that I didn't know I was doing. Tonight, when I flipped my bat, that was it. I was saying good-bye to baseball." And then, in the empty hotel lobby, he unburdened himself of months of pain and frustration.

"My eyesight never came back to normal," he disclosed. "When the pitcher holds the ball, I can't see his hand or the ball. I pick up the spin on the ball late, by looking away to the side. I don't know how I do it. I kept it away from the Red Sox."

Someone asked Tony how he managed to hit fifty-six home runs with one eye in two seasons with the Red Sox. "I had the support of my family, my teammates, and the fans," he said. "I figured if I worked harder, got more sleep than anybody, ate more steak than anybody, I could do it. You learn to live. But I had a lot of headaches because of the strain to see . . . my search for that damn baseball."

Of his Angels teammates, he declared, "I feel I've let the club down and I wouldn't be surprised if it felt the same way. I'm a loner. I don't hang around with anybody on this club. Maybe that's affected my teammates. I could say, 'Hey, you guys. I can't see out of my left eye. Back me up.' I hoped to gain respect out of what I've done in the past.

"When I first started playing baseball as a Little Leaguer, I always wanted to be the greatest right-handed hitter who ever lived. I carried that dream through life into the big leagues. But I don't have anything to prove now."

Tony returned to his room, packed his suitcase, and caught an 8:00 A.M. flight to Boston. He just wanted to go home. Sal, Teresa, and Richie were waiting for him as he stepped off the plane in the late afternoon at Logan. Baseball writer Joe Giuliotti of the *Herald* also waited and relayed a quote from Phillips: "Apparently his lack of success has been bothering him. The easiest way out is to quit." Tony signed an autograph for a young boy and stated, "I didn't quit. I retired. I could have told Phillips I didn't feel well and stayed with the club the rest of the year, collecting my eighty-thousand-dollar salary. I gave up forty thousand dollars by retiring at the halfway point of the season. Does that sound like quitting to you?"*

Like every scene in Tony's career, his retirement precipitated additional melodrama. When word of his predawn bugout reached New York, there was an explosion in the Red Sox clubhouse at Yankee Stadium. Billy boiled over. "Tony was traded because of one guy—over there," he fumed, gesturing in Yastrzemski's direction. Billy charged that Yaz "got rid of Pesky, Ken Harrelson, and Tony. I know I'm next. They all listen to number 8." Billy claimed the Yaz-Reggie Smith clique ran the Red Sox. "Yaz and Reggie are being babied, and the club better do something about it," he declared. He related a story from the previous

*Later, when emotions weren't running so high, Tony petitioned the Angels for the rest of his pay, claiming he was entitled to it because he retired with an injury, the bad eye. Already spending too much money on lawyers to handle Alex Johnson, California owner Gene Autry paid him.

summer, when Yaz failed to run out a ground ball and Tony reprimanded him from the on-deck circle. "Tony yelled at him, so Tony got traded," Billy asserted. He even brought up clubhouse man Don Fitzpatrick's pampering of Yaz.

The tribes were in open warfare, and Smith fired back, "I don't want to play with Billy anymore. He's a quitter." Yastrzemski said, "I don't know where Billy is coming up with all this. If the charges were true, I'd have to be the owner, general manager, manager, ticket salesman, and, if I had time, I'd get to play a little ball." Fitzpatrick wanted to know, "Why is he picking on a nobody?"

A harried Kasko stated, "I don't know what this is all about," then announced he was going away for the All-Star break and wouldn't tell anyone where he was going. General manager Dick O'Connell commented, "I wish their bats were as loquacious as their tongues." Owner Tom Yawkey observed, "Seems there are darned too many people talking out of turn." The Great Aunt ordered extra barrels of ink for the feud. Disgusted by it all, Teresa revealed: "I used to love baseball. We all did. But no more. Two of my sons have been ballplayers, but we kind of discourage the third one, Richie, from baseball. I couldn't take having another boy in baseball."

The storm prompted an extraordinary press conference on Wednesday, the day after the All-Star game. Yastrzemski sat at a table at the Parker House hotel in downtown Boston, with Billy on one side of him and Tony, who was no longer associated with the Red Sox, on the other. They were in street clothes—garish plaid sport jackets, dark shirts, light ties—and smiled uncomfortably. Yaz and Billy shook hands, like kids on the playground forced to make up by the teacher.*

The battle had forced the public to choose sides, and sentiment ran against the Conigliaros. There were doubts about the real reason for Tony's retirement. In California, Angels general manager Dick Walsh said: "He's a proud individual who was unhappy over the way he had been playing. I don't understand about the eye, though." Moses

---

*Billy had been correct: He was next. Immediately after the season Billy was traded, along with Joe Lahoud, Jim Lonborg, George Scott, Ken Brett, and Don Pavletich to the Brewers for Marty Pattin, Lew Krausse, and Tommy Harper.

*The look on Tony's face indicates frustration, among other emotions, as he appears in a strange press conference that took place the day after the 1971 All-Star Game. Also at the conference were Yaz and Billy Conigliaro, who joined Tony in an awkward moment of peacemaking and spin control. (*Boston Herald *archives photo)*

observed, "I think Tony was hurting, but I also think he was tired of baseball." And Red Sox lovers, showing more loyalty to the guy still hitting home runs for them than the guy who used to hit home runs for them, picked up on it. In a man-on-the-street interview in the *Record*, cab driver Steve Brown of Brighton said of the once-beloved Tony: "I think he's a faker and a crybaby. He probably likes baseball, but he's just not good enough anymore. His rationale for the public is that his eyes bother him."

Tony had sworn off any more eye exams, but he couldn't walk away with his image tattered. He returned to Dr. Charles Regan, now at the Massachusetts Eye and Ear Infirmary. There, he asked the doctor to make the results of his exam public. In a letter printed in the newspapers, Regan reported that Tony's left eye was worse. Looking straight at an object, his vision was 20-300. Looking a few degrees to either side, it was 20-30. In the past year the blind spot at the center of his vision had become 75 percent larger. His depth perception was severely skewed. "Your ability to use your two eyes together is now distinctly worse than it was a year ago," Regan wrote to Tony. And the public simmered down about calling Tony a quitter.

Tony, Richie, Jerry Maffeo, and Tony Athanas escaped to Hyannis on the Cape for the weekend. Richie remembers watching the tension drain from his brother as he dined and danced and golfed and let the sun warm him by the pool. "He was happy as hell to be home," Richie says. "He didn't want to be out there (in California)."

Tony was back where he belonged, among family and friends, making mischief. When Maffeo fell asleep on his back and snored loudly, Tony, Athanas, and Richie took turns trying to toss golf balls into his mouth. Then the three of them, giggling like schoolboys, picked up the cot Maffeo was sleeping on, carried it out of the room, and deposited it on the first green. "The sprinklers went off around him while he was out there," Richie recalls. Remembers Maffeo, "When I woke up, there were people putting around me."

In quieter moments, as Tony talked, Richie could tell his eyesight wasn't the real reason his brother walked away from baseball. Phillips, Walsh, and the fans were more right than they knew. Tony had fought, worked, pushed, concentrated, and struggled for so long, and the battle just didn't seem worth it anymore—not for a baseball team in the faraway suburbs of Orange County. "He missed his family," Richie explains. "If he hadn't been traded, if he had stayed with the Red Sox, I'm convinced he would have exceeded the thirty-six home runs and 116 RBIs he had the year before. The reason he didn't do well in California was 90 percent because he wasn't comfortable. Just being in a foreign place. He just wasn't into it anymore."

~16~

OLD FRIENDS WERE EVERYWHERE

TONY CONIGLIARO WAS TWENTY-SIX YEARS OLD AND DIDN'T KNOW WHAT TO DO NEXT. Like Sal, who raised chickens, hammered together music stands, and ran a doughnut shop in his scuffling days, Tony's mind went in a thousand different directions at once. When he was with the Red Sox, he had started a temp agency called Tony C's Girls. That was defunct, and now he wanted to open a baseball school. And he wanted to go to acting school—Paramount talked about a part for him in a new television series called *The Thunder Guys*. And he wanted to take another crack at the big screen.

In the back of his mind, as always, was baseball. A month after the nightmare in Oakland, he bunked at a friend's house in Beverly Hills and drove his Eldorado every night to exercise at the Sports Page, a combination bistro and private health club on the Sunset Strip. He was already mulling a comeback. He told the California press to make sure Lefty Phillips knew he wasn't bitter about "the man belongs in an institution" quote. It didn't cross his mind that Lefty might be bitter at him. He said, "I love this game. If there is a possibility of playing, I want to." But first, the left eye had to improve. Tony said his vision was so bad, he had to give up reading.

In November the Angels assigned him to their Pacific Coast League club in Salt Lake City, a technical move that left him exposed to any team that wanted to take a chance on him for the twenty-five-thousand-dollar waiver price. No one did. "If he decides that he wants to resume his career, we will bring him to spring training," said the Angels' new general manager, Harry Dalton.

In January, on his twenty-seventh birthday, Tony told the *Los Angeles Herald-Examiner,* "The chances are about fifty-fifty that I will play" in 1972 and "When I think of not playing baseball, it makes me sick." He recounted another visit to another Boston eye specialist, Dr. Henry Mosher, and said the eye that had tested 20-300 in July had improved to 20-30 (he likely angled his head again during the exam). As usual, he assessed his eyesight with confounding twists and muddling turns. After reporting vast improvement in his eye, he noted that if he returned, "It will be as a one-eyed player. I'll always have a blind spot in it." On February 25, Tony announced that Dr. Charles Regan had examined him, found a complete lack of depth perception, said the left eye was sensitive to glare and light, and recommended he not play baseball.

Tony's mind again went in a million different directions. He invested in a company that built Ramada Inns, did public relations for a Vermont-based land developing company, and bought a plot of land, a golf course, and a trailer park on the ocean in Nahant. He had big plans for the Nahant investments. He would remodel everything, open a first-rate nightclub and resort, and call it Tony C's. He would be in the middle of the action, with lots of noise and music and laughter and beautiful women. Whenever he felt like it, he could hop up onstage and sing. He could walk the premises, signing checks and nodding at the help like Humphrey Bogart in *Casablanca.*

Tony focused his considerable energies on the place. He loved barn board and wanted to decorate his nightspot with it, so he purchased a former tobacco barn near Hartford. In the middle of the winter he packed up a hammer, pliers, a screwdriver, and a hatchet, rounded up Bill Bates, Tony Athanas, Uncle Vinnie, Richie, and Billy, and motored to Connecticut to dismantle the barn and haul the pieces to Nahant.

They walked into the massive building, "and inside there was wire, twice as thick as coat hangers, strung from side to side, every two or three inches, the length of the barn," says Bates. "They used it to hang up the tobacco to dry. We looked at each other. How were we supposed to take this barn down?" They trudged out in the icy cold, every morning at 6:30. No one worked harder than Tony. "He worked twelve hours a day," Bates says, and Tony C's got its barn board.

Tony C's pro shop and nine-hole golf course, including the Third World cocktail lounge, opened in April 1972. The combination nightclub-health club opened in October. The club was a showplace of seventies-style bistro decor. The floors were blanketed with plush royal blue wall-to-wall carpeting. Round glass tables with leather swivel cocktail stools sprouted from the rugs. In front of the oversized fieldstone fireplace, bleacher-style stands were stacked up, so patrons could sit and gaze at the flickering flames as if they were watching the Sox at Fenway. The octagon-shaped bar had a glass top, illuminated from below by a black light. "At night," Richie recalls, "it glowed." There was a bandstand, a DJ's booth, and a Plexiglas dance floor over a pattern of spotlights. Huge windows looked out onto a breathtaking view of the slate blue waves of the Atlantic.

With the Vietnam war winding down, the streets calmer, and the political rhetoric less overheated, the masses were ready to party. On the forefront of the burgeoning club scene, Tony C's did a brisk business. For the first year it attracted a calm, over-twenty-five crowd. A Boston crooner named Bobby Vincent was a regular feature, singing lounge standards. Henny Youngman would stop by when he was in town. Merv Griffin cut a radio commercial for Tony.

One night in the fall Julie Markakis, who had recently ended her relationship with Hawk Harrelson, was out on the town with a female friend, and they decided to check out Tony's nightclub. When they walked in under the muted lights, they saw Sal, Teresa, Richie, Billy, and Tony, who waved them over to their table. Julie had always stayed in touch with Teresa, and she enjoyed seeing her again. She was also glad to see Tony. "It always tore at the heartstrings to see him," she admits.

Tony excused himself to take the stage to sing. Sal surveyed the table, and said, "Everyone, please, I have something to say." While his son crooned a saloon version of the Beatles' "Something," Sal said: "Julie, I have something to tell you. I can't apologize enough. I interfered in your life. I interfered in Tony's life as well. I should have just left well enough alone." The table was silent. Julie felt tears on her face. Tony sang "Color My World" and returned to his place at the table amid applause. Everyone there resumed talking, as if nothing had happened.

In 1973 Massachusetts dropped its legal drinking age from twenty-one to eighteen, and Tony C's began to draw a younger, rocking crowd. Tony, in his white cardigan sweater, dark pants, and white shoes, would move through the throng: Young girls with long straight hair, halter-tops, and slacks, would swoon. Rock bands were booked. The DJ stocked "Let's Get It On" and "We're an American Band" and "Keep On Truckin'." Richie, now in his early twenties, and his friends were regulars. One of his closest pals was Jason Angiulo, son of Gennaro Angiulo, reputed Mafia boss of Greater Boston, who owned a well-fortified residence not far from the Conigliaros in Nahant. Jason's frequent presence at Tony C's—he would often hop into the DJ's booth to spin records himself—fueled persistent rumors that the place was a front for the Mob. "It was guilt by association," Richie explains.

In the summer of 1973 residents on the road to Tony C's complained louder and louder that the nightspot was drawing crowds more and more the size and demeanor of those at Fenway Park. Cars filled with fun-seeking, blue-collar teens from Revere, East Boston, Chelsea, Lynn, and Swampscott began to roar up and down Willow Road. Beery kids clattered beer cans onto suburban driveways, bellowed obscenities in the night, and urinated on the trimmed lawns. Alcohol-induced fender benders became common. Monte Carlos and Camaros piloted by boozy teens strained their mufflers and jolted residents in the wee hours. Town selectmen began to badger the Alcoholic Beverage Control Commission about Tony C's liquor license. Tony told a reporter from the *Boston Globe* that he enjoyed the club but he would "give it all up tomorrow if I could go back to playing baseball." He also added that he never watched the Red Sox on television, because "it doesn't do me any good to watch, because I know I could still be out there."

Tony only went to Fenway to watch Billy, who had been sold during spring training to the Oakland Athletics, managed by Dick Williams.* He acted just like an older brother. During one game, the first time Billy played in nearly two months because of knee problems, he took a called strike three on a pitch by Bill Lee.

"How the hell can you take that pitch?" Tony nagged afterward.

"What? After not picking up a bat in a month?" Billy countered.

"How can you not swing at that?" Tony persisted.

"But I haven't picked up a bat in a month—"

"How could you take that pitch?"

Remembers Billy, "I couldn't believe it. Like Tony never struck out?"

---

*Billy reports Williams never mentioned Tony to him. "Not one word," Billy says. "But he never talked to me about anything."

Although Tony enjoyed Tony C's because he got to golf during the day and hang around women and music at night, he found that working as a saloon keeper was becoming a nuisance. The hours were long. Fights became common. One night Jerry Maffeo was on hand when a brawl erupted and, calling upon his years of experience working the door on the greater Boston nightclub scene, "We just locked them in and let them beat the crap out of each other." He didn't find out till the next morning that most of the combatants were his friends from the North End. On another night a policeman on security detail asked a disorderly twenty-year-old man from East Boston to leave the club, a scuffle ensued, and Tony stepped up to help. In the fracas he suffered a cut tendon in his hand. Injuries snared Tony, even far away from the ballfield.

Tony's mind wandered back to baseball. He was only twenty-eight. And for the 1973 season the American League had adopted the designated hitter rule, whereby a player would bat in place of the pitcher and not play in the field. "Perfect," thought Tony. On August 18, the sixth anniversary of the night he was beaned, he announced he was seriously thinking about a comeback. "I feel I've got five or six good years left and there are a lot of ballclubs who need a guy who can come in and get that clutch hit," he said. He added that he would love to return to the Red Sox, but "as it stands now, it appears the Boston front office doesn't want any part of me." The itch was there. In October he watched on television as his brother and the Oakland A's beat the New York Mets in the World Series. Billy would get a World Series ring, the envy of every player in America who pulls on a baseball uniform.

Technically, Tony was still on the Salt Lake City roster and available on waivers. He hoped the New York Yankees, who shopped for a designated hitter, would pick him up. At the baseball winter meetings in December, new Angels general manager Harry Dalton said Tony would be welcomed at the Angels' spring training. Then in February 1974 the Angels released him. He was available—for free, marked down from a twenty-five-thousand-dollar waiver price—to any team that wanted him. No one called. "It's 99 percent sure that I won't be playing this season," he conceded. "No one is interested in me."

Now he was twenty-nine years old, and in the summer of 1974, the tenth anniversary of his wonderful rookie season with the Red Sox, Tony realized that if he ever wanted to check back with his boyhood dream, he had to do it soon. It seemed like only yesterday that he was the brash kid on the Red Sox, the youngest to lead the league in home runs, the youngest in the American League to tally one hundred homers; but now he wasn't the youngest anymore. Boston was starting a rightfielder, Dwight Evans, who had been in grade school the day Tony homered in his first at-bat at Fenway Park. But Tony could feel young enough to try: After all, Yastrzemski was still adding layers to his legend at age thirty-five.

In October, Tony watched a World Series game between the Los Angeles Dodgers and the Oakland Athletics on television in Tony Athanas's apartment in the Harbor Towers in Boston. As Tony watched, he kept shaking his head.

"I could hit this guy," Tony mused, staring at the screen.

"Oh, this guy is nothing special. I could hit him," he told Athanas.

"I could hit *him*," Tony declared.

At last, Athanas asked, "Why don't you play next year?"

"No way," said Tony. "I haven't swung a bat in years." Athanas got up, hefted the *Baseball Encyclopedia* from the shelf, and announced he was going to look up how many home runs Babe Ruth hit after he turned thirty (in 1925). He hit forty-seven homers in 1926. He hit sixty in 1927. He hit fifty-four in 1928.

"Tony decided to make a comeback," says Athanas.

Tony telephoned Red Sox general manager Dick O'Connell, apologized for any nasty statements he might have uttered after the trade to California, and said he wanted to attempt another comeback with Boston. O'Connell graciously said no apologies were necessary and told Tony to go ahead and try out for the team in spring training. "If anyone can come back after being away for three years, it's Tony," O'Connell commented. "He has matured. He also has all the guts and determination in the world. We're pulling for him."

Tony went straight to work, reviving the muscles and reflexes that had rusted in the two years in the nightclub business. He took batting practice and shagged fly balls with Richie at a field in Swampscott. "He was smashing the ball all over the place," Richie says. He dug out the old lead bat and took hundreds of practice swings in the basement of his parents' home in Nahant. "He'd go down there before dinner," Richie recalls. "Then he'd go back down there after dinner." He worked out at Tony C's. He worked out indoors at Tufts and at Harvard. And he noticed something startling. The ball looked sharp. He could see the red stitches spin again. He could see . . . perfectly.

In November, Tony made an appointment with Dr. Regan, who reported startling news: Tony's left eye was 20-15. The glare sensitivity had diminished greatly. His binocular vision fell well within the normal range. The scar tissue had been reduced to "only a few specks like table pepper." The maddening blind spot that had helped push Tony onto the ledge in Oakland in the summer of '71 was "so small, that at any angle, the only thing he couldn't see would be an object the size of a period on this page." His eye was practically pre-1967 vintage. Now Tony had to work on the rest of him.

In December he trekked to Winter Haven, where the Red Sox issued him new bats, buckets of new baseballs, and granted him full use of the spring training facilities. Tony worked out for thirteen straight days. He hit, ran, and threw. He did calisthenics. He bulked up from 183 pounds to 190, his playing weight.

Someone kept count: In the course of his self-imposed boot camp, Tony carried the lead bat into the enclosed cage outside the Red Sox clubhouse to hit against the pitching machine and swung at three thousand balls. He used a wooden bat to swing at one thousand more. He enlisted players from Polk Community College to pitch to him. On his second day against human hurlers, he smacked seven balls over the wall at Chain o' Lakes Park. "I got blisters on blisters," Tony reported when he came home.

Tony turned thirty in January and returned to Winter Haven the next month to chase his boyhood dream once more. He was taking his toys out to play, one more time. Much had changed since the last time he had pulled on a Red Sox uniform. For example, the uniform was different. Instead of blue caps, the Red Sox now wore red caps with blue visors. Like many teams in the seventies, they had switched to ugly double-knit softball-style pullover jerseys and double-knit pants with wraparound fasteners instead of belts.

Tony had changed, too. Much of the boyish softness was gone from his face. He had half-moons under his eyes. His hair was shaggy and long, nearly covering his ears, and his wide sideburns extended to the bottoms of his earlobes. He also carried himself differently. "He wasn't as sure of himself," Rico Petrocelli recalls. "I don't think that, inside, he really knew whether he'd be able to do it."

There were few familiar faces in the old cinderblock clubhouse. Only Yastrzemski, Rico, Bob Montgomery, and Bill Lee were left from the roster of Tony's teammates in 1970. Darrell Johnson, the pitching coach who took Tony to the bullpen in 1968, had returned as manager. Johnny Pesky was back as first-base coach. Hawk Harrelson was the new color commentator on Red Sox television broadcasts and roamed the premises in a tall cowboy hat. The rest were young strangers, including the dynamic rookie duo of lefty-hitting Fred Lynn, twenty-three, and righty-hitting Jim Rice, twenty-two, the most promising Red Sox outfield prospects since, well, since Tony Conigliaro.

Tony competed for the designated-hitter job, which had yielded only ten home runs from a cast of players in 1974. He looked fit during early workouts, but when the exhibition schedule started, he suffered a pulled hamstring and a neck injury and was sidelined for eight days. He squirmed and fretted as he sat; longshot comeback kids can't miss too many days in spring training. "For the first few weeks he was down here, he was under terrific personal tension," O'Connell said. "You could see it in his face." One day Tony watched the Celtics on television and saw John Havlicek, who also had a bad hamstring, run up and down the floor. During half-time Tony telephoned Boston Garden and got Celtics trainer Frank Challant on the line and desperately asked what was his secret.

On March 16, Tony returned to action in a B-squad game against the Montgomery Tigers. On March 18, in Saint Petersburg, the Red Sox played the Mets, and the game was televised back to New York. Tony could still dance a little in the spotlight: With the Big Apple watching, he hit two doubles, a single, and a long, deep fly that the wind smothered and Gene Clines caught at the wall. In a B-game against Houston in Cocoa Beach, Tony went oh-for-four against Larry Dierker and Scipio Spinks. In a game against the Tigers in Lakeland he went oh-for-four against Joe Coleman and John Hiller. "I'm tired," Tony said. "but what is important is that I get good rips. And I did."

By the last week of March, Tony's chances of making the team were uncertain. The Red Sox desperately wanted to find a place in their

Conigliaro pulled off the incredible comeback with the Red Sox in 1975, making it onto the Opening Day roster in the starting lineup as designated hitter. But although Tony's sight in his left eye had almost totally healed, his physical skills had diminished. It wasn't long before young phenom Jim Rice had replaced Tony in the lineup. (Boston Herald archives photo)

lineup for Rice, who had won the International League Triple Crown and was *The Sporting News*'s Minor League Player of the Year the previous season. But with Fred Lynn, Juan Beniquez, Dwight Evans, and Rick Miller in the mix, there was no room in the outfield—even Yaz had shifted to first base. Rice and Tony would have to wrestle for the DH job.

There was no doubt which way the sentimental Great Aunt was rooting. Bill Liston wrote in the March 30 *Sunday Advertiser*: "Rarely have I encountered an athlete in any sport—except possibly Rocky Marciano, the late heavyweight boxing champion—with more dedication to clear the hurdles he faces. The conjecture here . . . is that Tony C will be wearing a Red Sox uniform on Opening Day."

On April 1 in Lakeland, Rice doubled home a pair of runs against the Tigers. Tony singled in five at-bats and struck out twice. With the bases loaded, he flied out to deep left (Liston reported that if the ball had been hit in Fenway, it would have cleared the wall). Now the scuttlebutt was that Tony would be asked to begin the season in the minor leagues, with the Red Sox's Triple-A team in Pawtucket, Rhode Island. The rumors and the suspense were killing him. Everything had been a lot easier when he was nineteen and telling Sal and Uncle Vinnie not to worry about his chances in Scottsdale. "I feel like I've had a hundred-pound weight on my shoulders," Tony said. "If they'd only tell me I've made it, I'm sure I'd be much looser and show them for certain that I can still hit."

One more time he grabbed destiny by the lapels. Against the Philadelphia Phillies on April 2 in Winter Haven, Tony cracked three hits, including a three-run home run, with four RBIs. Manager Darrell Johnson was asked if Tony's performance enhanced his shot at making the team. "It doesn't make a bit of difference," Johnson replied cryptically. Against the Minnesota Twins on April 3 in Orlando, Tony drilled two doubles with an RBI. He had five hits, three doubles, a homer, and five RBIs in two days, inflating his spring average to .246. In his game story Liston asked, "What else does the kid have to do?"

On the morning of April 4, Tony looked out the window of the team bus as it rolled through the flat, scrubby Florida landscape toward Tampa for an exhibition game against the Cincinnati Reds. Johnson strolled down the aisle, rocking with the motion of the bus. He stopped at Tony's seat, and over the roar of the engine told him he had made the team. "I was surprised and so happy and relieved that I didn't know what

to do," Tony said. "I wanted to jump up and start yelling or tell somebody, but I didn't. I don't really know who would have given a damn."

Back in Winter Haven Tony sat in a chair in front of his locker
and told the press he had big plans for 1975. He thought he could still
play the outfield, and he wasn't going to be content "to be a player
who hits ten homers and bats .250 or anything like that." Then he
called playfully across the room to Red Sox traveling secretary Jack
Rogers, "Hey, Jack, I need 175 free tickets for Opening Day. Can you
take care of me?"

Tony ended up hitting only .219 in the spring, but he had won
the job with his old impeccable timing, for he had one great week. It was
one of the proudest moments of his career. "I flat out beat Jim Rice for the
designated hitter's spot," Tony gloated three years later, as Rice sizzled
through his Most Valuable Player summer for the Red Sox. Says Richie:
"For him to go down there and beat out Rice, when he set his mind to it,
I think that was one of the most amazing things he did."

On a bright, chilly Tuesday afternoon, April 8, 1975, the Red Sox
opened against the Milwaukee Brewers at Fenway Park. The grounds
crew had labored hard over the weekend to shovel snow and slush out
of the grandstand and to squeeze water off the field. Red, white, and
blue bunting was strung on the box seats. Again, a birthday-party feeling was in the air. Tony was penciled into the starting lineup as the designated hitter. He was batting cleanup. He was home, back in the home
clubhouse, back at his old locker, back in the bright home whites,
which this season had a round Massachusetts Bicentennial patch on the
left sleeve. He pulled open the same old metal clubhouse door, with
the same old dents and dings from errant baseball bats; walked down
the same old steps, along the same old damp tunnel, and into the same
old dugout; and climbed out onto the same old field. He was on the
right side of the diamond again.

It was the same old wonderful Opening Day ritual, but for Tony,
it felt like a first date. Hank Aaron, who had shattered Babe Ruth's all-time
home-run mark just the year before, made his first appearance with the

Conigliaro meets newly crowned all-time home-run king Hank Aaron, now with the Milwaukee Brewers, on Opening Day 1975 at Fenway Park. Speculation persists that had Conigliaro never been beaned in 1967, he might have challenged Aaron's lifetime mark of 755 home runs. (AP/Wide World Photos)

Brewers. Before the game Aaron sought out Tony, who might have challenged the Hammer's record some day if the fates had been different, and said, "Just relax up there and be quick and I hope you have a great year." After batting practice and infield practice, the players left the field and the grounds crew tidied the dirt and the lawn. Both teams were introduced one by one over the public address system as they queued up on the white chalk along the base lines.

The Brewers were announced, and Aaron received a nice ovation. The Red Sox were announced, and the starters trotted out one at a time. Beniquez came first, then Lynn, then Yastrzemski . . . then Tony. The sellout crowd of 34,019 stood and cheered for a full minute. And the hard work in the basement in Nahant, in the gyms at Tufts and Harvard, and in the batting cage in Winter Haven, was worth every blister. The last time Tony was at Fenway, it was a rainy night, and he wore the ridiculous California Angels uniform, and the crowd was lukewarm toward him. Now the world was back to normal.

Duffy Lewis, hero of the 1912 Red Sox, threw out the first pitch. Tony wasn't in Anaheim anymore. In the first inning he stepped up against Brewers right-hander Jim Slaton with Yaz at first, and the crowd showered him with a forty-second standing ovation. "I was going to swing from my butt on that first pitch," Tony said, and he did, but missed. But now he was older and smarter, and with Yaz breaking from first on a three-and-one pitch, Tony saw the ball on the outside part of the plate and instead of trying to launch it into the screen, poked it into right field for a single.

The crowd stood and cheered him again. Old friends were everywhere. George Scott was playing first base for the Brewers, and the Boomer stuck out his hand and said, "I knew you could do it, T. C. I told all the guys you'd make it back. It's just too bad we're not all together on the Red Sox again." With Rico at bat, Tony broke for second base and Yaz broke from third, and the Brewers muffed the throw and both were safe on the startling double steal. It was only the twentieth stolen base of Tony's entire career. Between innings he huddled deep in a winter coat with the hood up—the DH job had a lot of downtime. In the third inning, with Yastrzemski on second and the Sox leading, 4-1, Tony bunted to try to move him to third. "I like to bunt in certain situations," Tony explained. "There was no sense in trying to hit a home run in the wind that was blowing today"—he was over thirty, all right. Tim Horgan wrote in the *Herald,* "Tony C can still make things happen, one way or the other." Tony was back, and so were his headaches: In the fifth inning he begged trainer Charlie Moss for a couple of aspirins.

Two days later in Baltimore Tony stepped to the plate against Orioles right-hander Mike Cuellar in the fifth inning with the game tied at 2-2. The irony was almost too much. In 1969 he had hit his first comeback home run at Memorial Stadium and logged his first Fenway at-bat against Cuellar. This time, six years later, Cuellar threw him a curve—the 1970 scouting report on Tony was still lying around American League clubhouses. Tony could see the spin now, though, and he smashed the ball over the left-field wall at the 360-foot marker into the bleachers. It was the Red Sox's first homer of the year. Yaz won the game with a home run in the twelfth, and people dreamed that the devastating one-two punch of 1967 might be revived. "Now if I can keep on doing that every so often, I'll be happy," Tony said.

But those days were gone forever. Boomers were turning thirty and watching their youth fade into history. Nixon was out, Vietnam had fallen to the Communists, and rock 'n' roll hits were now the stuff of B. J. Thomas and Tony Orlando and Dawn. Before April was out Tony pulled a hamstring, then injured his groin, and discovered it wasn't so easy to bounce back anymore. Meanwhile, the twenty-two-year-old Rice moved into the DH slot and showed off his devastating, short, quick swing.

Although Tony rarely got into the lineup, no one in the Red Sox clubhouse considered arranging a stretcher and crutches and fake blood in front of his locker. He was the DH on May 7 and on May 12, and he pinch-hit a couple of times. His average didn't crack .150. Rice was smashing the ball. Cecil Cooper also played some DH and smacked a few homers. Tony's comeback was fading, and one part of his dream still hadn't come true: He hadn't hit a comeback home run at Fenway Park, one of his favorite thrills in a baseball uniform.

In the third week of May the Athletics came to town, and Vida Blue was scheduled to start the Tuesday night series opener. On Tony's bizarre final night with the Angels, Blue's confounding deliveries had helped push Tony into near-madness and out of baseball. Four years later Blue was a hot pitcher again. He was 8-1 and had won six straight decisions. Tony wanted a rematch. "I'll get him," he told the Boston press on Sunday. "You just watch."

On May 20, an unseasonably sultry night at Fenway, Tony—now down to seventh in the batting order—stepped up against Blue in the second inning. Petrocelli was on first and Dwight Evans was on second. Blue delivered a fastball and Tony cracked a single to drive in Evans with the first run of the game.

In the fourth inning Tony led off and expected a fastball. Blue broke off a big, slow curve. Tony walloped it high into the night, reducing the ball to a white speck against the dark sky, just like the old days. The ball sailed over the wall, over the screen, and across Lansdowne Street. Tony touched first and clasped hands with coach Johnny Pesky, who was his manager the day he hit his first Fenway homer a thousand years earlier. Tony rounded the bases and the crowd of 17,201 cheered. "That's the longest and the hardest I've ever hit a ball," Tony offered. It was his eighty-seventh lifetime home run at Fenway Park, and it would be his last.

On June 14 the Red Sox were in Kansas City. The brass decided to promote infielder Denny Doyle from Pawtucket and needed to make room on the roster. Tony was ailing and hitting .123 with two homers and nine RBIs in twenty-one games. They asked him to report to the PawSox. O'Connell was on his way to Kansas City to talk to him about it personally. When he arrived, Tony was already gone.

Tony mulled the notion for a week, then joined Pawtucket, an hour's drive south of Boston down Route 95. For the first time since he was eighteen years old, he was a minor leaguer. He donned the tacky Paw-Sox jersey—red with white short sleeves, just like what they wear in beer softball leagues—with number 23 on the back. He dressed in clubhouses with chicken-wire lockers and sweaty concrete walls. He played in ballparks with garish billboards for outfield fences. He made road trips to Syracuse, Toledo, Richmond, and Columbus. At least there were no rickety bus rides, with breakdowns in the middle of the night on the road out of Wellsville.

Tony hoped for one more flash of drama. Maybe he would get hot and somebody would get hurt on the big club and they'd call him up again, and there would be another incredible chapter in his incredible story. But he was fresh out of miracles. His skills, once and for all, were

At first Conigliaro was reluctant to accept the demotion back to Triple-A ball, but he eventually relented and reported to the Pawtucket Red Sox. Here he is taking some swings in batting practice, giving it one more shot to win back the magical batting stroke that had been so productive. (AP/Wide World Photos)

gone. "He had lost those real good reflexes," recalls Joe Morgan, who managed Pawtucket that summer. "Any guy who threw real hard, he had trouble with." Says Buddy Hunter, then an infielder with Pawtucket: "He was dropping easy fly balls in the outfield. To see that, and to see him struggle, you felt sorry for him."

In Boston the Red Sox revived the fever of 1967. They roared past the Yankees and Orioles into first place, and the ballpark was filled night after night. Lynn (who would win the Rookie of the Year and Most Valuable Player awards by hitting .331, with twenty-one home runs and 105 RBIs) and Rice (.309, twenty-two, 102) blossomed into the amazing Gold Dust Twins.

Down on the farm Tony stayed in economy motels and ate in family restaurants and pulled on his socks in crummy clubhouses. And he made the best of it. Pawtucket manager Joe Morgan recalls only one disciplinary problem with the former teen idol and folk hero. The day after Tony was absent from a game, Morgan inquired, "Hey, where were you?"

"I was sick and there's no way I could have played," Tony replied.

"You still have to show up, no matter what," Morgan insisted. Tony, as always, didn't have to be told twice.

He didn't act like a man stuck with a dead dream. He had a spring in his step in the locker room. He laughed and joked with his teammates. He helped the younger kids with batting tips and told them stories about life in the big leagues. "Everybody looked up to Tony," Hunter says. "I always thought he would have made a great manager." In thirty-seven games he hit .203 with three homers and twelve runs batted in. Every day Hunter saw there was something special about him. It was the same thing people saw when he played with the Orient Sparks in East Boston. "I think he was excited to put on a uniform and get back out there and just play," Hunter recalls. "Even down there."

On Thursday, August 21, with less than a week left in the International League season, Tony declared, "I have had just about enough baseball because my body is falling apart," and he retired from baseball at a news conference at Tony C's. In September he took a job as a sportscaster with WJAR-TV in Providence. "Tony did an audition," said news director Arthur Alpert. "It showed that he knows his sports, he is very smart, and he is determined." When the Red Sox tangled with the Reds in the World Series, he sat in the press box and entertained the writers with second-guesses of Darrell Johnson's often-baffling maneuvers.

The Red Sox were back in the World Series, and, again, Tony was an outsider. "It was a lot tougher in 1967," he said. "I was younger then and it was a lot harder to take." Rice, who had broken a wrist when hit by a pitch in August, sat out the postseason, thus depriving the Red Sox of a big bat as had been the case with Tony in 1967. Tony buttonholed Rice one day and told him he knew exactly what he was feeling and to be proud of his great regular season. Rice didn't hear or retain a word of it: He was only twenty-two.

~17~

A Part of the Family

Tony Conigliaro hadn't held a regular job, with a boss and a set sched-ule, since he was a sales clerk at Sears in the winter of 1963–64. But he didn't wait his turn in sportscasting any more than he waited his turn in baseball. Providence was the minor leagues. However, after less than a year at WJAR, he signed a contract with ABC-TV, which assigned him to KGO-TV, their big-league affiliate in San Francisco.

Unlike the summer of 1964, Tony wasn't ready this time. He did sports features during the week and manned the sports anchor desk on weekends, and he was immediately branded just another jock enthusing about the scores. He was terrible. He spoke in clichés. He always seemed harried. His malaprops made him uncomfortable to watch. He identified Raiders tight end Dave Casper as George Casper. He mispronounced the names of California towns: San Joaquin became San JAWquinn.

Technical difficulties plagued him. He'd be talking about the World Series, and the Steelers-Bengals game would flash on the screen. Haywire playbacks made interview subjects sound like Donald Duck. Although they weren't his fault, the glitches contributed a comic air to his work. His Boston accent, charming to fans from Charlestown and Waltham and Worcester in the Fenway stands, made northern Californi-ans cover their ears. "I'm really trying to pronounce my *R*s a little bit," Tony said. "But it's been tough. Everything is ten yaRRRds, fifteen yaRRDs, and twenty yaRRRds. I get tired of holding that *R* and end up with a *yahd*." The station sent him to speech class at the American Con-servatory of Theater to purge the East Boston out of him.

Tony improved. He learned the broadcast business as if he were trying to come back from a near-fatal beaning. Not surprisingly, viewers began to respond to his charm. He wasn't smooth, but he came across as honest and genuine. He had a good rapport with athletes. The anchor work remained rough, but his features got better and better, eventually good enough to earn a local Emmy. As usual, he had fun. He'd cover a story at Oakland Raiders practice and end up playing catch with some of the players—and impressing owner Al Davis with his long, tight spirals. "He could have been a quarterback," Davis said.

Tony even learned to laugh about the gaffes. One day he participated in an Easter Seals celebrity golf tournament in a hard, relentless rain. Former basketball great Rick Barry quit after six holes. *Peanuts* cartoonist Charles Schulz begged off altogether. Joe DiMaggio lasted all eighteen and so did Tony. Thoroughly soaked, he showered in the clubhouse, then discovered he had neglected to bring a change of underwear. He wasn't going to put on the sopping wet ones, so he went without any. He hurried outside to do a live remote broadcast from the stormy course. As he spoke into the microphone in the downpour, rain washed away the ink from his notes. Then the papers slipped from his wet hands. He quickly bent over to pick them up, and his pants split wide open in the back, exposing his bare buttocks while he stood back up and resumed his live shot and the happy-talking anchor man in the dry studio chirped, "So, how's the weather out there?"

Tony was further away from baseball than ever—when he ran Tony C's, the game was always in the back of his mind—but he was happy. He thrived on exploring newness, and his life in northern California was something completely different. For the first time in his life he was away from his hometown year-round. He missed Sal, Teresa, Richie, and Billy, but otherwise he enjoyed the sensation. In the Bay Area he enjoyed enough television fame for people to wave on the streets and say hello in restaurants or agree to dinner and a movie. And Tony thoroughly enjoyed the recognition. But it wasn't like serving as a star slugger on the Red Sox in Boston, which sometimes was like being the Pope in the Vatican. Now he was a person, not just a personality.

The relentless schedule—practice today, game tonight, flight to Chicago tomorrow morning—that had ruled his baseball existence was gone. For the first time in his life he owned his own home, in Mill Valley.

Now he could stay put. For the first time in his life he bought his own dogs, golden retrievers named Cutty and Chivas. He was a young, single professional. He enjoyed going out on the town in his Cadillac Coupe DeVille, squiring beautiful women to discos in the city or to fern-choked restaurants up in the hills. "You know what was different about him?" says Dennis Gilbert, Tony's former Instructional League teammate and friend in California. "The guy was always—always—a gentleman. This was a guy who would run around and open up the passenger door for a woman. That was Tony."

The Bay Area was blatantly progressive, and Tony certainly could be old-fashioned. Billy came out to visit one time. The brothers were seated in a restaurant in Sausalito when the waiter approached with a folded-up piece of paper and said, "It's from one of the other diners." Tony had been getting that sort of overture since high school, and he smiled slyly at his jealous little brother as he opened the note. It began, "Dear Tony, I've seen you on television and I've always wanted to meet you. I wonder if it would be possible for us to meet sometime." Tony suddenly looked up at Billy in disgust, slapped the paper onto the tablecloth, jerked a thumb toward the door, and said, "Let's get out of here." Billy recalls, "The note was from a guy."

Not long into his career at KGO, Tony was assigned to do a feature on Clifford Ray, the Golden State Warriors center with bad knees. He took a camera crew to see Ray while he underwent therapy in Marin County. Tony interviewed Ray's exercise physiologist, a fellow in his early forties named Satch Hennessy, whose accent Tony immediately recognized. Hennessy was from Malden, Massachusetts, one town over from Revere. He had moved to California in 1965, but he was a New Englander through and through: Hennessy had acquired his nickname in childhood because his friends thought he shot a basketball like Boston Celtics great Satch Sanders.

Tony asked Satch if he could come back for treatment of his bursitis in his shoulder. After a few visits Tony was invited to the Hennessy house in Petaluma for dinner. Satch's wife, Shari, was Italian-American, a year younger than Tony, and liked to cook. Satch's children, Sean, nine; Kelly, two; and Lacey, one, loved to play. Tony was in heaven. He was attracted, more than anything else in the world, to a good family. He played ball with Sean, teased Kelly, made faces at Lacey, and kidded with Shari. Satch was surprised to see that the one-time slugger with a playboy image "had a lot of good fatherly qualities in him. He was great with kids. And kids liked him."

Tony became a regular. On weekends he would do his spot on the six o'clock news in San Francisco, race thirty-five miles north for dinner at the Hennessys, then hurry thirty-five miles south with a full belly for the eleven o'clock news. "We used to tease him, 'Tony, are you hungry or are you just lonely?' " Satch recalls. Tony telephoned just to say hello almost every day. He and his various girlfriends started joining the Hennessys on double dates.

A double date was scheduled for one Saturday night, but that morning Shari thought Kelly didn't seem quite right and took her to the pediatrician. The doctor thought she had some sort of infection and referred the Hennessys to a hematologist that afternoon. That night Satch telephoned Tony at his house in Mill Valley and canceled the double date.

"It's Kelly," Satch said. "She has leukemia."

Tony gasped, "I'm coming up there."

He sat up all night with Satch and Shari, talking when they needed to talk and saying nothing when they needed silence. "We hadn't known each other for very long," Satch recalls, "but he showed me a side of him that not too many people know about. And it was the real side of him."

Tony came to the house every day for the next two weeks. He baby-sat the kids when Satch and Shari needed to take Kelly to the doctor. He took Satch out for coffee. He took Shari to lunch. Mostly, he was just there. Over the months, as Kelly grew sicker and sicker, Satch watched nearly all of his friends fade away. Not many of them could deal with the grief of a beautiful little girl with a fatal illness. Tony, who knew what it was like to see friends disappear in hard times, stuck with the Hennessys closer than ever. It wasn't easy. He was there the day when Kelly lost her sight. She looked at Satch and said, "Daddy, I can't see." Tony went into the next room and sobbed uncontrollably.

On the steps in front of the house, in a coffee shop down the street, in a bar—where Tony would toy with a drink and almost never finish it—Satch and his new friend talked about nothing and everything. Tony had never been much of a talker. His brother Billy can't recall ever sitting down and having a deep conversation with him. But now, for the first time in his life, Tony wasn't climbing the baseball pyramid or serving as hometown legend. And for the first time since perhaps Freddie Atkinson, he had a friend who wasn't a running mate on the night scene. Tony had almost never talked about himself and his life. Now, at last, he had the time and the inclination to reflect.

Tony told Satch endlessly about his family, how close they were, and how much he loved them. "One thing about the Conigliaros," he said, "you take on one of us, you take on all of us." Satch felt as if he had known Sal, Teresa, Richie, and Billy long before he met them.

Tony talked about baseball. He told Satch the story of the time he slid into second base in Chicago and the umpire signaled he was out but hollered, "Safe!" Tony was standing on the bag, brushing the dirt off his uniform, when the umpire said, "Conigliaro, you're out." Tony said, "But you said I was safe." And the umpire said, "Yeah, but twenty thousand people saw me call you out."

He told Satch about his hitting tutorial with Ted Williams, who marched him to the batter's box and showed him that home plate was divided into ninety-six parts. "Satch, to this day, I can't tell you a thing he said," Tony told his friend. "I didn't know what the hell he was talking about." He told Satch about the time Darrell Johnson caught him walking out of a nightspot at 11:45, and Tony told his manager he had gone into the place to ask directions to Midnight Mass.

Tony talked about how hard he had worked. He told Satch about his trips to the basement in Swampscott, and how he would place a lit candle on a table, turn out the lights, and swing the bat to try to snuff out the flame without knocking over the candle. Tony talked about his career, and how he thought he could have broken Hank Aaron's home-run mark. "Satch, I didn't think much about it at the time," he said, "but looking back, I think I had the ability to be a Hall of Fame player."

Tony and Satch talked about bad things happening to good people. Why did he get hit in the head? Tony never complained, never sounded bitter, never said he got a raw deal, never blamed Jack Hamilton. "Why did I get hit in the eye?" Tony said. "Because I didn't duck. Things like that happen."

Satch and Shari Hennessy, circa 1978. Tony C became an extension of the Hennessy family. Although Satch and Tony knew each other a relatively short time before Tony's heart attack, many acquaintances mistook the good buddies for lifelong friends.

Lacey Hennessy tries getting "sexy" in this pose, done especially for cheering up Tony after he was disabled. The picture was taken in the backyard of the Conigliaros' family home in Nahant, Massachusetts, while the Hennessys were in town visiting Tony in the hospital. Richie Conigliaro's wife, Candy, "made up" Lacey for the "photo session." (Both photos courtesy of Satch Hennessy)

It was one of his most admirable traits—he never backed off. When Kelly died, the Hennessys invited family and a few friends to the funeral. Tony was there and helped carry the tiny white coffin out of the church. "He was my best friend in the real sense of the word," Satch remembers. "A lot of our friends bailed out. Tony hung in there. He didn't bail once."

Sean Hennessy loved baseball, and Tony would show up at the house and take the boy down to the park to hit and field and throw, just the way Uncle Vinnie had taken little Choo to Ambrose Park in Revere in the old days. Tony brought Sean to Candlestick Park to see Giants games and to the Oakland Coliseum to see the A's. He was among friends when he was with kids. Satch also was a teacher and dean of students at Marin Catholic High School in Kentfield. Tony would come to the school and work out with the baseball team and offer tips to the teen players. Far beyond the outfield wall at the school ballfield, on the other side of the street, about five football fields from home plate, was Saint Sebastian's Church. Tony would take batting practice against the high school pitchers and launch ball after ball over the fence, across the street, and off the wall of the priests' quarters alongside the church. An agitated priest would rush out the door in pursuit of the boys he thought were playing ball in his parking lot. Then he'd see Tony, a tiny speck with a bat on his shoulder on the distant ballfield, and wave.

In the summer of 1978, Tony was thirty-three, and he still loved to play. Satch didn't know Tony when he was a Red Sox hero, but he could see the competitive fire in his friend when he played golf or pickup basketball. Tony felt an old itch when he edited baseball highlights at KGO and watched Carl Yastrzemski, six years older than he, make diving catches for the Red Sox, and Willie McCovey, seven years older than he, swat home runs for the Giants.

Red Sox fan Dick Johnson, who had thrilled to Tony's comeback when he was in junior high in Worcester, Massachusetts, was fresh out of college and bumming around the country when he and his older brother took in a Giants-Padres doubleheader at Candlestick. There was a home-run-hitting contest between games, and the public address announcer said, "Will Tony Conigliaro please report to the field?" and the two New Englanders looked at each other in anticipation. "Tony walks out. He's wearing this garish polyester outfit," Johnson recalls. "He hands his checked sport coat to the bat boy and gets into the cage and he hits six of ten pitched balls out of the ballpark. It brought a tear to my eye, to think of what might have been." For a brief moment, one more time Tony wondered what might have been, too, and told the newspapers, "I think I can do it again because I have the natural ability plus the capacity to push my body so hard that I can make up for the more than two years I've been away." He said maybe Bill Veeck, the noted risk-taker who owned the Chicago White Sox and once signed a midget as a pinch-hitter, might want him. But Tony let the notion fade. He knew better. One day he was at the gym and watched Satch work out with weights.

"God, Satch, I don't know how you bench press that much," Tony said.

"That's all right," Satch countered. "I can't hit a curveball."

"Neither can I," Tony said. "If I could, I'd still be out there playing."

Because they both had Greater Boston accents and spent so much time together, people assumed Satch and Tony had been boyhood chums. Tony grew close to Shari, too. She was a great cook, she was pretty, and she was upbeat and unflappable. Tony became part of the family. He was at the house on Christmas, Easter, and Thanksgiving. He'd tell Satch and Shari to go out for dinner or to a movie while he watched the kids. He badgered the giggling Lacey about marrying him someday. "I'm not going to let you marry Tony," Satch would tell her in mock horror. "He's an Italian." Tony would drop by and ask Shari to get a bite to eat, and on the way out the door, he'd beg her to run away to Tahiti with him, while Satch stood there smirking and saying, "You make a pass at her, you keep her."

In the summer of '78 Shari was diagnosed with breast cancer. Satch's other friends seeped away again, but Tony edged closer. "Satch, whatever you need," he said, "tell me how I can help."

But Tony knew what to do without asking. He joked and smiled, even though it wasn't easy. "He was a typical Italian—very emotional," Satch says. "He had his bladder in his eyes." Without telling Satch, Tony hired a top cancer specialist to examine Shari. He helped with the kids, but mostly he was wonderfully underfoot. With Satch busy tending to his wife, Tony spent extra time with Sean.

"Tony, who was the toughest person you ever saw?" Sean asked one day. "Bob Gibson?"

"Nope," answered Tony.

"George Scott?"

"No."

"Who, then?"

"Your mother," Tony answered. "Your mother is the toughest person I've ever known. When you get older, I hope you know it. She's tough in all the ways that really count."

When Shari underwent a double mastectomy and lost all her hair to chemotherapy, Tony asked her more often than ever to run away to Tahiti with him. "She was ravaged by this disease," Satch says, "and Tony made her feel still attractive."

Into the winter and spring, as Shari's condition worsened, Satch and Tony passed long hours talking. It was the only thing Satch really needed. They talked about marriage. Tony said he couldn't do it until he was absolutely certain he would remain faithful to his wife. He was no moralist, but he had seen many married teammates catting around on the road over the years and he had found it distasteful. Sitting in his house with his two children and his dying wife in a bed in the next room, Satch told him, "Tony, this is what marriage is all about."

Tony talked about his young, brash days. "He told me he was extremely cocky. All mouth," Satch remembers. "He also felt the beaning did a lot to knock that out of him. He said that for the first time in his life, he had felt vulnerable."

Tony talked about religion. He went to Mass every Sunday. "I was given a lot of athletic ability," he told Sean. "If I don't know where it came from, it doesn't mean much." He hated it when athletes blessed themselves before shooting a free throw or stepping up to bat. "That's not religion, that's superstition," he said. Satch quoted Saint Augustine—"Pray like everything depends on God. Work like everything depends on you"—and Tony loved it. "He was a lot deeper than his public image led people to believe," says Satch.

Tony talked about living and dying. One day in the summer, when Shari's condition had deteriorated, Tony spent a long time in the room with her, then joined Satch outside on the front steps. "Satch," he declared quietly, "if I ever get like that, you've got to promise me you'll pull the plug on me."

"I promise you," Satch said.

"That's not living," Tony said.

Shari mapped out the details of her funeral, and she excluded Tony from her list of pallbearers. "Tony is a blubberer," she told Satch. "I don't want him blubbering all over my casket." When Tony got the news, he was livid, and burst into her room and swore he wouldn't cry. Shari relented. She died on August 30, 1979. She was thirty-three, one year younger than Tony. He wore dark glasses as he carried her coffin, and he held back his tears, just as he promised. Later, he told Satch, "When Shari died, I felt like part of me died with her."

One week into the 1980s, Tony turned thirty-five. His Big Chill generation was approaching middle age. His face had a few more lines. His black hair, layer cut and brushed back, parted in the middle in the fashion of the day, had a few gray strands. Long ago he had sensed his own mortality, but Kelly and Shari Hennessy and the mirror were relentless reminders.

He had always been something of a hypochondriac, but now he concentrated harder than ever on his health and his body. He was teenaged slim—he could still eat a million banana buckets at Roland's and not gain an ounce—but he worked hard to stay in shape. He would lace up combat boots and run five or six miles a day through the hills in Novato, where he had purchased a home with a little land. He embraced every fad and stay-well system that came along: vitamin supplements, bee pollen, garlic pellets. He hated to be around cigarette smoke. The kid who used to think eating smart was a steak for dinner every night bought into a health-food store in San Anselmo. He worried constantly about aches and pains. If he read in the newspaper that a medical study had found that a percentage of men suffered heart attacks after going to the bathroom, he was on the phone to Satch or back home to Bill Bates, asking what he should eat and do to avoid such a calamity. "The stupider the thing was, the more he worried about it," Satch says.

Once Tony had told Satch about his dating habits: "When I was a young guy, it was my determination to screw everything in creation."

"Well?" said Satch.

"Well," smiled Tony, "I did put a dent in it."

But now he started to wonder if there was more to romance than flashy women and recreational sex. Sal had advised against marrying Julie when he was nineteen because he wanted his son to sample life before settling down. After nearly twenty years on the go-go scene, Tony thought he might be missing something else in life.

Tony went to a show at the Hyatt in San Francisco one night, was enchanted by a singer named Georgia Elliot, and asked her for a date. A decade younger than Tony, Georgia was petite, with short dark hair and an upbeat, outgoing personality—sometimes, she reminded Satch of Shari. She and Tony would banter and joke and kid each other relentlessly. Tony was clearly in love for the first time in a long time. One day he told Satch, "I haven't felt this way about anybody since Julie." Satch was sure Tony and Georgia would get married.

In February 1980, Tony was fired by KGO. Angry and hurt, he claimed he had an unwritten agreement with ABC-TV into 1984 and threatened to sue. The television news world is arbitrary, fickle, and intensely political—Tony was merely squeezed out the same way a hundred other weekend sports anchors are across the country. The brass customarily concocts a reason for it afterward. "Tony's not happy because he's been let go, which is understandable," an anonymous source told the *San Francisco Chronicle*. "But . . . was he a workaholic? No. Did he have his facts and figures straight all the time? No. Did he give 110 percent? No, maybe 90. Unfortunately, there are people in television who can do that and get by, but Tony isn't one of them."

Two months later he was picked up by KRON to work the weekend sports desk, fill in during the weekday until a regular sports anchor was hired, and do sports features. "I think Tony is very good, and he'll get better," KRON news director Jean Harper said. But it was not a stable position. KRON was searching for a new sports director, and Tony knew enough about broadcasting to know that once the new boss took over, no one was safe. And he was right. In August, KRON hired Jan Hutchins as its new sports anchor and sports director. Tony was told he would stay on as the anchor on Mondays and Tuesdays, but he was uneasy. Six months later KRON replaced its news director, Mike Ferring, who reshuffled the sports department and showed Tony the door. "He is not the man for the long term," Ferring declared. But Tony's dismissal prompted a flood of protesting cards and letters from viewers. As usual, Tony had a following. But he didn't have a job. He was finished with television.

"I worked very hard in TV and got nowhere," he noted. "I can take a hint." He was searching again, and by the summer of 1981 money was tight. He had skillfully jumped from home to home, but a fire at one of his places and a dip in the real estate market cost him dearly. He interviewed for a job as a hitting instructor for the San Francisco Giants, who never got back to him. He traded in the Cadillac for a Honda Civic, the first non-gas-guzzler he had ever owned. When Billy came for a visit, they had to watch where they went out to eat. Tony's budget had no room for gourmet dinner checks. Bad luck was back. NBC invited him to be the color commentator on a backup *Game of the Week* in San Francisco. The day before the telecast, when he was playing pickup basketball, he took an errant elbow in the chin, which opened a cut on his tongue, making it difficult to talk. He had to cancel. It was one of the few times his friends saw him depressed.

Out of work, without focus, and worried, Tony felt Georgia drifting away from him. By the fall of 1981 they had split. "There was no big blowup, no big fight," says Satch. "They just broke up." But when Satch visited Tony's house, the only photograph he saw was a framed shot of Georgia.

Tony started spending time in Los Angeles, bunking in a small room in the Beverly Hills home of his friend Dale Gribow, jogging in a park elbow to elbow with sweaty beautiful people in Spandex tights. He began exploring the sports agent business with Gilbert, his old baseball chum who was making it big in life insurance. Tony would try anything. He developed a vitamin supplement system specifically for flight attendants and even telephoned Julie Markakis, who had flown for Eastern, to enlist her help.

On November 4, Tony was at Cedar-Sinai hospital in Beverly Hills when Gilbert's daughter was born. Gilbert asked Tony to be Ashlee's godfather. In turn, Tony asked if he could carry her out of the hospital when it was time to go home. Gilbert saw Tony's smile—that old, enchanting smile—as he carried the swaddled bundle, and he thought his friend would make a great father.* ✓

Tony waited for his luck to change. He and Athanas took a trip to Las Vegas and sat through comedian Slappy White's lounge act for five straight nights. On the first four nights White announced that Tony was in the audience. The spotlight fell on his seat, and Tony stood and waved. On the last night White introduced Nancy Sinatra, who stood there in the spotlight—sexy, big-haired, white go-go boots, Frank's daughter—while Tony stared. Then Slappy White said, "And there's someone else here I'd like to introduce . . ." and Tony coiled in his seat. He would stand, wave to the crowd, and look over from his spotlight to Nancy Sinatra in her spotlight and establish eye contact and he would be on his way.

"Please give a big hello—" said White, and Tony gripped the arms of his chair.

"—to Sandler and Young!" whooped Slappy White, and Tony slumped into his seat.

---

*Given his sexual escapades, he may well have already been a father. Two years after Tony's death, in 1992, a tall, teenaged girl with big brown eyes knocked on the door of the Conigliaro home in Nahant and announced she was Tony's daughter. Teresa and Richie were stunned. The girl said her mother, who had not been involved in a serious relationship with Tony, had told him she was pregnant, but Tony doubted his paternity. "And knowing the way he was," Richie says, "if he thought there was any chance the child was his, he would have embraced her, no matter how it had happened." Tony never met the girl. Still, Richie and Teresa have maintained contact with her, on the chance she is Tony's daughter. "I wish there was a way we could know for sure," Richie continues. "She would be the only thing we have left of him."

~18~

TIME TO GO HOME

IN LATE DECEMBER 1981 MUD SLIDES RAVAGED TONY CONIGLIARO'S HEALTH-FOOD
STORE. He started to wonder if that Saint Augustine stuff was so much
hooey. Then word came from Boston that Hawk Harrelson, of all people,
was leaving his color commentator's job on Red Sox telecasts. Tony was
welcome to try out for the opening.

It would be perfect for him. He would be back with his beloved Red
Sox. He would do running commentary on baseball games, which he had
done many times, including being in the press box at the 1975 World Series.
That came a lot more naturally to him than staring into a camera to read Little League scores from San Rafael. It would be like another comeback. He
could develop a following among a whole new generation of Red Sox fans.

"This is a tremendous opportunity for you," Satch Hennessy
told him.

"Satch, there's nothing to keep me here anymore," Tony said. "It's
time to go home."

Tony flew to Boston to celebrate the holidays at his parents'
house in Nahant and tried out for the WSBK job on Thursday, January 7,
1982, his thirty-seventh birthday. The audition took place at the station's
studios in Brighton. Tony and veteran Red Sox play-by-play man Ned
Martin watched a tape of a game and simulated a broadcast. Tony was terrific. He looked good on the air, sounded sharp, and offered solid hardball insight. Martin, who knew Tony from his playing days, thought the
former kid slugger looked well, if a little tired.

Late that afternoon Jerry Maffeo was on the job as night manager
at Jason's, a trendy nightspot and restaurant in the Back Bay, when WSBK

general manager Joe Dimino walked in. He and Maffeo had become friends not long after Dimino's arrival in Boston, and the two sat down to dinner. Dimino chitchatted about the Sox telecast auditions and how he had tried out former Red Sox catcher Bob Montgomery and former Red Sox outfielder Tony Conigliaro for the job. Dimino, a non-New Englander who had been nowhere near Kenmore Square in the summer of 1967, commented he liked Tony's work, and he had all the right qualities for the job, but "no one around here knows who he is anymore."

Maffeo dropped his fork into his plate. "What did you say?"

"No one knows him," repeated Dimino.

Maffeo threw his napkin on the table, told Dimino to "come with me," and led him around the restaurant, accosting diners in midbite.

"Hey," Maffeo asked a guy selected at random, "in baseball, who's T. C.?"

"Tony Conigliaro," the patron replied, as if it were a stupid question, "the best ballplayer who ever came out of Boston."

They moved to another table. "Who's Conig?" Maffeo demanded, and the diner answered without hesitation, "Tony Conigliaro. Homered in his first time up at Fenway."

Later that evening Dimino and Maffeo were at the bar and Billy, Athanas, and Tony piled through the door amid their night on the town to celebrate Tony's birthday. Dimino and Maffeo joined the party, which lasted until 1:00 A.M. "We laughed all night," Maffeo recalls. "And I swear on my mother's soul, Dimino turned to Tony at the end and said, 'Tony, you've got the job.' "

On Friday, Tony went for a six-mile run in Nahant. That night he and Athanas headed into Boston for the Celtics-Philadelphia 76ers game at Boston Garden. The winter air was brisk, and as they left the Garden, Tony produced a wool watch cap and pulled it way down over his ears.

"What's with the hat?" Athanas inquired.

"Hey, it's freezing," Tony answered. "I don't want to catch anything."

Tony and Athanas met their dates for pizza at Regina's in the North End, and Athanas noticed that his pal, uncharacteristically, left a slice uneaten on his plate. Then the two couples headed to Seaside, a bar in Faneuil Hall. They weren't there long when Tony announced he wasn't feeling well and thought he ought to call it an early night.

There was a lot to do on Saturday morning. Tony was booked on a 10:00 A.M. flight out of Logan for Atlanta, where he would meet sports agent Mike Trope. Whatever happened with the TV job, Tony was going to manage the new baseball division in Trope's Los Angeles-based International Sports Management, Inc. Tony planned to go from Atlanta to Puerto Rico and Venezuela to scout potential clients, then head back to San Francisco to get his affairs together for the move east. He was sure he was coming home. He even knew where he wanted to live. The house next door to Sal and Teresa was for sale.

"Hey, Ma," he called to Teresa, on his way out the door to the airport, "I might be moving back home. What do you say if I live right next door to you? How would you like that?"

His mother laughed.

"Ma, you gotta think positive," Tony declared, and he was gone. Teresa went and got a cigarette; Tony hadn't allowed her to smoke one in the house the whole time he was there.

From the day he left for Bradenton in his black suit with white socks in the fall of 1962, through the glorious summers with the Red Sox, through the Saturday he staggered home from the Angels, through his trips back from San Francisco, Tony was usually chauffeured to and from the airport by Sal. But this morning his father needed to go to Suffolk Downs to check on his racehorses. So Tony eased into the passenger seat of Billy's 1980 silver gray BMW 320i, and his brother drove the car out onto Route 1-A for the fifteen-minute run to Logan.

They were near the horse track, just over the hill from where they grew up, when Billy asked, "You ever figure out who that girl was?" A woman had called the night before while Tony was out, and Teresa hadn't taken the message. Tony made a wheezing sound. Billy glanced over. His brother's arms were tight against his chest and his fists were clenched.

"Come on," Billy laughed, "don't kid me. Did you ever find out who that girl was?" Then he saw a tear ooze out of Tony's eye and run down his cheek, and he knew something was seriously wrong.

"*Tony!*" Billy yelled. His brother struggled to breathe. "*Tony!*" His brother slumped into the seat. Billy's mind raced. There was some sort of walk-in clinic in East Boston, but he wasn't sure where it was. They weren't far from Logan, and there were usually ambulances parked around the terminals, but the airport was a maze, and he could get lost there searching for help. Massachusetts General Hospital, about five miles away in Boston, was the place to go.

Billy was dating a nurse there, so he knew the route by heart. He opened up the throttle on the BMW and roared down Route 1-A at nearly eighty-five miles per hour. When he reached the toll booth at the entrance to the Sumner Tunnel, he slowed enough to holler, "*Hospital!*" and raced through without paying. It was Saturday morning, so traffic was light—on a weekday during rush hour it would have taken two hours to inch into the city—and Billy weaved and darted around cars through the two-lane tunnel.

Emerging out of the tube in the gray winter daylight, Billy gunned and raced and stopped and gunned up again—Tony slumped forward once, and Billy reached over with his right hand to prop him up—through the narrow streets to the hospital. He jolted to a halt outside the emergency entrance, bolted from the car, stuck his head through the automatic sliding doors, and hollered for help. Nurses and orderlies ran out and lifted Tony from the car onto a gurney. Billy heard one of the nurses say, "I'm not getting a pulse." It was a little before 9:30 in the morning.

After they rushed Tony out of sight, Billy asked for Dr. Roman DeSanctis, the renowned cardiologist who had treated Sal through a triple-bypass operation four years earlier. DeSanctis arrived shortly and was confronted with a desperate situation. "We had a tremendous time getting his heart going again," he remembers. Emergency-room physicians had zapped him with electrical impulses several times, but each jolt was followed by a flat line on the heart monitor. DeSanctis ordered Tony be taken to the catheritization lab to have an intra-aortic balloon inserted into the heart, a drastic last resort.

DeSanctis found Billy in the waiting room and told him they had restarted Tony's heart but his condition was still serious. "We did not hold out much hope that he would survive the next twenty-four hours," DeSanctis says. Billy knew Tony's brain had been deprived of oxygen for at least six minutes, and he knew that brain damage occurs at five minutes. But at least he wouldn't have to inform Sal and Teresa that their son was dead. Billy told DeSanctis he wanted to go get his father. Before he left, he asked the doctor to give him two nitroglycerin pills for Sal to take when he heard the news.

Billy walked briskly through the concourse at Suffolk Downs, desperately demanding of ushers, "Where's my father?" and they directed him to one of the dining rooms.

"What are you doing here? Who is it?" Sal asked, when he saw his agitated, pale son approach. "Your mother?" Billy handed him the nitro pills.

"It's Tony," Billy said. "He's sick."

"What do you mean, sick?" Sal said. "Was there an accident? What happened?"

"Take the pills," Billy ordered. Then he told his father that Tony had suffered a heart attack.

Sal was staggered. As he hurried out of the track with Billy, he thought, "My God, what else can happen to the kid?"

The news flashed over the radio and reporters began to show up at Mass General, but the family requested little information be given out. Friends, family, former teammates, and fans were incredulous. "I happened to be driving my car past Logan when I heard it on the radio," George Scott recalls. "I had to pull over to the side of the road for a moment and think it over. It was hard to understand."

Tony was only thirty-seven, in terrific shape, didn't smoke, and barely drank. "It's extremely rare," DeSanctis says, "but it happens." Tony had been under stress in his life, but worry could not have caused the massive coronary. He had no underlying heart disease and no virus. In his family history Sal had had heart problems and Tony had a touch of high blood pressure. His cholesterol level might have been sky high. In 1982 it was not yet standard procedure to measure it in heart attack victims. In the absence of an autopsy, DeSanctis can only guess that Tony had been carrying a harmless clot on the wall of the artery that ruptured, causing a blockage that stopped the heart. The less likely explanation was that Tony suffered a heart spasm.

By Monday it was clear that Tony's heart was not the main concern. Although he was still in danger, his heart beat stronger and stronger and there was very little permanent damage. (Tony would suffer no heart

problems in the remaining eight years of his life.) But he was in a deep
coma, and there was significant brain damage.

Sal, Teresa, Billy, Richie, Uncle Vinnie, Aunt Phyllis, and assorted
cousins, aunts, and uncles had streamed to the hospital Saturday night.
They stayed there to keep vigil, shuttling between their homes, the hospital cafeteria downstairs, and the waiting room in the intensive care
unit. At the end of the first week, a neurologist examined Tony, then met
with Sal, Billy, and Richie (Teresa declined to sit in). Tony had greatly
diminished brain function, he informed them, and they should expect no
significant neurological recovery. Billy didn't like the guy's bow tie, and
he surely didn't like what he was saying. "The idiot," Billy thought to
himself. "He doesn't know Tony."

Later, Sal, Richie, and Billy met with Dr. DeSanctis, who asked
what they wished if Tony suffered another life-threatening episode. Did
they want aggressive measures to save him? The Conigliaros looked at
each other as if it were the most ridiculous question they had ever heard.
"Of course," Sal said. "Do everything you can."

It was a painful, tense time for the family. Their anguish was so
intense that they could barely speak to one another. Sal snapped at
Richie. Richie snapped at Billy. Someone would wonder out loud what
would have happened if he had gotten to the hospital quicker, and Billy
would bristle because he felt he was being second-guessed. Actually, Billy
sometimes second-guessed himself. In reality, his quick thinking and
quick driving saved his brother's life. Virtually the only way Tony could
have avoided brain damage was to have suffered the heart attack in
Dr. DeSanctis's waiting room.

Slowly, during the first five weeks after the attack, Tony emerged
from his deep coma into semiconsciousness. By the end of February he
could respond to simple commands, look in a certain direction, and open
and close his eyes. He could move enough to burn the three thousand
calories per day he was fed through a tube in his stomach. This looked
like great news when it appeared in the newspapers, but in fact Tony's
doctors were disappointed. The neurologist was right. He just wasn't going
to get much better. "There are times when a physician comes close to crying
when he sees situations like this," DeSanctis said. "It's a terrible tragedy."

The Conigliaros didn't buy it. Doctors could be wrong. They had
been wrong when they said Tony would never play baseball again after he

was hit in the eye, and they were wrong about this. On March 1, Tony was moved from Mass General to the Shaughnessy Chronic Disease Rehabilitation Center in Salem, close to Nahant. He couldn't walk or talk, he barely moved, and he had a tracheostomy, or a surgical hole in his throat to help him breathe, yet the family thought it time for them and for Tony to get down to work.

Patients recovering from a coma need stimulation from familiar places, objects, or people. Tony was assigned Room 215 because it faces the North Shore: On a clear day he could see Swampscott, where he and his family used to live—if he were cognizant of any of that. Billy brought over his brother's favorite Rodney Dangerfield tapes, attached earphones to Tony's head, and played them over and over. The family contributed Tony's old Penn-Tone 45s, hoping "Little Red Scooter" would help bring him out of the coma.

Visitors would help the most, and the family left a list, updated daily, of ten people who were allowed admittance to the room. Many of Tony's friends and former teammates had visited at Mass General, but there had been little of Tony to see. Now they came to the Shaughnessy, expecting to find improvement and hoping they could do something, anything to enhance it.

Mike Ryan came by and said, "C'mon, Roomie, I've got a couple of broads outside." Tony squeezed his hand and gave him a funny smile, but Ryan wasn't even sure if Tony knew who he was. Julie Markakis showed Tony a ring he had given her in high school, and he moaned and smiled and cried. Luis Tiant sat in a chair next to Tony's bed with a big black cigar in his mouth. Sal said, "Tiant's here," and other people thought they saw a glimmer of recognition in Tony's face. And some people thought they saw nothing at all.

Bill Bates brought along his four-year-old son, led him near the bed, and said, "Hey, Anthony. This is Brandon Anthony Bates." Tony moaned. "He was in and out," Bates recalls. Tony Athanas, Mike Andrews, Gerry Moses, Rico Petrocelli, George Scott, Jerry Maffeo, and others visited. If they wanted to be wishful thinkers, they could convince themselves he was tickled by their jokes or cried because he was sad. They saw what they wanted—and needed. Uncle Vinnie got close to Tony's face one day and said, "For chrissakes, kid, will you snap out of it? There's going to be a party down at the club for you in a couple weeks. What fun's it gonna be, us having a few drinks down there, and you stuck in here?" And Vinnie was sure the kid looked straight at him and smiled.

As the second son, Billy stepped up to take a leading role in the care of his brother. A month after the heart attack, he went to California to sell Tony's home and car, straighten out his paperwork, and pack up his belongings to ship them back home. Billy was glad he wasn't as emotional as his brothers, but he wobbled when he saw Tony's license with his photo on it and notes in Tony's handwriting.

Billy was determined to round up all the help he could get. An avid reader of science and near-science, he had summoned a Russian faith healer when Tony was at Mass General. The short, balding man with a Boris Badanov accent had moved his hands around Tony's head and heart and lungs, then shook his head and said, "I can't get any kind of response. I can't help you." Now at the Shaughnessy, Billy was willing to turn to just about anything. He called in a holistic healer and tried an acupuncturist. He tried low-voltage electrical stimulation and nutrient treatments, which meant an unwieldy Myoflex machine had to be lugged into the room.

He even enlisted Laurie Cabot, the official witch of Salem, who appeared in Room 215 wearing a black cloak, white face makeup, and black eye makeup. "I'm pretty open-minded," Billy explained. His father was not. Sal walked into Tony's room during one of the witch's sessions and bellowed, "What the hell is that?" When Billy told him, Sal exploded, "Don't be ridiculous! Get her out of here!"

Medical doctors and witch doctors alike produced only small improvements—a smile here, a laugh there. Everyone had come to expect majestic drama out of Tony, but this time there was no neurological home run. If Tony were ever going to snap out of it and shock the medical word, it would have been the day a vaguely familiar middle-aged woman stuck her head into Room 215 and introduced herself as Sister Ernestina, Tony's old tormentor from Saint Mary's. No longer a nun, she was married with children of her own. "If Tony knew it was you," Teresa said, "he'd get up out of that bed and smack you," but Tony didn't budge.

The Conigliaros lavished on Tony love, prayers, and lots of attention. On May 24 they thought they had finally been blessed with results.
Billy was at home when he got the exciting news from his mother: Tony
had spoken.

Billy raced to the Shaughnessy, hoping to find the miracle of his
brother sitting up and chatting. The real story was that Tony had been
doing breathing exercises with his respiratory therapist and she thought
he *looked* like he wanted to talk. She closed off the trachea and he said,
"Hi." He also said, "yes," "no," and "hospital."

It was hardly the Gettysburg address, but Tony's utterances were
enough to spark a blizzard of wishful thinking. The Great Aunt got word
of it, a press conference was assembled at the Shaughnessy, and headlines shouted: "Tony's Speech Amazes His Doc" and "Tony C Speaks: 'Hi,
Mom.' " It was called a miracle. It was 1969 all over again. But no one read
the fine print. Dr. Maxmillian Kaulbach, Tony's cardiologist, said, "There
is reason to be more optimistic about the outcome, but caution should be
used because his chances for full recovery are extremely unlikely." The
public, however, read the headlines and half-expected to see Tony coming
back as a DH the next spring. They wanted him back so badly that they
saw mirages. "You know what I think?" Uncle Vinnie predicted. "I think
he's going to walk out of here."

On June 7 a limousine pulled up outside the Shaughnessy and
out stepped a man with tinted glasses, slicked-back hair, and a nylon
warm-up jacket. It was Al Davis, the owner of the Oakland Raiders. He
had befriended Tony in the Bay Area. Davis knew precisely what the
Conigliaro family was going through. In 1979 his wife, Carol, had suffered a heart attack and was in a deep coma for thirteen days before she
awoke and asked, "What happened?" She eventually achieved a 98
percent recovery.

When Davis walked into his room, Tony grinned. Everybody
agreed it was because he recognized him. Davis sat for ninety minutes
telling stories about Vida Blue, Marcus Allen, and Charlie Finley. Tony
laughed and smiled and nodded. Later, Davis told a reporter from *Sports
Illustrated,* "The main thing for them to remember is that it gets lonely.

It's human nature to be very concerned at first, then have that concern slack off."

The Conigliaros never slacked off. Daily, from nine in the morning until eleven at night, at least one member of the family was in the room with Tony. There was stress on all of them. Teresa prayed. Richie talked to Tony normally, as if they were sitting in the backyard in Swampscott about to play catch. Billy tried throwing a sponge ball to him. After work at the Triangle Tool and Die Company, Sal would go straight to Tony's bedside, then go home to eat dinner and go straight to bed, only to get up the next morning and start the routine all over again. Often while at the Shaughnessy, he would go out into the hall to smoke a cigarette and try to compose himself.

They all struggled to stay upbeat, the way Tony always did. To think of Tony was sad, and the sadness followed them everywhere. Adding to their pain were the cruel rumors, which they got wind of almost immediately after the heart attack: Tony—young, apparently healthy, and a Bay Area resident the previous six years—must have been dabbling in cocaine. The rumors could persist because there was no clinical way to prove or disprove it. Dr. DeSanctis says, "There was absolutely no indication he was involved with drugs. I was always very comfortable there was nothing in the way of drugs involved here."

People close to Tony, the health fanatic-hypochondriac, agree the notion is out of the question. "Tony Conigliaro never did drugs," Bill Bates insists. "That is incontrovertible. No one in the world can prove differently." That was true in Boston, and it was true in the zonked-out world of southern California in the early eighties. Dale Gribow, the Los Angeles attorney who had Tony as a housemate in the months leading up to the heart attack, remembers Tony's fitness fetish, which included grueling daily jogs to Coldwater Park in Beverly Hills. If there were drugs around, Tony just said no. "For people in our age group, coke and pot were very prevalent, especially here in California," Gribow says. "He was so antidrug. Tony and I had numerous conversations about it. He wouldn't go near a girl who was into that. He wouldn't even date a girl who smoked." Gribow remembers a young party girl sizing up the two non-smoking, nontooting, barely drinking bachelors and saying, "What, are you guys Mormons or something?"

Before long the family could see that Al Davis had been right; it could get lonely. There were fewer visitors than at the beginning. At least the great avalanche of get-well cards, letters, religious medals, flowers, trinkets, T-shirts, paintings, and baseball figurines from the general public helped; and the flow never stopped. "It was the stuff from strangers, people we didn't even know, that got us through it sometimes," Billy says. The Conigliaros didn't really blame anyone who couldn't bear to see Tony so severely impaired. To visit him could be painful. Satch Hennessy came east and brought his daughter Lacey, now six years old, to Room 215.

"Tony, it's me, Lacey," she said. "Your girlfriend. We're going to get married."

Tony was gripped by a coughing jag, and his trachea piece whistled out of his throat and shot across the room. Crying, Lacey turned to Teresa and sobbed, "I don't think I want to marry Tony anymore."

Later, Satch was alone in the room with Tony and whispered, "Tony, I know I made a promise to you many years ago. But there isn't any plug for me to pull."

Into the fall and over the winter, Tony was in and out of hospitals with respiratory problems and pneumonia. A lung was in danger of collapsing. But wishful-thinking stories persisted. One of them, in November, was headlined "New Signs of Progress for Tony C". The progress, as reported by a nurse at the Shaughnessy, was that Tony could hold a pencil (but couldn't write anything), could move all four limbs, and he "scratched his own nose." Tony's progress was disheartening. He spent his thirty-eighth birthday at the Shaughnessy attached to a respirator. Sal brought over a cake. "We'll see if he can blow out the candles," he said. "We know he won't be able to eat it."

In the spring of 1983 Tony's health insurance from AFTRA (American Federation of Television and Radio Artists) and the major-league players union (he had surprised everyone by keeping up payments on both) ran low. The stay at Mass General alone had cost fifty-eight thousand dollars. Now the Shaughnessy and other medical expenses were running close to four thousand dollars a week. Many of Tony's friends were eager to help, and a gala benefit concert was planned for Symphony Hall.

Someone was needed to line up heavy hitters from the entertainment world. Merv Griffin surprised everyone by not helping at all. Billy turned to an old roommate, agent Ed Kleven, who was once road manager for Dionne Warwick. Warwick was glad to pitch in. She and Tony went way back; she had been a backup singer on one of his 45s in the midsixties. "An Evening for Tony C". was held on April 15. Marvin Hamlisch played the piano; Warwick and Frank Sinatra sang; and Ted Williams, Bobby Orr, Joe DiMaggio, Willie Mays, Ben Davidson, Gerry Moses, Mike Andrews, Rico Petrocelli, and Al Davis schmoozed to raise $230,000.

The Conigliaros got help from all over. Bumper stickers reading "I Pray for Tony C" began to appear on the North Shore. Satch Hennessy took an armload of them home with him, and they started to appear on cars in northern California. Satch also organized a benefit for Tony at Marin Catholic High School, which was well attended by Bay Area friends who felt far away and helpless. Two months after the Symphony Hall extravaganza, the Red Sox staged "Tony C Night" at Fenway, including a reunion of the 1967 team (Yaz was sure to show as he was still in the Red Sox lineup), with the net proceeds of the game with the Tigers going to Tony's medical fund. It was a nice gesture, and it raised about one hundred thousand dollars. But the evening was spoiled. That night Red Sox co-owner Buddy LeRoux, the team's former trainer, attempted to wrest away full control of the team from co-owners Haywood Sullivan and Mrs. Jean Yawkey. He was even going to resurrect Dick O'Connell as general manager. The whole mess stole headlines from Tony's tribute and spawned years of lawsuits. While the soap opera unfolded at Fenway, Tony recuperated at Mass General from an operation to remove part of his left lung.

Just before the holidays in 1983 Tony was moved to his parents' home in Nahant. For the next six years, when he wasn't in hospitals for treatment of various ailments, he lived either with Billy or with Sal and Teresa. It would strain all of them to the breaking point.

*Billy Conigliaro holds the plaque honoring his older brother at Fenway Park's Tony C Night on June 6, 1983. But it really wasn't the Tony C Night it should have been: That same night Red Sox co-owner Buddy LeRoux, the team's former trainer, trashed the dignity of the proceedings by trying to wrest away control of the team from Haywood Sullivan and Jean Yawkey. (*Boston Herald *archives photo)*

Tony required round-the-clock nurses, as well as myriad therapists and rehabilitation specialists. It was like constantly having a houseful of guests. There was always a stranger in the kitchen, somebody using the bathroom, somebody asking how the can opener worked. And Tony wasn't getting better. As time went by, unspoken despair settled in with the Conigliaros. They put on brave faces for visitors, who were fewer and fewer in number; but they weren't so sure anymore: Maybe Tony wasn't going to get better.

Somehow they pushed on. They craved something, anything, about which to get enthusiastic. They desperately wanted to see Tony walk. In February 1984 he underwent extensive surgery at Mass General to loosen his heel cords and Achilles tendons, which had tightened during his long stays in bed. Day after day, with a therapist on one side and Billy on the other, Tony was escorted outside for "walks" in the driveway. They refused to give up. In the winter they bundled Tony in a heavy coat and earmuffs and kept trying, shuffling along the icy blacktop while Tony strained and sweated. Sal made braces for his son's legs in the shop at the Triangle Tool and Die Company. When they didn't help, he went back and worked on another design. Then another. Finally, Billy gently asked his father to stop making braces.

On his fortieth birthday, four years after the heart attack, Tony still couldn't eat or walk by himself, and could barely talk. Any hopeful sign of improvement was immediately followed by long, seemingly endless stalemates. Hennessy had returned for a visit once when Tony was back in the Shaughnessy for a treatment. When an attractive nurse entered Tony's room, Satch remarked, "Hey, Tony, how do you stand it with all these ugly nurses around here? I wouldn't be able to look at them." Slowly and deliberately, Tony said, "Satch . . . you're . . . full . . . of . . . shit." But the next moment his eyes would again be vacant.

Good days meant that Tony hadn't thrown up, or gotten agitated and wrestled a nurse, or had a coughing fit. The coughing was the worst. Tony would hack and gurgle and wheeze for hours straight, and the terrible sound would echo all through the house, sometimes all night. Sal and Teresa would lie in bed listening, knowing their son was suffering. "Sometimes at night, I sit there looking at him," Sal said. "And he looks so great. But the brain . . . ? I must have asked the question a thousand times: 'Why?' "

Billy knew how his parents suffered. He was in the construction-carpentry business, remodeling homes and reselling them, and he tried to have Tony live with him as often as he could. The coughing kept him awake at night, too, and he filled in when a nurse quit, called in sick, or just didn't show up. When he wasn't tending to Tony or arranging his brother's care, Billy struggled with insurance forms, wrote letters to Medicare, or argued on the telephone with a clerk at the Major League Players Association. Says Bill Bates: "Billy was there every single day for him. Every single day. He gave up his life to take care of his brother."

For Billy it was a matter of willpower: He tried not to think about what had happened, even when Tony was in the next room, gagging for two straight hours. Some thoughts he simply avoided. It was why Billy couldn't bring himself to go to Fenway for a Red Sox game. "I'd sit there looking back, thinking how good things used to be," he said.

In the fall of 1986, Sal, who had undergone another bypass, suffered chest pains and Billy rushed him to Mass General. Billy recalled driving up to the same entrance, parking in the same spot, and sitting in the same waiting area the day Tony had his heart attack. Not long afterward Tony suffered an unusually severe coughing spell, and there was Billy, again racing down Route 1-A, weaving through the tunnel, and delivering Tony to the same emergency room entrance. They even wheeled Tony into the same treatment room. It got to where Billy couldn't dodge the thoughts anymore. He wondered if Tony wouldn't have been better off had he died the day of the heart attack.

All of the Conigliaros suppressed such grievous thoughts, but sometimes they bubbled out. One day Billy was driving Sal home from a family wedding, and suddenly his father started to cry.

"Dad, what's the matter?"

"Billy, this thing with Tony, I can't handle it," Sal wept. "I can't beat it. All my life, whenever I've had a problem at home or at the shop, I'd work it out. Resolve it. But this . . . there's nothing we can do, and it's so damn frustrating. When you have a son . . . oh, it's hard to explain, but it's a hundred times worse when it's your son than it is when it's someone you happen to know. When it's your own son, it just eats away at you."

On July 5, 1987, Sal went to Suffolk Downs to check out his horses. He was in the stable area when he felt a sharp pain in his chest.

He collapsed onto the soft dirt. Four days later he died at Mass General at age sixty-four. No one told Tony. "I don't think he would have known the difference," Billy says.

Billy came downstairs in his home and there was Tony, talking and laughing and full of life, walking across the floor, getting something to eat, perfectly normal, right back to the way he used to be. Billy was overwhelmed with joy, but then he wondered how on earth he would explain to Tony that he had sold his car and house out in California. Then Billy woke up and lay there recovering from the same old dream. It was just a dream. Tony would never be his old self again.

As time passed and Tony didn't get better, as he developed infection after infection and was rushed to the hospital over and over—Billy began to hope that his brother would die. "I felt so bad for him," Billy says. "He couldn't eat. He couldn't talk. He'd have spasms. He'd grab you and shake you and he'd look you in the face and there was terror in your eyes. It was such torture for him."

Billy didn't want to hear any more wishful thinking, because he had reached the conclusion that blind optimism was doing Tony no good. A cousin called from New Jersey and said he had a vision that if they took Tony to Lourdes on a certain date, he would be cured. Billy fought not to hang up on him. There was a time when he might have bundled Tony onto a plane for France, "three or four months after he got sick, maybe. But not after seven years."

As he watched his brother suffer, Billy was sure now: He would have been better off dying in the BMW that day. Also, Billy was having thoughts that scared him. He telephoned a nurse friend, tiptoed around the subject, then finally came out and asked if there were any way he could help Tony die without going to jail. Billy's friend gently talked him out of it.

One week into the nineties, Tony turned forty-five, but there was no cake or celebration. There were prayers that he would go in peace. The next month he again developed pneumonia and was back in Salem hospital. On a dreary Saturday morning, Uncle Vinnie, his son, Vinnie Jr., and Billy went to the hospital to visit. Tony wheezed and barked, and Uncle Vinnie couldn't take it anymore. He went home, waited for the call, and prayed to God that Tony would finally give up.

"I was cross-country skiing that day," recalls Gale Carey, who had grown up in Natick, Massachusetts, in the sixties, loving the Red Sox. She was one of the thousands who never met Tony but felt touched by him. "All of a sudden I smelled what must have been wood smoke, but for some reason it reminded me of incense in a Catholic church. I thought to myself, 'Something's happened.' When I got home I found out Tony C had died."

People reached back to remember his life and their own life. They went back, to shaggy haircuts, cool sideburns, and one more home run at Fenway; to tie-dyed shirts and acid rock, and a joyous romp around the bases on Opening Day in Baltimore; to draft card notices and the Summer of Love and a young man face down at home plate; to the Beatles on *Ed Sullivan,* and a teenager hitting a home run after one pitch on the home field. They went back to convertible rides on the Lynnway, and a kid in a Catholic school uniform tie, signing with a big-league team at the kitchen table; to Ike and baseball cards and long fly balls off the supermarket wall in East Boston; back to dungarees and PF Flyers and a small boy with his shirt inside out, running by himself to the park first thing on a summer morning, because all he really wanted to do was play.

ᘒ BIBLIOGRAPHY ᘓ

Books
Conigliaro, Tony, with Jack Zanger, *Seeing It Through*. New York: Macmillan, 1970.
Reynolds, Bill, *Lost Summer*. New York: Warner, 1993.
Williams, Dick, and Bill Plaschke, *No More Mr. Nice Guy*. New York: Harcourt Brace Jovanovich, 1990.

Magazines
McCallum, Jack, "Faith, Hope, and Tony C," *Sports Illustrated*, July 5, 1982.
Mulvoy, Mark, "Now Playing Right Field," *Sports Illustrated*, April 7, 1969.

Newspapers
Boston Herald, articles, 1960-90.
Boston Record-American, articles, 1962-72.
Boston Sunday-Advertiser, articles, 1964-67.
Boston Traveler, articles, 1962-67.
Boston Globe, articles, 1962-90.
New York Times, articles; 1964, 1983.
San Francisco Chronicle, articles, 1976-81.
Los Angeles Times, articles, 1970-71.

～ INDEX ～